Cite T

Study Skills

Academic Success
Academic Writing Skills for International Students
The Business Student's Phrase Book
Cite Them Right (11th edn)
Critical Thinking and Persuasive Writing for Postgraduates
Critical Thinking Skills (3rd edn)
Dissertations and Project Reports
Doing Projects and Reports in Engineering
The Employability Journal
Essentials of Essay Writing
The Exam Skills Handbook (2nd edn)
Get Sorted
Great Ways to Learn Anatomy and Physiology (2nd edn)
How to Begin Studying English Literature (4th edn)
How to Use Your Reading in Your Essays (3rd edn)
How to Write Better Essays (4th edn)
How to Write Your Undergraduate Dissertation (3rd edn)
Improve Your Grammar (2nd edn)
The Mature Student's Handbook
Mindfulness for Students
The Macmillan Student Planner
The Personal Tutor's Handbook
Presentation Skills for Students (3rd edn)
The Principles of Writing in Psychology
Professional Writing (3rd edn)
Skills for Success (3rd edn)
Stand Out from the Crowd
The Student Phrase Book
The Student's Guide to Writing (3rd edn)

Study Skills Connected
The Study Skills Handbook (5th edn)
Study Skills for International Postgraduates
Studying in English
Studying History (4th edn)
Studying Law (4th edn)
Studying Physics
The Study Success Journal
Success in Academic Writing (2nd edn)
Smart Thinking
Teaching Study Skills and Supporting Learning
The Undergraduate Research Handbook (2nd edn)
The Work-Based Learning Student Handbook (2nd edn)
Writing for Engineers (4th edn)
Writing History Essays (2nd edn)
Writing for Law
Writing for Nursing and Midwifery Students (3rd edn)
Write it Right (2nd edn)
Writing for Science Students
Writing Skills for Education Students
You2Uni: Decide, Prepare, Apply

Pocket Study Skills

14 Days to Exam Success (2nd edn)
Analyzing a Case Study
Blogs, Wikis, Podcasts and More
Brilliant Writing Tips for Students
Completing Your PhD
Doing Research (2nd edn)
Getting Critical (2nd edn)
Managing Stress
Planning Your Dissertation (2nd edn)
Planning Your Essay (2nd edn)
Planning Your PhD
Posters and Presentations

Reading and Making Notes (2nd edn)
Referencing and Understanding Plagiarism (2nd edn)
Reflective Writing
Report Writing (2nd edn)
Science Study Skills
Studying with Dyslexia (2nd edn)
Success in Groupwork
Successful Applications
Time Management
Where's Your Argument?
Writing for University (2nd edn)

Research Skills

Authoring a PhD
The Foundations of Research (3rd edn)
Getting to Grips with Doctoral Research
Getting Published
The Good Supervisor (2nd edn)
The Lean PhD
PhD by Published Work
The PhD Viva
The PhD Writing Handbook
Planning Your Postgraduate Research
The Postgraduate Research Handbook (2nd edn)
The Professional Doctorate
Structuring Your Research Thesis

Career Skills

Excel at Graduate Interviews
The Graduate Career Guidebook (2nd edn)
Graduate CVs and Covering Letters
Graduate Entrepreneurship
How to Succeed at Assessment Centres
Social Media for Your Student and Graduate Job Search
Work Experience, Placements and Internships

Cite Them Right

The Essential Referencing Guide

Eleventh revised and expanded edition

Richard Pears & Graham Shields

 macmillan international HIGHER EDUCATION

 RED GLOBE PRESS

Contents

Section H ▶ Institute of Electrical and Electronics Engineers (IEEE) referencing style **157**

Section I ▶ Modern Humanities Research Association (MHRA) referencing style

Welcome to the eleventh edition of *Cite them right*. We hope that it will guide you in referencing for your academic work. Our experience in university libraries with students and academics has allowed us to understand more clearly where students struggle with referencing, and their queries fuel the need to clarify or refine examples and to create new ones. We are grateful to our readers for their continuing feedback and reviews on the usefulness of *Cite them right*. Your many positive reviews encourage us. We hope that you will continue to provide constructive suggestions in the future.

New and revised material

New sections and additions include:

♦ New section for Institute of Electrical and Electronics Engineers (IEEE) referencing style.
♦ Chicago section rewritten for the 17th edition of *The Chicago manual of style*.
♦ MLA section rewritten for the 8th edition of the *MLA handbook*.
♦ Expanded APA, MHRA, OSCOLA and Vancouver sections.
♦ New examples of Harvard referencing for citing body art, book cover blurb, case analyses, cinemagraphs, circuses, collages, GIS maps and datasets, House of Commons Library reports, intranet documents, letters to the editor, LIDAR, musicals, NICE guidelines, paragraphs in web pages, Periscope, product reviews, screenshots, sewing and knitting patterns, silhouettes, streaming services, systematic reviews, Snapchat, WhatsApp, and working papers.

♦ We are treating all published reports, including those in databases (E8), as publications, so they will have titles in italics.
♦ We only use italics for the titles of publications, not for the names of corporate bodies (such as BBC and Amazon) nor for social media platforms (such as Facebook and Snapchat).
♦ We have changed the format of additional contributors to sources (including translators, choreographers and directors) to initial, surname, to read more clearly in the references.

How to make the best use of *Cite them right*

You are *not* expected to read it from cover to cover.

Everyone should read **Sections A–D**, which cover the basics about referencing, quotations and avoiding plagiarism. These will provide you with a much clearer understanding of where you can find the elements that need to be referenced, and the confidence to set them out correctly in your text and reference list.

Section E, the main body of the book, details a comprehensive range of source materials and provides specific examples of how they should be referenced using the Harvard (author-date) referencing style. This system originated in the USA, but has become one of the most widely used referencing style internationally due to its simplicity and ease of use. However, there is no single authority to define 'Harvard'; hence, there are many versions, with slight variations, of the system in use. The alternative title, 'author-date', arises from the fact that the in-text citations follow the format of using the author's surname and the date of publication (where available) to link with the full reference details in the reference list/bibliography.

Use the **Contents** or **Index** pages to identify the type of source you need to reference (for example, ebook, web page, government publication), then follow the advice and example(s) on the relevant page(s).

Sections F–L provide examples for referencing the most commonly used sources in the American Psychological Association (APA), Chicago, Institute of Electrical and Electronics Engineers (IEEE), Modern Humanities Research Association (MHRA), Modern Language Association (MLA), Oxford University Standard for Citation of Legal Authorities (OSCOLA) and Vancouver styles.

A **Glossary** is included to explain the meaning of certain terms used in the text. These words appear in bold when they first occur within each section.

Richard Pears and Graham Shields, 2019

Acknowledgements

The authors would like to thank:

Debbie Cesvette for information on the citation of *Written questions and answers*.

Colleagues at Durham University Library, and staff and students at other academic institutions for their support, constructive feedback and suggestions.

Our Editor Suzannah Burywood, Georgia Park, Senior Production Editor, and Richard Wong, Digital Development Editor, for his work on the online version of *Cite them right*.

The publishers would like to thank the following for permission to reproduce copyright material:

Getty Images/iStockphoto, p. 6; Getty Images, pp. 16, 24, 27, 219; Blend *Images – RF*, p. 20; Digital Vision, p. 31; iStock.com/bigtunaonline, p. 60; iStock.com/bazza1960, p. 75; ImageSource, p. 87; E+, p. 131; David Travis, p. 135; iStockphoto, p. 152; http://www.jupiterimages.com, p. 162; Getty Images/Blend Images, p. 170; Getty Images/Science Photo Library RF, p. 192; Nick Fewings, p. 184; Kimberly Farmer, p. 195; Rob Girkin, p. 227; Jubal Kenneth Bernal, p. 243.

Section A
What is referencing?

Referencing is the process of acknowledging other people's work when you have used it in your assignment or research. It allows the reader to locate your source material as quickly and easily as possible so that they can read these sources themselves and verify the validity of your arguments. Referencing provides the link between what you write and the evidence on which it is based.

You identify the sources that you have used by citing them in the text of your assignment (called **citations** or **in-text citations**) and referencing them at the end of your assignment (called the **reference list** or **end-text citations**). The reference list only includes the sources cited in your text. It is not the same thing as a **bibliography**, which uses the same referencing style, but also includes all material (for example, background readings) used in the preparation of your work.

Why reference?

There are a number of important reasons why you need to reference. Referencing allows you to:

♦ Demonstrate that you have read widely on the subject and considered and evaluated the writings of others
♦ Show your tutor the evidence of your research, and thereby appreciate your contribution to the topic
♦ Establish the credibility and authority of your ideas and arguments

♦ Enable the reader to locate the original material you used
♦ Give credit to the original author/creator
♦ Enable the reader to form their own views on the value of your sources and how you have interpreted them
♦ Distinguish between your own ideas and opinions, and those of others
♦ Highlight relevant points by quoting, paraphrasing or summarising from the original text (see Section C)
♦ Achieve a better mark or grade
♦ Avoid **plagiarism** (see 'What is plagiarism?' on page 4)

Every academic institution requires its students to reference in their work, and your tutors will expect you to do this accurately, clearly and concisely. Your university or institution should issue you with guidelines on how they expect you to reference in your particular subject area. Follow these guidelines carefully.

When should you reference?

You are expected to reference every time you use someone else's work or ideas in your own work. There are no exceptions to this rule, and it applies to all your work, including assignments, essays, presentations, dissertations, and other research or publications. It is very important that when undertaking your research, you systematically record and save full details of all the resources that you have used, and it is vital that you save these sources at the time that you use them. Otherwise, it can be very difficult (or even impossible) to locate these resources again at a later date.

What should you reference?

You should reference *all the sources* that you use for your assignment or research and maintain records for all of them. Any information that you copy and paste, repeat word for word, paraphrase or summarise must be acknowledged by referencing it. This includes all information available on the **internet**. Students commonly believe, erroneously, that because it is available online, they are not required to acknowledge it. There are numerous reference management software tools available (some free) that can help you to manage the referencing process. Be aware, though, that even if you use these tools, you must still double-check your citations and references to ensure that they appear in a consistent style and follow your institution/tutor's guidelines.

Your aim should always be to reference reliable sources of information. These may include books (printed and ebooks), journal articles, web pages, conference papers, newspaper articles, lecture notes, government publications, videos, legal material and reports. This list can be extended, depending on the subject you are studying and the nature of the source material in your area.

In the era of 'fake news', it is vital that you consider how reliable the sources are, because newspaper and magazine articles, websites, blogs, tweets, wikis, and popular or social media can be unreliable or weak sources of information. They may simply offer someone's opinion on a topic, but may also be deliberate misinformation to mislead or change your opinion. Always try to locate academic sources that substantiate the original material. In many cases, this may be peer-reviewed books or articles (also referred to as 'refereed' or 'scholarly'). This means that they are written by experts in their field and then reviewed by several other experts (or an editorial board) to ensure quality and accuracy before the

material is published. All of these scholarly sources will have references to show you where the authors sourced their evidence. If a written or online source does not have references, think carefully before using it in academic work. Scholarly publications will also provide details of the author's experience, and in many instances which institution they work for, enabling you to check that they are who they say they are.

Students often struggle to understand which version of a source they should reference. *You should always reference the version of the information source that you have actually used* (see also 'What about secondary referencing?' on page 3). The reason for this is clear – a journal or newspaper article may appear in both print and electronic formats, and the two versions may vary. If using visual sources, be clear to your reader about what you have seen: a painting in a gallery is seen as the painter intended, but if reproduced in a book or online it may have been cropped or digitally altered. If you saw the image online, cite the online version.

When looking at sources online, it can sometimes be difficult to identify what kind of source you are looking at. This is particularly true if you have retrieved results from internet search engines, which can provide direct links to PDFs. The PDF is not the information source; it is only one means of delivering information to you online. You will need to determine if you are looking at a journal article, a book chapter or a section of a larger report by checking for authors, section or chapter headings, or page numbers, then use the appropriate format for citing the source.

If you have included an appendix in your assignment or research, it should be clearly labelled with a letter (A) or number (1). If it contains information from other sources, these should be cited in-text in the appendix, with full references given at the end of the appendix as a separate reference list.

What about secondary referencing?

In some cases, you may want to refer to a source that is mentioned or quoted in the work you are reading. This is known as **secondary referencing**. It is important that, whenever possible, you cite and reference the primary source of your information. For example, if you read about a study by Harvey (primary source) in a book by Lewis (secondary source), you should try to locate and read the original work by Harvey. This will enable you to check for yourself that Harvey has not been misinterpreted or misquoted by Lewis. If you cannot locate the primary source (in this case Harvey), you cannot include it in your reference list. You can only cite it in your text. In your essay or assignment, you should cite both sources and use the phrase 'quoted in' or 'cited in', depending on whether the author of the secondary source is directly quoting or summarising from the primary source.

Harvard examples

Harvey (2015, quoted in Lewis, 2018, p. 86) provides an excellent survey …

White's views on genetics (2014, cited in Murray, 2018) support the idea that …

APA example

Harvey (as cited in Lewis, 2018) provides an excellent survey …

You then include Lewis and Murray in your reference list (and Harvey and White only if you have read them).

Once again, if you are unable to read the primary sources, you can only cite them in your text (as in the examples).

What about referencing common knowledge?

There is no need to reference things that are considered **common knowledge**. This is generally defined as facts, dates, events and information that are expected to be known by someone studying or working in a particular subject area or field. The information or facts can be found in numerous places and are likely to be widely known (for example, that London is the capital city of England). Such information does not generally have to be referenced.

However, as a student, you may have only just started to study a particular subject and be unaware of what is regarded as common knowledge. In order to decide if the material you want to include in your work constitutes common knowledge, you need to ask yourself the following questions:

♦ Did I know this information before I started my course?
♦ Did this information or idea come from my own brain?

If the answer to either or both of these questions is 'no', then the information is not common knowledge to you. In these cases, you should cite and reference the sources. So, if you are unsure whether something is common knowledge, it is always advisable to cite and reference it.

What about referencing anecdotal or personal experience?

Anecdotal sources can be very compelling, particularly in the field of medicine. The primary weakness of anecdotes and personal stories is that they cannot be verified. Although in most cases you would not reference anecdotal sources of information, you may still use these sources and include them as an appendix to your main text. It is very important that you are aware of confidentiality and are absolutely certain that you have permission to use the material (see 'What about referencing confidential information?' below). Clearly, if you have recorded someone recounting their story or anecdote, then you can include the transcript as an appendix to your work (with the interviewee's permission).

You can speak from personal experience in contexts such as personal responses, opinion pieces or reflective papers, and in many subjects this approach is positively encouraged and expected. Experience and opinions are important in your writing because a large part of academic writing is demonstrating that you have understood the foundation of knowledge on which your contributions stand. Once again, though, to back up your opinions or responses, you should always try to support your viewpoints and experiences with substantiating scholarly material.

What about referencing confidential information?

There may be times when you need to use a source of information that is confidential (for example, medical, legal or business material). This information is, by its very nature, unpublished and not in the public domain. In most cases, your tutor will offer guidance on whether you can use the information and reference it. If you decide to use confidential sources, you should always obtain permission from those who might be affected by its inclusion in your work. Similarly, it is regarded as good practice to ask for permission from the sender of information via personal communications (see Section E28).

In some cases, you may be able to anonymise the documents or sources, allowing you to refer to them for argument or statistical purposes. For example, in healthcare subjects, you could use terms such as 'patient X' or 'placement hospital'. See Section E27 for more details on how to reference confidential information.

What is plagiarism?

Plagiarism is a term that can often frighten students. It conjures up all kinds of negative thoughts, and yet it is relatively easy to avoid by following good academic practice. The term itself describes the unacknowledged use of someone else's work. This includes material or ideas from any (published or unpublished) sources, whether print, electronic (even if freely available on the internet) or audiovisual. Using the words or ideas of others without citing and referencing them would be construed as plagiarism, and is a very serious academic offence. At the end of the day, it is regarded as the stealing of intellectual property.

The following are all considered forms of plagiarism:

♦ Presenting any part of someone else's work as your own. This includes the work of other students, paying for work to be written by someone else and handed in as your own work (using so-called 'essay mills' or ghostwriters), and visual material (such as photographs you obtained online and haven't given credit to the creator)

♦ Using a source of information word for word (without quotation marks)
♦ Paraphrasing or summarising material in your assignment without acknowledging the original source through in-text citation and reference (see Section C)
♦ Altering a few words of someone else's work but retaining their sentence structure – for example, 'The company made a profit'/'The firm made a profit'
♦ Audio plagiarism: copying lyrics or parts of a music composition within your own work
♦ Visual plagiarism: making minor alterations to another person's images or designs without crediting the original source
♦ 'Recycling' a piece of your own work that you have previously submitted for another module or course (that is, self-plagiarism)
♦ Citing and referencing sources that you have not used
♦ Using too many quotations so that your work is little more than the work of others (even if referenced), held together by linking sentences you have written
♦ Collusion: working with another person to produce an assignment and not declaring this

How can you avoid plagiarism?

In most cases, students plagiarise unintentionally. Poor organisation and time management, as well as a failure to understand good academic practice or follow the published university guidelines, are often to blame. Through rigorous preparation and careful checking of your institution's advice and guidelines on referencing, you should be confident that you will not be accused of plagiarising.

The following advice can help:

♦ Manage your time and plan your work – ensure that you give yourself enough time to prepare, read and write
♦ Maintain clear notes and records of all the sources you use as you use them – it can prove very difficult to locate sources later
♦ Be organised – keep all of your notes and references until your assignment has been graded/marked
♦ When paraphrasing an author's text, ensure that you use your own words and a sentence structure that is sufficiently different from the original text (see Section C)
♦ In your notes, highlight in colour/bold any **direct quotations** you want to use in your assignment – this will help to ensure that you use quotation marks alongside an appropriate reference when you are writing up your work
♦ Allow enough time to check your final draft for possible referencing errors or omissions (for example, check that all your in-text citations have a corresponding entry in your reference list, and vice versa)

Plagiarism detection software

Some institutions use software such as Turnitin to identify where words, phrases or sentences in your text have been taken from other sources. This software compares a student's assignment against a database of the text of books, articles, websites and previous student assignments, and provides a marked-up version of the student's work showing matches with text stored in the database. This software should not alarm you if you have followed guidance from your tutors and in *Cite them right*. The marked-up version of your text will identify where you have used quotation marks around any phrases or sentences taken directly from the original sources as quotations and provided in-text citations (or footnote numbers). It will also note in-text citations where you have paraphrased or summarised another author's work. The software will highlight in a different colour where words and phrases match text in its database but no references have been given in your text, which may be instances of plagiarism. Often this software is used for formative assignments to teach students how to incorporate the works of other authors in their own academic writing, but can be used in disciplinary proceedings where deliberate plagiarism is suspected.

Section B
How to cite

Setting out citations

When you cite, you are referring to someone else's work or ideas in the text of your essay or assignment. It is often called in-text citing.

It is important to remember that **citations** in your assignments must be included in the final word count.

In-text citations give the brief (abbreviated) details of the work that you are quoting from, or to which you are referring in your text. These citations will then link to the full **reference** in the **reference list** at the end of your work, which is arranged in alphabetical order by author. Works cited in appendices, but not in the main body of your text, should be included in a separate reference list at the end of your appendix. It is important to note that **footnotes** and **endnotes** are not used in Harvard and other author-date referencing styles.

There are several ways in which you can incorporate citations into your text, depending on your own style and the flow of the work. However, a tutor or supervisor may advise you on their preferred format. You can see from the examples below how you can vary the use of citations in your text.

Your citations should include the following elements:

♦ Author(s) or editor(s) surname/family name

♦ Year of publication
♦ Page number(s) if required (always required for **direct quotations**)

If you are quoting directly or using ideas from a specific page or pages of a work, you should include the page number(s) in your citations. Insert the abbreviation p. (or pp.) before the page number(s).

> ### Example
>
> Harris (2018, p. 56) argued that 'nursing staff …'

If your citation refers to a complete work or to ideas that run through an entire work, your citation would simply use the author and date details.

> ### Example
>
> In a recent study (Evans, 2018), qualifications of school-leavers were analysed …

Citing one author/editor

Cite the author/editor.

> ### Example
>
> In his autobiography (Fry, 2014) …

Citing a corporate author

Cite the name (or initials, if well known) of the corporate body. For corporate bodies with long names where you wish to make clear what their initials stand for, you should write out the name in full the first time you use it and use the abbreviation for the citation. Be consistent in using the abbreviation each time to ensure that all your references appear correctly in your reference list.

Examples

… as shown in its annual report (BBC, 2016).

… the popularity of visiting historical monuments (English Heritage, 2014).

… in claims made by the United Nations Framework Conference of Climate Change (UNFCCC, 2014) …

Citing two authors/editors

Both are listed.

Example

Recent educational research (Lewis and Jones, 2018) …

Citing three authors/editors

All three are listed.

Example

In an important study of the subject (Hill, Smith and Reid, 2014) …

Citing four or more authors/editors

When citing four or more authors/editors in academic assignments, you should *either* cite the first name listed followed by **et al.** (meaning 'and others'):

Example

In-text citation

Research on nanostructures by Cutler *et al.* (2011) …

Reference list

Cutler, J. *et al.* (2011) 'Polyvalent nucleic acid nanostructures', *Journal of the American Chemical Society*, 133(24), pp. 9254–9257. doi:10.1021/ ja203375n.

Or, if your institution requires referencing of all named authors:

Example

In-text citation

Research on nanostructures by Cutler, Zhang, Zheng, Auyeung, Prigodich and Mirkin (2011) …

Reference list

Cutler, J., Zhang, K., Zheng, D., Auyeung, E., Prigodich, A.E. and Mirkin, C.A. (2011) 'Polyvalent nucleic acid nanostructures', *Journal of the American Chemical Society*, 133(24), pp. 9254–9257. doi:10.1021/ ja203375n.

If you are writing for a publication, you should follow the editor's guidelines, as you may be required to name all the authors, regardless of the number, to ensure that each author's contribution is recognised.

Citing a source with no author/editor

Where the name of an author/editor cannot be found, use the title (in italics). Do not use 'Anon.' or 'Anonymous'.

Example

In a groundbreaking survey (*Health of the nation*, 2011) …

Citing multiple sources

If you need to refer to two or more publications at the same time, these can be separated by semicolons (;). The publications should be cited in chronological order (with the earliest date first). If more than one work is published in the same year, then they should be listed alphabetically by author/editor.

Example

A number of environmental studies (Town, 2013; Williams, 2015; Andrews *et al.*, 2017; Martin and Richards, 2018) considered …

Citing sources published in the same year by the same author

Sometimes you may need to cite two (or more) publications by an author published in the same year. To distinguish between the items in the text, allocate lower-case letters in alphabetical order after the publication date.

Example

In his study of the work of Rubens, Miller (2006a) emphasised the painter's mastery of drama. However, his final analysis on this subject (Miller, 2006b) argued that …

In your reference list, the publications would look like this:

Example

Miller, S. (2006a) *The Flemish masters*. London: Phaidon Press.

Miller, S. (2006b) *Rubens and his art*. London: Killington Press.

Citing different editions of the same work by the same author

Separate the dates of publication with a semicolon (;), with the earliest date first.

Example

In both editions (Hawksworth, 2015; 2018) …

In your reference list, the publications would look like this:

Example

Hawksworth, S. (2015) *Company law*. 3rd edn. Oxford: Oxford University Press.

Hawksworth, S. (2018) *Company law*. 5th edn. Oxford: Oxford University Press.

Citing multiple sources by the same author

Put the sources in chronological order in your in-text citations and reference list, as in the examples below.

Example

Research by one author (Singh 2017; 2018) …

OR

Research by Singh (2017; 2018) …

In your reference list, the publications would look like this:

Example

Singh, S. (2017) 'Sikh costume', *Indian Journal of Design*, 22, pp. 47–52.

Singh, S. (2018) *Religion in India*. Delhi: Scholars Press.

Citing sources with multiple authors

If you want to cite a book edited by Holmes and Baker that has, for example, 10 contributors and does not specify who wrote each section or chapter, follow the format of citing using the editors' names.

Example

Recent research (Holmes and Baker, 2009, pp. 411–428) proved …

NB See Section E1.10 for the relevant information on citing and referencing when the author's name is given for a specific chapter or section.

Citing sources when one author has worked with other authors for some publications

For the same lead author, single-author works precede works with multiple authors. Furthermore, the order of the reference list entries for works with the same lead author is determined alphabetically according to the second author's surname (and so on if there are more co-authors).

Example

Anderson, J. (2009) …

Anderson, J. (2017) …

Anderson, J. and Atherton, P. (2018) …

Anderson, J. and Bell, T. (2015) …

Citing a source with no date

Use the phrase 'no date'.

Example

In an interesting survey of youth participation in sport, the authors (Harvey and Williams, no date) …

Citing a source with no author or date

Use the title and 'no date'.

Example

Integrated transport systems clearly work (*Trends in European transport systems*, no date).

Citing a web page

If you are citing a **web page**, it should follow the preceding guidelines, citing by author and date where possible, by title and date if there is no identifiable author, or, as in the example below, by **URL** or **DOI** if neither author nor title can be identified.

Example

The latest survey of health professionals (http://www.onlinehealthsurvey.org, 2018) reveals that …

For more details on how to cite and reference web pages, see Section E10.

Using illustrations in your text

In some subjects, you may be required to provide graphics or illustrations within your assignments (for example, graphs in mathematics or diagrams of experiments). Your tutor or department should provide a guide, perhaps in a module handbook, for how your work is to be presented (for example, fonts, referencing style, word count and how any illustrations are to be incorporated). There may also be subject-specific regulations from a professional body. *Cite them right* is not intended to replace any departmental regulations, nor can it provide guidance to cover the full range of academic subjects its readers are studying. If you are unsure about how you should present illustrations in your academic work, you should ask your tutor for guidance.

If no guidance is available from your tutor, we suggest that you number each illustration in the order that they are used in your work, and provide a caption that describes the illustration, beginning the caption with Figure, then the number, then the description. If you have used an illustration from someone else's work, conclude the caption with, in round brackets, 'Source:' and the details of where the illustration came from. If possible, and definitely if your work is going to be published, you should obtain written permission from the creator of the illustration to reuse their work.

Example

The magnificent ruins of Dunstanburgh Castle (Figure 1) stand on a promontory jutting out into the North Sea near Embleton in Northumberland.

Figure 1. Dunstanburgh Castle, Northumberland (Source: Richard Pears)

The castle was built for Thomas, Earl of Lancaster, between 1313 and 1322, but was in ruins by the end of the sixteenth century …

Section C
How to quote, paraphrase and summarise

Setting out quotations

Quotations should be relevant to your arguments and used judiciously in your text. Excessive use of quotations can disrupt the flow of your writing and prevent you from demonstrating your understanding and analysis of the sources you have read. Your tutor will prefer to read your own interpretation of the evidence.

Bear in mind that **direct quotations** are also counted in your assignment's total word count.

Short direct quotations (up to two or three lines) should be enclosed in quotation marks (single or double – be consistent) and included in the body of your text. Give the author, date, page number (if available) or URL that the quotation was taken from. When citing direct quotations from sources without pagination (for example, ebooks, online journal articles, web pages), use the information that you have to help the reader locate the quotation. For example, you may use a paragraph number if provided, or you can count down paragraphs from the beginning of the document.

Examples

'If you need to illustrate the idea of nineteenth-century America as a land of opportunity, you could hardly improve on the life of Albert Michelson' (Bryson, 2004, p. 156).

Lomotey (2018, para. 4) said 'the children remained calm like professionals'.

Longer quotations should be entered as a separate paragraph and indented from the main text. Quotation marks are not required.

Example

King describes the intertwining of fate and memory in many evocative passages, such as:

> So the three of them rode towards their end of the Great Road, while summer lay all about them, breathless as a gasp. Roland looked up and saw something that made him forget all about the Wizard's Rainbow. It was his mother, leaning out of her apartment's bedroom window: the oval of her face surrounded by the timeless gray stone of the castle's west wing!
>
> (King, 1997, pp. 553–554)

Quoting material not in English

You should always quote in the language which appears in the source that you are reading. Cite the original author and use quotation marks (or indent for longer quotes as above).

Example

'… que nunca sabemos lo que tenemos hasta que se nos ha escapado' (Delibes, 2010).

If quoting from a translated work, you should cite the original author and quote the text in the language in which it appears in the item you are reading.

Example

In-text citation

'Daniel realised that his future was inextricably linked with his village' (Delibes, 2013).

Reference list

Delibes, M. (2013) *The path*. Translated by B. Haycraft and J. Haycraft. London: Dolphin Books.

If you translate some foreign-language text into English yourself and include it in your work, you should not present this as a quotation. However, you must acknowledge the original source.

Example

In-text citation

Delibes (2010, p. 56) notes that you do not know what you have until it is gone.

Reference list

Delibes, M. (2010) *El camino*. Madrid: Destino.

Making changes to quotations

Omitting part of a quotation

Indicate this by using three dots … (called an **ellipsis**).

Example

'Drug prevention … efforts backed this up' (Gardner, 2007, p. 49).

Inserting your own, or different, words into a quotation

Put them in square brackets [ ].

Example

'In this field [crime prevention], community support officers …' (Higgins, 2008, p. 17).

Pointing out an error in a quotation

Do not correct the error; instead write **[sic]**.

Example

Williams (2008, p. 86) noted that 'builders maid [*sic*] bricks'.

Retaining/modernising historical spellings

Decide to either retain the original spelling or modernise the spelling, and note this in your text.

Examples

'Hast thou not removed one Grain of Dirt or Rhubbish?' (Kent, 1727, p. 2).

'Have you not removed one grain of dirt or rubbish?' (Kent, 1727, p. 2, spelling modernised).

Emphasising part of a quotation

Put the words you want to emphasise in italics and state that you have added the emphasis.

Example

'Large numbers of *women* are more prepared to support eco-friendly projects' (Denby, 2014, p. 78, my emphasis).

If the original text uses italics, state that the italics are in the original source.

Example

'The dictionary is based on *rigorous analysis* of the grammar of the language' (Soanes, 2015, p. 2, original emphasis).

Paraphrasing

When you **paraphrase**, you express someone else's writing in your own words, usually to achieve greater clarity. This is an alternative way of referring to an author's ideas or arguments without using direct quotations from their text. Used properly, it has the added benefit of fitting more neatly into your own style of writing and allows you to demonstrate that you really do understand what the author is saying. However, you must ensure that you do not change the original meaning, and you must still cite and reference your source of information.

Example

Harrison (2007, p. 48) clearly distinguishes between the historical growth of the larger European nation states and the roots of their languages and linguistic development, particularly during the fifteenth and sixteenth centuries. At this time, imperial goals and outward expansion were paramount for many of the countries, and the effects of spending on these activities often led to internal conflict.

Note that if you are paraphrasing ideas from a specific page or pages, you should include page references in your citation so that your reader can locate the original text, as in the Harrison example above.

Summarising

When you **summarise**, you provide a brief statement of the main points of an article, **web page**, chapter or book. This brief statement is known as a summary. It differs from paraphrasing in that it only lists the main topics or headings, with most of the detailed information being left out.

Example

Nevertheless, one important study (Harrison, 2007) looks closely at the historical and linguistic links between European races and cultures over the past five hundred years.

Section D
How to reference

Points to note

Students often find it difficult to differentiate between the terms **reference list** and **bibliography**.

The reference list is the detailed list of **references** cited in your assignment. It includes the full bibliographical information on sources so that the reader can identify and locate the work/item.

A bibliography also provides a detailed list of references, but includes background readings or other material you may have consulted, but not cited, in your text.

You should always check with your tutors whether they require you to include a reference list, a bibliography or both (where you would provide a reference list and a separate bibliography of background readings). Either way, both are located at the end of your essay/piece of work. In the Harvard system, they are always arranged in alphabetical order by the author's surname/family name or, when there is no author, by title. For **web pages** where no author or title is apparent, the **URL** address should be used.

The fundamental points are that the reference links with your **citation** and includes enough information for the reader to be able to readily find the source again.

Example

In-text citation

In a recently published survey (Hill, Smith and Reid, 2018, p. 93), the authors argue that …

Reference list

Hill, P., Smith, R. and Reid, L. (2018) *Education in the 21st century*. London: Educational Research Press.

It is important that in your references, you follow the format exactly for all sources, as shown in each example. This includes following the instructions consistently regarding the use of capital letters, typeface and punctuation.

Using referencing software

Many library catalogues and subscription databases have facilities for you to save bibliographic information about sources and export this to use in your assignments. Ask your library staff about this, as it will ensure that you have all of the relevant information, such as volume and page numbers, required to produce a reference at the end of your work, though you will usually need to rearrange the elements of the reference to the referencing style that you are using.

If you are working on a long assignment such as a dissertation or thesis with scores of references to save, or if you are likely to use references to the same sources in several pieces of work (for example, journal articles you are writing), you may wish to use referencing software. There are many products available, including EndNote, RefWorks, Mendeley and Zotero. Each has a range of functions in addition to storing references. Some products will convert your references into different referencing styles, if, for example, a tutor wishes you to use a different style to other tutors, or if you are writing for a journal that has its own house style. Some of the products also enable you to tag or add comments to sources and to share lists or comments with your colleagues. Your institution may have a preferred product and provide guidance to use this, or there are many guides to referencing software available online.

There are also referencing generators freely available online. We advise that you use these cautiously, and ask tutors and librarians if they are good enough for academic work. Referencing software that your institution subscribes to (for example Endnote and RefWorks) generally provides accurate references, but some free online reference generators have, in the authors' experience, provided incorrect citations and this led to some students being penalised for using incorrect references in their work.

Non-English naming conventions

Across the world, there are several practices for naming individual people, including given name followed by family name (for example, John Smith), family name followed by given name (for example, Smith John), given name alone (for example, John) and given name followed by father's name (for example, John son of James). Within one country, there may be several naming conventions employed by different ethnic groups.

When referencing names of authors in your work, you may be required to use a

preferred naming convention. If in doubt, ask for advice from tutors or publishers, or copy the authors' expressions of their names. The principle followed in *Cite them right* (as with other authorities) is to place the family name first in the citation, followed by the initials of given names. The following examples show the complexity of this issue.

Arabic names

The given name precedes the family name. For example, Najīb Maḥfūz would be referenced as:

Example

Maḥfūz, N. (1980) *Afrāḥ al-qubbah* (Wedding song). al-Fajjālah: Maktabat Miṣr.

Yusuf al-Qaradawi would be referenced as:

Example

Qaradawi, Y. (2003) *The lawful and the prohibited in Islam*. London: Al-Birr Foundation.

Tariq Ramadan would be referenced as:

Example

Ramadan, T. (2008) *Radical reform: Islamic ethics and liberation*. Oxford: Oxford University Press.

When a man has completed the Hajj pilgrimage to Mecca, he may include Hajji in his name (for example, Ragayah Hajji Mat Zin). Follow the order for the person's name given in the publication. For example, Ragayah Hajji Mat Zin would be referenced as:

Example

Zin, R. H. M. (2008) *Corporate governance: role of independent non-executive directors*. Bangi: Institut Kajian Malaysia dan Antarabangsa, Universiti Kebangsaan Malaysia.

Burmese names

Individuals are usually referenced by the first element of their name. For example, Aung San Suu Kyi would be referenced as:

Example

Aung, S.S.K. (1991) *Freedom from fear and other writings*. London: Viking.

Chinese names

Traditionally, the family name is the first element of the individual's name, and when citing use this first, as with Western names. For example, Hu Sen appears as Sen Hu in Western convention on the book title page, but in Chinese tradition would be referenced as:

Example

Hu, S. (2001) *Lecture notes on Chern-Simons-Witten theory*. Singapore and River Edge, NJ: World Scientific.

Zhang Boshu would be referenced as:

Example

Zhang, B. (1994) *Marxism and human sociobiology: the perspective of economic reforms in China*. Albany, NY: State University of New York Press.

If the author has adopted the convention of placing family name last, invert the elements

as with Western names. For example, Sophia Tang would be referenced as:

Example

Tang, S. (2009) *Electronic consumer contracts in the conflict of laws*. Oxford: Hart Publishing.

Indian names

The given name precedes the family name. For example, Mohandas Gandhi would be referenced as:

Example

Gandhi, M.K. (1927) *An autobiography, or, the story of my experiments with truth*. Translated from the original in Gujarati by M. Desai. Ahmedabad: Navajivan Press.

Japanese names

The family name precedes the given name. For example, Kenzaburō Ōe would be referenced as:

Example

Ōe, K. (1994) *The pinch runner memorandum*. Armonk, NY: M.E. Sharpe.

Note that many Japanese authors are known by given name then family name (for example, Kenzaburō Ōe).

Malaysian names

Malay names may have a given name followed by a patronym or father's name (for example, Nik Safiah Nik Ismail). Some names may have the family name followed by given names.

Portuguese names

In Portuguese naming conventions, individuals have a given name followed by their mother's family name and then their father's family name. Reference the father's family name first. For example, Armando Gonçalves Pereira would be referenced as:

For names with particles (for example, de), reference this after the initials of the given names. For example, André Luiz de Souza Filgueira would be referenced as:

Spanish names

Traditionally, Spanish/Latin American individuals have a given name followed by their father's family name and then their mother's family name. When referencing these compound names, use the father's family name, following conventions for Western, Arabic and many other naming styles. For example, Pedro Vallina Martínez would be referenced as:

Thai names

The given name is followed by the family name. For example, Piti Disyatat would be referenced as:

Vietnamese names

Individuals are referenced by their family name, the first element of their names. For example, Võ Nguyên Giáp would be referenced as:

Names with particles/prefixes

These are names that include, for example, d', de, de los, le, van and von.

It is difficult to provide definitive examples for all names with particles/prefixes, as each language has its own rules. As mentioned above, where possible, copy the authors' own expressions of their names from the publication you are viewing, and if in any doubt use the internet or library catalogues to confirm the details.

Elements that you may need to include in your references

Generally, the elements for inclusion for any source should be self-evident. Use the 'citation order' listed with the examples to help you identify the elements you should be looking for. When referencing some of the most commonly used sources, try the following:

♦ *For books*: look on the title page or back of the title page (verso)
♦ *For printed journal articles*: look at the beginning of the article or at the table of contents of the journal issue
♦ *For electronic journal articles*: look at the top of the first page (before or after the article title)
♦ *For web pages*: look at the top and bottom of the first page, the logos and, for the URL, in the **address bar** at the top of your screen

Authors/editors

♦ When referencing four or more authors/ editors in academic assignments, you should reference the first name followed by **et al.** (meaning 'and others') – for example, Harris, G.R. *et al.* (2016). This replicates your citation (see 'Citing four or more authors/editors' in Section B), unless your institution requires you to list all authors
♦ If you are writing for a publication, you should follow the editor's guidelines, as you may be required to name all the authors in your reference list, regardless of the number, to ensure that each author's contribution is recognised
♦ Put the surname/family name first, followed by the initial(s) of given names – for example, Hill, P.L.

NB For non-English names, see 'Non-English naming conventions' on page 18.

♦ Some publications are written/produced by corporate bodies or organisations, and you can use this name as the author – for example, the National Trust (see also the guidance given in 'Citing a corporate author' in Section B). Note that the corporate author may also be the publisher
♦ If the publication is compiled by an editor or editors, signify this by using the abbreviation (ed.) or (eds) – for example, Parker, G. and Rouxeville, A. (eds)
♦ Do not use 'Anon.' if the author/editor is anonymous or no author/editor can be identified. Use the title of the work

Year/date of publication

♦ Give the year of publication in round brackets after the author/editor's name – for example, Smith, L. (2014)

- If no date of publication can be identified, use (no date) – for example, Smith, L. (no date)

Title

- Use the title as given, together with the subtitle (if any) – for example, *Studying and working in Spain: a student guide*

Edition

- Only include the edition number if it is not the first edition. Only include the edition number if it is not the first edition. If it is a revised edition, write rev. edn. See also Section E1.1
- Edition is abbreviated to edn (to avoid confusion with the abbreviation ed. or eds for editor or editors) – for example, 3rd edn, rev. edn, 4th rev. edn

Place of publication and publisher

- Only required for printed books, reports, etc.
- Separate the place of publication and the publisher with a colon – for example, London: Initial Music Publishing
- If there is more than one place of publication, include only the most local
- For places of publication in the United States, add the abbreviated US state name (unless otherwise obvious) – for example, Cambridge, MA: Harvard University Press
- If a source is unpublished, please refer to Section E25

Series/volumes (for books)

- Include series and individual volume number, if relevant, after the publisher – for example, Oxford: Clio Press (World Bibliographical Series, 60)

Issue information (for journals, magazines and newspapers)

- When provided, you need to include the following information in the order:
  - volume number
  - issue/part number
  - date or season

For example, 87(3), or 19 July, or summer.

Page numbers

- Page numbers are only required in the reference list for chapters in books, and serial (journal/magazine/newspaper) articles
- The abbreviation p. is used for single pages and pp. for more than one – for example, London: River Press, pp. 90–99. Note that page numbers are not elided (for example, pp. 90–9), but written in full

ISBNs

- Although International Standard Book Numbers (ISBNs) represent unique identifiers for books and eliminate confusion about editions and reprints, they are not commonly used in references

Uniform Resource Locators (URLs)

- When using the URL address for web pages, you can shorten it, as long as the route remains clear
- After the URL, include the date you accessed the online source – for example, (Accessed: 14 Feb 2015) – unless there is a digital object identifier (DOI)

Digital object identifiers (DOIs)

♦ DOIs tag individual digital (online) sources. These sources can range from ebooks and journal articles to conference papers and presentations. They include a number identifying the publisher, work and issue information. The following example shows how the DOI replaces the URL in the reference. Note that because the DOI is the permanent identifier for the source, it is not necessary to include an accessed date. In your reference lists, DOI is always written in lower case

Example

Horch, E.P. and Zhou, J. (2012) 'Charge-coupled device speckle observations of binary stars', *Astronomical Journal*, 136, pp. 312–322. doi:10.1088/0004-6256/136/1/312.

♦ You or your reader can locate a source by entering its DOI in an internet search engine

Journal articles using article numbers and DOIs

♦ Some publishers now use article numbers instead of issue and page numbers
♦ The reference to the article includes the number of pages in the article
♦ Note that to see the page numbers, you may need to open the PDF version of the article. If this is not available, you may need to refer to the section number, or even number the

paragraphs, and cite one of these for your reference (for example, section 2.2, paragraph 3)

Example

Bond, J.W. (2008) 'On the electrical characteristics of latent finger mark corrosion of brass', *J. Phys. D: Appl. Phys*, 41, 125502 (10pp). doi:10.1088/0022-3727/41/12/125502.

Social networking websites

Hashtags # are a common sight now on Twitter, Facebook, Instagram, Crowdfire, Tumblr, Viber, LinkedIn, The Dots and other platforms, and you may wonder how to cite and reference them. The answer is that you do not. This is because, just like your research on a database, finding and searching with the right hashtag is part of your research methodology. So, you can simply describe it in your text: for example, 'During the 2015 migrant crisis in Europe I searched *Twitter* and *Instagram* for the hashtags #refugees, #migrants and #asylumseekers appearing between September 1, 2015 and October 15, 2015'. Your reader can then try to replicate the search if they wish to follow your evidence. To reference any tweets, posts or photographs that you find on social networking sites you should follow the relevant examples.

If you wish to refer to a specific time within a video, use a time code in your in-text reference, with the format minutes:seconds. See the example in Section E10.8d.

Non-Roman scripts

You may need to reference sources that are not in Roman script as part of your work, for example Chinese and Arabic sources. It is recommended that you provide a translation of the title of the work in square brackets after the title in the original script.

You may also need to transliterate from the original language into Roman script. Chinese is transliterated into Pinyin and syllables are aggregated according to a Modern Chinese word dictionary. Arabic is transliterated according to the Library of Congress transliteration.

Example: Chinese book with Chinese script

Pu, S. (1982) 聊斋志异 [*Strange stories of Liaozhai*]. Taiyuan: Shanxi Renmin Chubanshe.

Example: Chinese book with transliterated script in Pinyin

Pu, S. (1982) *Liao zhai zhi yi* [*Strange stories of Liaozhai*]. Taiyuan: Shanxi Renmin Chubanshe.

Example: Arabic books with Arabic script

Hussein, T. (1973) المجموعة الكاملة لمؤلفات الدكتور طه حسين [*The complete collection of Dr. Taha Hussein's works*]. Beirut: Dār al-Kitāb al-Lubnānī.

Example: Arabic book with Romanised script

Hussein, T. (1973) *al-Majmū'ah al-kāmilah li-mu'allafāt al-Duktūr Tāhā Husayn* [*The complete collection of Dr. Taha Hussein's works*]. Beirut: Dār al-Kitāb al-Lubnānī.

Sample text and reference list using Harvard (author-date) referencing style

NB This text makes extensive use of references for illustrative purposes only.

Text

A comparative study conducted by Bowman and Jenkins (2011), on properties built within the last twenty years and older houses, clearly illustrated the financial and environmental benefits of investing time and money in improving home insulation. A recent survey (Thermascan, 2012) and video (Norman, 2012) underlined that as much as a third of the heat generated in homes is lost through the walls or the roof as a result of poor insulation.

An article by Hallwood (2016) was fulsome in its praise of the work of organisations such as Tadea and the Energy Saving Trust in producing public information packs providing guidance on cavity wall and loft insulation. Further studies show that the amount of energy needed to heat our homes can have an ever-increasing impact on both the environment and family finances (BBC, 2017; Department of the Environment, 2018; Hampson and Carr, 2017). However, Kirkwood, Harper and Jones (2011, pp. 49–58) criticised the conflicting information regarding installation costs and the subsequent savings to be made.

Energy companies have emphasised the benefits for customers to 'supply their own energy with technologies such as solar panels and ground source heat pumps' (British Gas, 2012, p. 8). However, the conflict between expensive sustainable energy and family economic constraints has been examined by Young (2012). What remains clear is that by finding ways in which we can significantly reduce our home running costs, we can simultaneously substantially reduce our carbon footprint (Strathearn, 2013).

Reference list

NB This list incorporates bubble captions to identify the type of source being referenced, which are used for illustrative purposes only.

BBC (2017) *Energy use and the environment*. Available at: http://www.bbc.co.uk/energy (Accessed: 18 August 2018).

web page — see Section E10

Bowman, R. and Jenkins, S. (2011) 'Financial and environmental issues and comparisons in new and old build properties', in Harris, P. (ed.) *Studies on property improvements and environmental concerns in modern Britain*. London: Pinbury, pp. 124–145.

chapter in edited book — see Section E1.10

British Gas (2012) *A green light to save you more*. Eastbourne: British Gas.

company pamphlet/booklet — see Section E1.18

Department of the Environment (2018) *Energy and the environment in Britain today*. Available at: http://www.doe.gov.uk (Accessed: 18 August 2018).

online government report — see Section E13.2

Hallwood, L. (2016) 'The good work of sustainable energy organisations continues', *The Times*, 20 June, pp. 20–21.

electronic or print newspaper article — see Section E2.4

Hampson, P. and Carr, L. (2017) 'The impact of rising energy use on the environment: a five-year study', *Journal of Energy and Environmental Issues*, 53(5), pp. 214–231.

(electronic or print journal article)
see Section E2.1

Kirkwood, L., Harper, S. and Jones, T. (2011) *The DIY culture in Britain: costs for homes and the nation*. Available at: http://www.amazon.co.uk/kindle-ebooks (Accessed: 18 August 2018).

(signifies the date you viewed the source)

(ebook) — see Section E1.3

Norman, L. (2012) *Heat loss in houses*. Available at: http://www.youtube.com/watchheatlosshouseclm (Accessed: 18 August 2018).

(YouTube video) — see Section E22.5

Strathearn, G. (2013) *Energy and environmental issues for the 21st century*. Basingstoke: Palgrave Macmillan.

(print or electronic book)
see Section E1

Thermascan (2012) *A report into costs and benefits relating to heat loss in homes*. Birmingham: Thermascan.

(printed report) — see Section E8

Young, L. (2012) *Sustaining our energy: challenges and conflicts*. Available at: http://books.google.com (Accessed: 18 August 2018).

(ebook) — see Section E1.3

Top 10 tips

1. *Be aware*: if you don't already know, check with your tutor which referencing style you are expected to use.
2. *Be positive*: used properly, references strengthen your writing, demonstrating that you have spent time researching and digesting material and produced your own opinions and arguments.
3. *Be decisive* about the best way to cite your sources and how you balance your use of direct quotations, paraphrasing and summarising (read about these in Sections B and C).
4. *Be willing to ask for help*: library/ learning resource staff can offer support with referencing and academic skills.
5. *Be organised*: prepare well and keep a record of all potentially useful sources as you find them.
6. *Be prepared*: read Sections A to D before you begin your first assignment.
7. *Be consistent*: once you have established the referencing style required, use it consistently throughout your piece of work.
8. *Be patient*: make time and take your time to ensure that your referencing is accurate.
9. *Be clear*: clarify the type of source you are referencing and check the appropriate section of *Cite them right* for examples.
10. *Be thorough*: check through your work and your references before you submit your assignment, ensuring that your citations all match with a full reference, and vice versa.

Checklist of what to include in your reference list for the most common information sources

	Author	Year of publication	Title of article/chapter	Title of publication	Issue information (volume/part numbers if available)	Place of publication	Publisher	Edition	Page number(s)	URL/DOI	Date accessed/downloaded
Book	✓	✓		✓		✓	✓	✓			
Chapter from book	✓	✓	✓	✓		✓	✓	✓	✓		
Ebook	✓	✓		✓						URL if required	✓
Journal article (print and electronic)	✓	✓	✓	✓	✓				✓	DOI if required	
Web page	✓	✓		✓						✓	✓
Newspaper article (print and electronic)	✓	✓	✓	✓	✓				✓		

Section E
Harvard referencing style

NB Before looking at specific examples in this section, you should ensure that you have read Sections B, C and D.

E1 Books (including ebooks, comic and motion books, and graphic novels)

NB For audiobooks, see Section E1.4.

The increasing availability of ebooks in identical form to print has rendered the distinction between the versions unnecessary. If the online source includes all the elements seen in print versions (that is, publication details, edition and page numbers), reference in the same way as print.

Only include the edition number if it is not the first or revised edition (see Section E1.1)

E1.1 Printed books

Citation order:

♦ Author/editor
♦ Year of publication (in round brackets)
♦ Title (in italics)
♦ Place of publication: Publisher
♦ Series and volume number (where relevant)

Example: book with one author

In-text citation

According to Bell (2014), the most important part of the research process is …

Reference list

Bell, J. (2014) *Doing your research project*. Maidenhead: Open University Press.

Example: book with two or three authors

In-text citation

Goddard and Barrett (2016, p. 17) noted that 'teenagers are vulnerable'.

Reference list

Goddard, J. and Barrett, S. (2016) *The health needs of young people leaving care*. Norwich: University of East Anglia, School of Social Work and Psychosocial Studies.

Example: book with four or more authors

In-text citation

This was proved by Young *et al.* (2015, pp. 21–23) …

Reference list

Young, H.D. *et al.* (2015) *Sears and Zemansky's university physics*. San Francisco, CA: Addison-Wesley.

Or, if your institution requires referencing of all named authors:

Young, H.D., Freedman, R.A., Sandin, T.R. and Ford, A.L. (2015) *Sears and Zemansky's university physics*. San Francisco, CA: Addison-Wesley.

Example: book with an editor

In-text citation

The formation of professions was examined in Prest (2014).

Reference list

Prest, W. (ed.) (2014) *The professions in early modern England*. London: Croom Helm.

Example: book with author(s) and editor(s)

In-text citation

Orksun (2017, p. 22) stated …

Reference list

Orksun, B. (2017) *Healthcare management*. 7th UK edn. Edited by B. Jones and D. Kirk. London: Medical Press Ltd.

Example: book with no author

In-text citation

The Percy tomb has been described as 'one of the masterpieces of medieval European art' (*Treasures of Britain and treasures of Ireland*, 1990, p. 84).

Reference list

Treasures of Britain and treasures of Ireland (1990) London: Reader's Digest Association Ltd.

For second, later and revised editions use the following:

Citation order:

♦ Author/editor
♦ Year of publication (in round brackets)
♦ Title (in italics)
♦ Edition (edition number and/or rev. edn.)
♦ Place of publication: Publisher

♦ Series and volume number (where relevant)

(See also Section E1.2)

Example: later edition

In-text citation

The excellent study by Waugh (2015) …

Reference list

Waugh, D. (2015) *The new wider world*. 5th edn. Cheltenham: Nelson Thornes.

Examples: revised edition

In-text citation

The beautiful work by Moxon (2013) …

Reference list

Moxon, J. (2013) *The art of joinery*. Rev. edn. Fort Mitchell, KY: Lost Art Press.

In-text citation

Steinberg's analysis (2016, p. 45) …

Reference list

Steinberg, E.L. (2016) *Court music of Henry V*. 4th rev. edn. Oxford: Oxford University Press.

E1.2   Reprint and facsimile editions

For reprints and facsimile editions of older books, the year of the original publication (not the place of publication or publisher) is given, along with the full publication details of the reprint or facsimile.

Citation order:

♦ Author/editor
♦ Year of original publication (in round brackets)
♦ Title of book (in italics)
♦ Reprint or Facsimile of the …

- Place of reprint or facsimile publication: reprint or facsimile publisher
- Year of reprint or facsimile

Example: reprint

In-text citation

One of the first critics of obfuscation (David, 1968) …

Reference list

David, M. (1968) *Towards honesty in public relations*. Reprint. London: B.Y. Jove, 1990.

Example: facsimile

In-text citation

… his perfect blend of adventure, magic and fantasy (Tolkien, 1937).

Reference list

Tolkien, J.R.R. (1937) *The Hobbit*. Facsimile of the 1st edn. London: HarperCollins, 2016.

E1.3 Ebooks

When an ebook looks like a printed book, with publication details and pagination, you should reference as a printed book (see Section E1.1).

Citation order:

- Author/editor
- Year of publication (in round brackets)
- Title of book (in italics)
- Place of publication: Publisher

Example

In-text citation

In their analysis, Hremiak and Hudson (2011, pp. 36–39) …

Reference list

Hremiak, A. and Hudson, T. (2011) *Understanding learning and teaching in secondary schools*. Harlow: Pearson Longman.

On some personal electronic devices, specific ebook pagination details may not be available, so use the information you do have, such as loc, %, chapter/page/paragraph – for example, (Richards, 2012, 67%), (Winters, 2011, ch. 4, p. 12).

Citation order:

- Author/editor
- Year of publication (in round brackets)
- Title of book (in italics)
- DOI *or* Available at: URL (Accessed: date)

Example

In-text citation

Arthur's argument with the council was interrupted by the Vogon Constructor Fleet (Adams, 1979, loc 876).

Reference list

Adams, D. (1979) *The hitchhiker's guide to the galaxy*. Available at: http://www.amazon.co.uk/kindle-ebooks (Accessed: 29 January 2018).

E1.4 Audiobooks

Citation order:

♦ Author/editor
♦ Year of publication/release (in round brackets)
♦ Title of book (in italics)
♦ Narrated by (if required)
♦ Available at: URL
♦ (Accessed: date)

Example

In-text citation
Covering 2000 years of medical history, Cunningham (2007) …

Reference list
Cunningham, A. (2007) *The making of modern medicine*. Available at: http://www.audiogo.com/uk/ (Accessed: 18 March 2018).

E1.5 Historical books in online collections

If you are reading a scanned version of the printed book, complete with publication information and page numbers, reference in the same manner as the print book (see Section E1.1). This includes books available in subscription collections, such as Early European Books and Eighteenth Century Collections Online, and freely available sites, including Google Books, Internet Archive and HathiTrust Digital Library.

Some early printed books do not have a publisher as they were privately printed. Record the information given in the book in your reference.

Citation order:

♦ Author/editor
♦ Year of publication (in round brackets)

♦ Title of publication (in italics)
♦ Place of publication: printing statement

Example

In-text citation
Adam's measured plans (Adam, 1764) …

Reference list
Adam, R. (1764) *Ruins of the palace of the Emperor Diocletian at Spalatro in Dalmatia*. London: Printed for the author.

E1.6 Ancient texts

If citing an ancient text that existed before the invention of printing, reference it as a manuscript (see Section E30) or reference the published (and translated) edition you have read.

Citation order:

♦ Author
♦ Year of publication (in round brackets)
♦ Title of book (in italics)
♦ Translated from the [original language] by … (if relevant)
♦ Edition (only include the edition number if it is not the first edition)
♦ Place of publication: Publisher
♦ Series and volume number (where relevant)

Example

In-text citation
The classic tale by Homer (1991) …

Reference list
Homer (1991) *The Iliad*. Translated from the Greek by R. Fagles. Introduction and notes by B. Knox. London: Penguin Books.

E1.7 Translated books

Reference the translation you have read, not the original work.

Citation order:

- Author/editor
- Year of translated publication (in round brackets)
- Title of book (in italics)
- Translated from the [original language] by …
- Place of publication: Publisher

Example

In-text citation

Delibes (2013, pp. 4–11) vividly describes childhood in a Spanish village …

Reference list

Delibes, M. (2013) *The path*. Translated from the Spanish by G. Haycraft and R. Haycraft. London: Dolphin Books.

E1.8 Books in languages other than English

If referencing a book in its original language, give the title exactly as shown in the book.

Citation order:

- Author/editor
- Year of publication (in round brackets)
- Title of book (in italics)
- Place of publication: Publisher

Example

In-text citation

Her depiction of middle-class lifestyles (Beauvoir, 1966) …

Reference list

Beauvoir, S. de (1966) *Les belles images.* Paris: Gallimard.

E1.9 Text extracts from an authored book

You may be given an extract from a book that is less than a whole chapter.

Citation order:

- Author
- Year of publication of book (in round brackets)
- Title of book (in italics)
- Place of publication: Publisher
- Extract Page numbers of extract

Example

In-text citation

At least one author (Fenwick, 2014, pp. 160–164) …

Reference list

Fenwick, H. (2014) *Civil liberties and human rights*. London: Routledge Cavendish. Extract pp. 157–168.

E1.10 Chapters/sections of edited books

Citation order:

- Author of the chapter/section (surname followed by initials)
- Year of publication (in round brackets)
- Title of chapter/section (in single quotation marks)
- 'in' plus author/editor of book
- Title of book (in italics)
- Place of publication: Publisher
- Page reference

Example

In-text citation

The view proposed by Franklin (2012, p. 88) …

Reference list

Franklin, A.W. (2012) 'Management of the problem', in Smith, S.M. (ed.) *The maltreatment of children*. Lancaster: MTP, pp. 83–95.

E1.11 Multi-volume works

E1.11a Volumes of whole multi-volume works

Citation order:

- Author/editor
- Year of publication (in round brackets)
- Title of book (in italics)
- Volumes (in round brackets)
- Place of publication: Publisher

Example

In-text citation

Butcher's (1961) guide …

Reference list

Butcher, R. (1961) *A new British flora* (4 vols). London: Leonard Hill.

When citing a single volume of a multi-volume work, add the title of the relevant volume as a subtitle after the title.

Example

In-text citation

Part 3 of Butcher's work (1961) …

Reference list

Butcher, R. (1961) *A new British flora. Part 3: lycopodiaceae to salicaceae*. London: Leonard Hill.

E1.11b Chapters in multi-volume works

Citation order:

- Author of the chapter/section (surname followed by initials)
- Year of publication (in round brackets)
- Title of chapter/section (in single quotation marks)
- 'in' plus author/editor of book
- Title of book (in italics)
- Place of publication: Publisher
- Page numbers of chapter/section

Example

In-text citation

In analysing ports (Jackson, 2000) …

Reference list

Jackson, G. (2000) 'Ports 1700–1840', in Clark, P. (ed.) *Cambridge urban history of Britain: Vol. 2 1540–1840*. Cambridge: Cambridge University Press, pp. 705–731.

E1.11c Collected works

Citation order:

- Author/editor
- Year(s) of publication of collection (in round brackets)
- Title of book (in italics)
- Volumes (in round brackets)
- Place of publication: Publisher

Example

In-text citation

His collected works (Jung, 1989–1995) provide …

Reference list

Jung, C.G. (1989–1995) *Gesammelte Werke* (24 vols). Olten: Walter Verlag.

E1.12 Anthologies

Citation order:

- Editor/compiler of anthology (surname followed by initials)
- Year of publication (in round brackets)
- Title of book (in italics)
- Place of publication: Publisher

Example

In-text citation

In his collection of humorous poems, West (1989) …

Reference list

West, C. (compiler and illustrator) (1989) *The beginner's book of bad behaviour*. London: Beaver Books.

For *a line of a poem/prayer within an anthology*, use the following citation order:

- Author of the poem/prayer (surname followed by initials)
- Year of publication (in round brackets)
- Title of poem/prayer (in single quotation marks)
- 'in' plus author/editor/compiler of book
- Title of book (in italics)
- Place of publication: Publisher
- Page reference

Example

In-text citation

'The lion made a sudden stop

He let the dainty morsel drop' (Belloc, 1989, p. 89).

Reference list

Belloc, H. (1989) 'Jim', in West, C. (compiler and illustrator) *The beginner's book of bad behaviour*. London: Beaver Books, pp. 88–92.

E1.13 Lines within plays

Citation order:

- Author (surname followed by initials)
- Year of publication (in round brackets)
- Title (in italics)
- Edition information
- Place of publication: Publisher
- Act.scene: line

Example

In-text citation

'I prithee do not mock me fellow student' (Shakespeare, 1980, 1.2: 177).

Reference list

Shakespeare, W. (1980) *Hamlet*. Edited by Spencer, T.J.B. London: Penguin, 1.2: 177.

NB If referencing *a live performance*, see Section E21.

E1.14 Bibliographies

Although print **bibliographies** have been largely replaced by electronic sources for current information, they may provide commentary and highlight earlier writings.

Citation order:

- Author/editor
- Year of publication (in round brackets)
- Title (in italics)
- Edition (only include the edition number if it is not the first edition)
- Place of publication: Publisher
- Series and volume number (where relevant)

Example

In-text citation

Ushpol (1958) noted the key research …

Reference list

Ushpol, R. (1958) *Select bibliography of South African autobiographies*. Cape Town: University of Cape Town, School of Librarianship.

E1.15   Printed reference books

The citation order for these reference sources generally follows the guidance given in E1.1. However, when distinct authors or editors are identified for specific sections, follow the guidance given in E1.10.

Citation order:

◆ Author/editor
◆ Year of publication (in round brackets)
◆ Title (in italics)
◆ Place of publication: Publisher
◆ Series and volume number (where relevant)

Example

In-text citation

Beal (2008, p. 171) identified the meaning of 'Folio'.

Reference list

Beal, P. (2008) 'Folio', *A dictionary of English manuscript terminology: 1450 to 2000*. Oxford: Oxford University Press.

Example: with author and editor

In-text citation

Byrd (2011) examined …

Reference list

Byrd, D. (2011) 'Phonetics', in Hogan, P.C. (ed.) *The Cambridge encyclopedia of the language sciences*. Cambridge: Cambridge University Press.

Examples: with no authors

In-text citations

The definition (*Collins beginner's German dictionary*, 2014, p. 21) …

Reference list

Collins beginner's German dictionary (2014) New York: Collins.

Example: editor but no section authors

In-text citation

The financial analysis ('Balance of payments', 2008) …

Reference list

'Balance of payments' (2008) in Darity, W.A. (ed.) *International Encyclopedia of the Social Sciences: Volume 1*. 2nd edn. Detroit, MI: Macmillan Reference USA, pp. 238–241.

E1.16 Online reference books

As with other print sources, a growing number of reference books are now available as ebooks or online-only sources. As with other examples where print and online versions exist, be careful to reference the version you have used.

E1.16a Reference sources only available online

There are many online-only dictionaries and thesauri.

Citation order:

- Author/editor (if available)
- Year of publication (in round brackets)
- Title (in single quotation marks)
- Series and volume number (where relevant)
- Available at: URL (Accessed: date)

Example

In-text citation
The definition of 'Citation' (2019) …

Reference list
'Citation' (2019) Available at: https://www.dictionary.com/browse/citation (Accessed: 16 January 2019).

E1.16b Books published in print and online, and updated at different times

In this case, the online version is updated regularly but the print version is not updated until a new edition is published, so the online version differs from the printed version. Replace publication details with:

- DOI *or* Available at: URL (Accessed: date)

Example: printed reference work that is being updated online

In-text citation for print version
Rutherford's contribution (Badash, 2004) …

Reference list for print version
Badash, L. (2004) 'Rutherford, Ernest, Baron Rutherford of Nelson (1871–1937)', in *Oxford dictionary of national biography*. Oxford: Oxford University Press, pp. 381–389.

In-text citation for online version
Rutherford's contribution (Badash, 2008) …

Reference list for online version
Badash, L. (2008) 'Rutherford, Ernest, Baron Rutherford of Nelson (1871–1937)', in *Oxford dictionary of national biography* (2004). Available at: http://www.oxforddnb.com/view/article/35891 (Accessed: 25 January 2019).

E1.17 Sacred texts

E1.17a The Bible

There is a well-established system for citing references from the Bible in your text. This uses the book name, chapter and verse (but not page number, as this will vary between printings). It also avoids stating authors, as the actual authorship of some books is unclear.

NB The publisher and publication date are not required.

Citation order:

- Book of the Bible
- Chapter: verse
- Holy Bible (not in italics)
- Version of the Holy Bible

Example

In-text citation

The Beatitudes (Matthew 5: 3–12) …

Reference list

Matthew 5: 3–12, Holy Bible. New International Edition.

E1.17b   The Torah

Citation order:

♦ Torah (not in italics)
♦ Book
♦ Chapter: verse

Example

In-text citation

The reply (Shemot 3: 14) is the most profound …

Reference list

Torah. Shemot 3: 14.

E1.17c   The Quran

Citation order:

♦ Quran (not in italics)
♦ Surah (or chapter): verse
♦ Year of publication (in round brackets)
♦ Translated by …
♦ Place of publication: Publisher

Example

In-text citation

'And ease for me my task' (Quran 20: 26).

Reference list

Quran 20: 26 (2010) Translated by M. A. S. Abdel-Haleem. Oxford: Oxford University Press.

E1.18   Pamphlets

Citation order:

♦ Author/editor
♦ Year of publication (in round brackets)
♦ Title (in italics)
♦ Place of publication: Publisher
♦ Series and volume number (where relevant)

Example

In-text citation

Bradley's pamphlet (1994) gave instructions in the use of …

Reference list

Bradley, M. (1994) *CD-ROMs: how to set up your workstation*. London: ASLIB.

E1.19   Exhibition catalogues

Citation order:

♦ Author of catalogue
♦ Year (in round brackets)
♦ Title of exhibition (in italics)
♦ Location and date(s) of exhibition
♦ [Exhibition catalogue]

Example

In-text citation

Urbach (2007, p. 8) noted the demands for reform …

Reference list

Urbach, P. (2007) *Reform! Reform! Reform!* Exhibition held at the Reform Club, London 2005–2006 and at Grey College, Durham University, March 2007 [Exhibition catalogue].

E1.20 Event programmes (including printed concert, theatre and sports programmes)

Citation order:
♦ Author of programme (if known, or use performers)
♦ Year (in round brackets)
♦ Title of event (in italics)
♦ Location and date(s) of event
♦ [Event programme]

Example

In-text citation

The Avison Ensemble (2015, p. 2) were formed in 1988.

Reference list

Avison Ensemble (2015) *The concerto in England – Handel and his contemporaries*. The Sage, Gateshead, 9 October [Event programme].

E2 Serials (journal/magazine/ newspaper articles – print and electronic)

Many serials have print and online equivalents (either with all details the same or with small variations, for example page numbers). Or they may just be available online or in print editions. As always, you should reference the version that you are using. Students and tutors can access academic journal articles through password-protected institutional databases, but other readers may not have access to these. Therefore, as long as the serial reference provides enough bibliographic information for the article to be located by the reader, other elements – for example, [Online], database title, and URL – no longer need to be included. However, include the URL or DOI if you are using an article that is only available online (see the example below).

E2.1 Journal articles

Citation order:
♦ Author
♦ Year of publication (in round brackets)
♦ Title of article (in single quotation marks)
♦ Title of journal (in italics – capitalise first letter of each word in title, except for linking words such as and, of, the, for)
♦ Issue information (that is, volume (unbracketed) and, where applicable, supplement or part number, month or season (all in round brackets))
♦ Page reference (if available)

If accessed online:

♦ DOI *or* Available at: URL (Accessed: date)

Example: electronic or print or both

In-text citation

In their review of the literature (Norrie *et al.*, 2012) …

Reference list

Norrie, C. *et al.* (2012) 'Doing it differently? A review of literature on teaching reflective practice across health and social care professions', *Reflective Practice*, 13(4), pp. 565–578.

Or, if your institution requires referencing of all named authors:

Norrie, C., Hammond, J., D'Avray, L., Collington, V. and Fook, J. (2012) 'Doing it differently? A review of literature on teaching reflective practice across health and social care professions', *Reflective Practice*, 13(4), pp. 565–578.

Example: electronic article with DOI

In-text citation
Shirazi's review article (2010) …

Reference list
Shirazi, T. (2010) 'Successful teaching placements in secondary schools: achieving QTS practical handbooks', *European Journal of Teacher Education*, 33(3), pp. 323–326. doi:10.1080/02619761003602246.

Example: electronic article with no print equivalent (URL and no DOI)

In-text citation
Barke and Mowl's excellent study (2016) …

Reference list
Barke, M. and Mowl, G. (2016) 'Málaga – a failed resort of the early twentieth century?', *Journal of Tourism History*, 2(3), pp. 187–212. Available at: http://www.tanfonline.com/full/1755182.2016 (Accessed: 23 April 2018).

If you are specifically referencing the abstract of a journal article, your **citation** would make this clear – for example, 'The abstract highlights … (Rodgers and Baker, 2013, p. 34)'. Note that the reference would follow the same format as for a journal article because the page reference would take the reader to the abstract.

If referencing a whole journal issue, use the following:

Citation order:

- Issue editor (if given)
- Year of publication (in round brackets)
- Title of issue (in single quotation marks)
- Title of journal (in italics – capitalise first letter of each word in title, except for linking words such as and, of, the, for)
- Issue information (that is, volume (unbracketed) and, where applicable, supplement or part number, month or season (all in round brackets))

If accessed online:
- DOI *or* Available at: URL (Accessed: date)

Example: whole journal issue (electronic or print)

In-text citation
In the recent special issue (Harrison, 2018) …

Reference list
Harrison, P.R. (ed.) (2018) 'Alzheimer's – a transmissible disease?', *Trends in Medical Sciences*, 64(3).

NB For electronic whole journal issues with no print equivalent, follow the example above, adding DOI *or* URL (Accessed: date).

For prepublication articles in digital repositories, see Section E7.3.

E2.2 Systematic reviews

Citation order:

- Author (surname followed by initials)
- Year of publication (in round brackets)
- Title and any subtitle (in single quotation marks)
- Database name (in italics)
- Issue number
- Article number (CD …)
- DOI *or* Available at: URL (Accessed: date)

Example: whole journal issue (electronic or print)

In-text citation

Following a systematic review (Pasquali *et al.*, 2018) …

Reference list

Pasquali, S. *et al.* (2018) 'Systemic treatments for metastatic cutaneous melanoma', *Cochrane Database of Systematic Reviews*, 2, CD011123. doi:10.1002/14651858.CD011123.pub2.

E2.3 Magazine articles

Citation order:

- ◆ Author
- ◆ Year of publication (in round brackets)
- ◆ Title of article (in single quotation marks)
- ◆ Title of magazine (in italics – capitalise first letter of each word in title, except for linking words such as and, of, the, for)
- ◆ Issue information (that is, volume (unbracketed) and, where applicable, part number, month or season (all in round brackets))
- ◆ Page reference (if available)

If accessed online:

- ◆ DOI *or* Available at: URL (Accessed: date)

Example: electronic or print article

In-text citation

Bletcher discussed body image (2017, p. 9) …

Reference list

Bletcher, K. (2017) 'Matters of the heart', *Heart Matters,* (August/September), pp. 9–11.

Example: electronic article with no print equivalent (URL and no DOI)

In-text citation

Brealey sought tips from experts … (Brealey, 2016).

Reference list

Brealey, S. (2016) 'Returning to work after a heart attack', *Health of the Heart*, 6(3), pp. 65–72. Available at: https://bhf.org.uk/healthoftheheart/work (Accessed: 14 September 2018).

If referencing a whole magazine issue, use the following:

Citation order:

- ◆ Issue editor (if given)
- ◆ Year of publication (in round brackets)
- ◆ Title of issue (in single quotation marks)
- ◆ Title of magazine (in italics – capitalise first letter of each word in title, except for linking words such as and, of, the, for)
- ◆ Issue information (that is, volume (unbracketed) and, where applicable, part number, month or season (all in round brackets))

If accessed online:

- ◆ DOI *or* Available at: URL (Accessed: date)

Example: whole magazine issue

In-text citation

In the recent special issue (Woods, 2018) …

Reference list

Woods, L.R. (ed.) (2018) 'Searching for dark matter', *Trends in Astronomy*, (June/July).

NB For electronic whole magazine issues with no print equivalent, follow the guidance given in Section E2.1 for electronic whole journal issues using the DOI *or* Available at: URL (Accessed: date).

E2.4   Newspaper articles

Where the author (byline) of a newspaper article is identified, use the following citation order:

♦ Author/byline
♦ Year of publication (in round brackets)
♦ Title of article (in single quotation marks)
♦ Title of newspaper (in italics – capitalise first letter of each word in title, except for linking words such as and, of, the, for)
♦ Edition if required (in round brackets)
♦ Day and month
♦ Page reference (if available)

If accessed online:

♦ DOI *or* Available at: URL (Accessed: date)

Example: electronic or print article

In-text citation
Financial incentives were offered to graduates (Mansell and Bloom, 2018).

Reference list
Mansell, W. and Bloom, A. (2018) '£10,000 carrot to tempt physics experts', *The Guardian*, 20 June, p. 5.

When referencing a *regional newspaper article*, include the edition to distinguish it from others with the same title.

Example: electronic or print regional newspaper article

In-text citation
House prices fell by 2.1 per cent last month (Old, 2019).

Reference list
Old, D. (2019) 'House price gloom', *Evening Chronicle* (Newcastle edn), 26 January, p. 25.

NB Where no author (byline) is given, use the following citation order:

♦ Title of newspaper (in italics – capitalise first letter of each word in title, except for linking words such as and, of, the, for)
♦ Year of publication (in round brackets)
♦ Title of article (in single quotation marks)
♦ Day and month
♦ Page reference

Example: electronic or print article – no author

In-text citation
The article (*The Times*, 2018, p. 7) reported …

Reference list
The Times (2018) 'Bank accounts', 14 June, p. 7.

NB If you are specifically using the online version of a newspaper, which often varies from the print edition (for example, no pagination), then you would reference it using the URL.

Example: printed news articles accessed online

In-text citation

US-led air strikes appeared to be imminent (Roberts and Ackerman, 2013).

Reference list

Roberts, D. and Ackerman, S. (2013) 'US draft resolution allows Obama 90 days for military action against Syria', *The Guardian*, 4 September. Available at: http://www.theguardian.com/world/2013/sep/04/syria-strikes-draftresolution-90-days (Accessed: 9 September 2018).

NB If you are citing several articles published in the same year, use a, b, c and so on after the year – for example, *The Times* (2018a).

If you are referencing *letters* or *leading articles/editorials*, you would note this in your citations. When referencing a *section of a newspaper*, where page numbering may well be the same as in the main newspaper, give the section as a subtitle.

Example: letter

In-text citation

In the opinion of Anderson (2019, p. 7) …

Reference list

Anderson, I. (2019) 'Social media aren't to blame', *The Guardian: Journal*, 9 February, p. 7.

Example: leading article

In-text citation

In the leading article (*The Independent*, 2012, p. 28) …

Reference list

The Independent (2012) 'Grace in defeat', 27 January, p. 28.

Example: section

In-text citation

A recent article (*The Guardian*; G2, 2018, p. 14) …

Reference list

The Guardian: G2 (2018) 'Hope springs eternal', 24 July, p. 14.

If referencing a *whole newspaper issue*, use the following.

Citation order:

♦ Title of newspaper (in italics – capitalise first letter of each word in title, except for linking words such as and, of, the, for)
♦ Year of publication (in round brackets)
♦ Edition if required (in round brackets)
♦ Day and month

If accessed online:

♦ DOI *or* Available at: URL (Accessed: date)

Example: whole newspaper issue

In-text citation

Yesterday's copy of the newspaper (*The Independent*, 2018) …

Reference list

The Independent (2018) 17 April.

If referencing an article in an online-only newspaper use the following:

Citation order:

- Author
- Year of publication (in round brackets)
- Title of article (in single quotation marks)
- Title of news source (in italics and capitalise first letter of each word in title, except linking words such as and, of, the, for)
- Edition if required (in round brackets)
- Day and month
- DOI *or* Available at: URL (Accessed: date)

Example: articles in online-only newspapers

In-text citation

Cuthbertson (2019) queried Bitcoin's rise.

Reference list

Cuthbertson, A. (2019) 'Bitcoin price surge', *Independent*, 9 February. Available at: https://www.independent.co.uk/life-style/gadgets-and-tech/news/bitcoin-price-latest-cryptocurrency-market-value-explained-a8770501.html (Accessed: 10 February 2019).

E3 Conferences

E3.1 Full conference proceedings

Citation order:

- Author/editor
- Year of publication (in round brackets)
- Title of conference: subtitle (in italics)
- Location and date of conference
- Place of publication: Publisher

Example

In-text citation

The conference (Jones, 2018) …

Reference list

Jones, T. (ed.) (2018) *Small firms: adding the spark: the 23rd ISBA national small firms policy and research conference*. Robert Gordon University, Aberdeen, 15–17 November. Leeds: Institute for Small Business Affairs.

E3.2 Full conference proceedings published in journals

These are often published as special issues or journal supplements and are referenced as follows.

Citation order:

- Title of conference, location and date (if included) (in single quotation marks)
- Year of journal publication (in round brackets)
- Title of journal (in italics – capitalise first letter of each word in title, except for linking words such as and, of, the, for)
- Issue information (that is, volume (unbracketed) and, where applicable, supplement or part number, month or season (all in round brackets))

If accessed online:

- DOI *or* Available at: URL (Accessed: date)

NB You only need to include the URL or DOI if the journal issue is only available online.

Example

The quality of all the papers ('Proceedings of the higher education technology conference', 2017) …

'Proceedings of the higher education technology conference, University of Edinburgh, 23–25 March 2017' (2017) *Learning Online*, 27(4).

E3.3 Individual conference papers

Citation order:

♦ Author of paper
♦ Year of publication (in round brackets)
♦ Title of paper (in single quotation marks)
♦ Title of conference: subtitle (in italics)
♦ Location and date of conference
♦ Place of publication: Publisher
♦ Page references for the paper

Example

Cook (2014) highlighted examples …

Cook, D. (2014) 'Developing franchised business in Scotland', *Small firms: adding the spark: the 23rd ISBA national small firms' policy and research conference*. Robert Gordon University, Aberdeen, 15–17 November. Leeds: Institute for Small Business Affairs, pp. 127–136.

E3.4 Individual conference papers published in journals

Citation order:

♦ Author of paper
♦ Year of publication (in round brackets)
♦ Title of paper (in single quotation marks)
♦ from the Conference title, location and date (if included) (in round brackets)
♦ Title of journal (in italics – capitalise first letter of each word in title, except for linking words such as and, of, the, for)
♦ Issue information (that is, volume (unbracketed) and, where applicable, supplement or part number, month or season (all in round brackets))
♦ Page references for the paper

If accessed online:

♦ DOI *or* Available at: URL (Accessed: date)

NB You only need to include the URL or DOI if the journal paper is only available online.

Example

The groundbreaking study (Pilsen, 2017) …

Pilsen, G. (2017) 'Online learning in higher education in China' (from the Proceedings of the higher education technology conference, University of Edinburgh, 23–25 March 2017), *Learning Online*, 27(4), pp. 42–57.

E3.5 Papers from conference proceedings published online

Citation order:

♦ Author
♦ Year of publication (in round brackets)
♦ Title of paper (in single quotation marks)
♦ Title of conference: subtitle (in italics)
♦ Location and date of conference
♦ Page references for the paper (if available)

If accessed online:

♦ DOI *or* Available at: URL (Accessed: date)

Example

In-text citation

A recent paper (Mendes and Romão, 2018) …

Reference list

Mendes, L. and Romão, T. (2018) 'Children as teachers', *Proceedings of the 8th international conference on advances in computer entertainment technology*, Lisbon, 8–11 November. doi:10.1145/2071423.2071438.

E4   Theses

Citation order:

♦ Author
♦ Year of submission (in round brackets)
♦ Title of thesis (in italics)
♦ Degree statement
♦ Degree-awarding body

If accessed online:

♦ DOI *or* Available at: URL (Accessed: date)

Examples

In-text citations

Research by Tregear (2013) and Parsons (2014) …

Reference list

Parsons, J.D. (2014) *Nutrition in contemporary diet*. PhD thesis. Durham University. Available at: http://etheses.dur.ac.uk/846 (Accessed: 14 August 2018).

Tregear, A.E.J. (2013) *Speciality regional foods in the UK: an investigation from the perspectives of marketing and social history*. Unpublished PhD thesis. Newcastle University.

E5   Protocols, regulations and guidelines

These tend to relate to official procedures, rules and guidance from health, government and other corporate bodies – for example, the National Institute for Health and Care Excellence, NICE.

For scientific and technical standards, see Section E18.1.

Citation order:

♦ Author
♦ Year of publication (in round brackets)
♦ Title (in italics)
♦ Series or publication number (if given)
♦ Place of publication: Publisher

If accessed online:

♦ DOI *or* Available at: URL (Accessed: date)

Examples

In-text citations

The hospital's guideline (Great Ormond Street Hospital for Children, 2017) …

The updated guidance (NICE, 2016) …

Reference list

Great Ormond Street Hospital for Children (2017) *Bone marrow biopsy*. Available at: http://www.gosh.nhs.uk/health-professionals/clinical-guidelines/bone-marrow-biopsy (Accessed: 18 February 2019).

NICE (2016) *Hypertension in adults: diagnosis and management*. CG127. Available at: https://www.nice.org.uk/guidance/cg127 (Accessed: 21 February 2018).

E6 Teaching materials, including lecture notes and virtual learning environments (for example, Blackboard, PebblePad and MOOCs)

You should always check with your tutor whether or not you are allowed to refer to course materials in your own work. It is more academically correct to refer to published sources.

Personal learning environments/spaces (such as PebblePad) are often known as 'eportfolios' or 'webfolios'. They generally include a collection of electronic information (coursework, images, multimedia, hyperlinks and other electronic files) demonstrating the student's learning record and evidence of achievements. In many cases, eportfolios are now retained within university **virtual learning environments (VLEs)**, which means that they are not easily accessible to anyone outside the VLE. External hosts such as PebblePad can offer solutions to this problem, although issues relating to confidential information may persist (see Section E27).

In eportfolios, a multitude of different types of information may be referenced. However, the reference will always relate to the web page of the user/student's work. For more specific examples, see http://www.pebblepad.co.uk.

VLEs and collaboration suites such as Blackboard are used in further and higher education as stores for course documents and teaching materials, and for discussions between students and tutors and between students themselves. You will need to distinguish what you are citing (for example, a tutor's notes, a journal article, text extracted from a book and digitised for use in VLEs, or an item from a discussion board). Note in the examples below that the URL gives the access point to the VLE because a reader would need login details to locate the item being cited.

E6.1 Live lectures

NB For speeches see E24.1.

Citation order:

- Author/speaker
- Year (in round brackets)
- Title of lecture (in single quotation marks)
- Medium (in square brackets)
- Module code: module title (in italics) (if known)
- Institution or venue
- Day/month

Example

In-text citation
Points of interest from the lectures (Brown, 2018) …

Reference list
Brown, T. (2018) 'Contemporary furniture' [Lecture]. *DE816: Interior Design*. Northumbria University. 21 April.

E6.2 Recorded lectures

Citation order:

- Author/speaker
- Year (in round brackets)
- Title of lecture (in single quotation marks)
- Medium (in square brackets)
- Module code: module title (in italics) (if known)
- Institution or venue
- Day/month
- Available at: URL (Accessed: date)

Example

In-text citation

Points of interest from the lectures
(Brown, 2018) …

Reference list

Brown, T. (2018) 'Bridge construction
techniques' [Recorded lecture].
ENG1145: Fundamental engineering.
Durham University. 21 March. Available
at: http://duo.dur.ac.uk (Accessed: 21
April 2018).

E6.3　Tutors' handouts

Citation order:

♦ Tutor
♦ Year of distribution (in round brackets)
♦ Title of handout (in single quotation
　marks)
♦ Module code: module title (in italics)
♦ Institution
♦ Unpublished

Example

In-text citation

The tutor's handout (Hadley, 2018) …

Reference list

Hadley, S. (2018) 'Biomechanics:
introductory readings'. *BM289: Sport
biomechanics*. University of Cumbria.
Unpublished.

E6.4　Tutors' lecture notes in VLE

Citation order:

♦ Author or tutor
♦ Year of publication (in round brackets)
♦ Title of item (in single quotation marks)
♦ Module code: module title (in italics)
♦ Available at: URL of VLE (Accessed:
　date)

Example

In-text citation

The tutor's notes (Hadley, 2018) …

Reference list

Hadley, S. (2018) 'Biomechanics:
introductory readings'. *BM289: Sport
biomechanics*. University of Cumbria.
Available at: https://mylearning.cumbria.
ac.uk (Accessed: 7 April 2018).

E6.5　PowerPoint presentations

Citation order:

♦ Author or tutor
♦ Year of publication (in round brackets)
♦ Title of presentation (in single quotation
　marks)
♦ [PowerPoint presentation]
♦ Module code: module title (in italics)
♦ Available at: URL of VLE (Accessed: date)

Example

In-text citation

The excellent presentation (Booth,
2017) …

Reference list

Booth, L. (2017) 'History of
radiography' [PowerPoint presentation].
*MISR4004: Patient care skills: an
introduction to human sciences*.
University of Cumbria. Available at:
https://mylearning.cumbria.ac.uk
(Accessed: 7 April 2018).

E6.6　Learning support materials

Sometimes you will access, and need to
reference, material from modules not
produced by tutors (for example, skills
modules produced by learning support
teams).

Citation order:

♦ Author
♦ Year of publication (in round brackets)
♦ Title of item (in single quotation marks)
♦ Title of support/skills module (in italics): subtitle (if required) (in italics)
♦ Available at: URL of VLE (Accessed: date)

Example

In-text citation ▶

… and this module allows you to test your own skills (University of Cumbria, Library and Student Services, 2018).

Reference list ▶

University of Cumbria, Library and Student Services (2018) 'Skills evaluation tools', *Skills@cumbria: assess your skills.* Available at: https://mylearning.cumbria.ac.uk (Accessed: 18 October 2018).

E6.7 Journal articles

For journal articles where you have all the required elements for the reader to track the article down, you should simply cite and reference the article as in Section E2.1.

E6.8 Extracts from books digitised for use in VLEs

You may be given an extract from a book. If it is an extract, cite it as in Section E1.9, or if it is a chapter from an edited book, cite it as in Section E1.10.

E6.9 Messages from course discussion boards

Citation order:

♦ Author
♦ Year of publication (in round brackets)
♦ Title of message (in single quotation marks)

♦ Title of discussion board (in italics)
♦ 'in'
♦ Module code: module title (in italics)
♦ Available at: URL of VLE (Accessed: date)

Example

In-text citation ▶

It is advisable to check which referencing style is required (Thomas, 2018).

Reference list ▶

Thomas, D. (2018) 'Word count and referencing style', *Frequently Asked Questions discussion board*, in *PHYS 2011: Housing Studies*. Available at: http://duo.dur.ac.uk (Accessed: 14 October 2018).

E6.10 Massive online open courses (MOOCs)

Citation order:

♦ Producer
♦ Year of publication (in round brackets)
♦ Title of course (in italics)
♦ [MOOC]
♦ Available at: URL of MOOC (Accessed: date)

Example

In-text citation ▶

… in relation to the University's MOOC (University of Bradford, 2016).

Reference list ▶

University of Bradford (2016) *How to save energy* [MOOC]. Available at: https://www.bradford.ac.uk/mooccourses/energy26934/progress (Accessed: 10 July 2018).

E7 Digital repositories

Many academic and learned institutions maintain digital repositories of the research undertaken by their members, and make digital copies (eprints) of book chapters, journal articles and conference papers available via the internet. Digital repositories are useful sources of new research and are often heavily cited in scientific literature.

If the book or article has already been published, reference it as the publication. Repositories can also be used by authors to present their articles to readers before traditional publication processes, such as **peer review**, have been completed. Peer review can take many months, by which time the value and opportunities raised by the new information may be lost. This form of rapid publication is common in the sciences, where early notice and discussion of new research is essential. If the articles are available before the item has been peer-reviewed, they are known as 'preprints'.

As with all internet-based sources, be clear what you are referencing. If it is a book, chapter or article that has already been published, reference it as you would the printed source, as in the book and conference paper examples below. However, if it is only available online use the URL (or DOI). If it is a prepublication article, conference, working paper or presentation that has not been peer-reviewed or formatted by publishers, or is a draft of a work that was published later, be clear that you are referencing the preprint, as this may be different from the later publication. Give the DOI or URL and accessed date and use [Preprint] to highlight to your reader that you have read the preprint, not the final approved article.

E7.1 Books in digital repositories

Reference books and journal articles in repositories as you would for print versions (unless they are only available online, in which case use the URL or DOI).

Examples

In-text citation

Previous PhD candidates provided useful advice (Cook and Crang, 2013).

Reference list

Cook, I. and Crang, M. (2013) *Doing ethnographies*. Norwich: Geobooks.

In-text citation

The research process highlighted ... (James and Phelps, 2014).

Reference list

James, P.R. and Phelps, J. (2014) *The dynamic research process*. Available at: http://archivos.com/18736 (Accessed: 23 November 2018).

E7.2 Conference papers in digital repositories

If the conference paper is only available online, give the URL or DOI.

Citation order:

♦ Author
♦ Year of publication (in round brackets)
♦ Title of paper (in single quotation marks)
♦ Title of conference: subtitle (in italics)
♦ Organisation or company (if stated)
♦ Location and date of conference
♦ Available at: URL (if required) (Accessed: date) *or* DOI (if available)

Examples

Price (2015) disputed the theory …

Price, P.B. (2015) 'Life in solid ice?', *Workshop on life in ancient ice*, Westin Salishan Lodge, Gleneden Beach, Oregon, 30 June to 2 July 2015.

Brandt (2015) argues strongly that …

Brandt, P.D. (2015) 'Global warming: fact or fiction?' *Our climate, our future*, New York, 24–27 April 2014. Available at: http://www.arxiv.org/abs/1478.3356 (Accessed: 15 September 2018).

E7.3 Prepublication journal articles online or in digital repositories

Citation order:

♦ Author
♦ Year (in round brackets)
♦ Title of article (in single quotation marks)
♦ To be published in (if this is stated)
♦ Title of journal (in italics – capitalise first letter of each word in title, except for linking words such as and, of, the, for)
♦ Volume and issue numbers (if stated)
♦ [Preprint]
♦ Available at: URL (Accessed: date) *or* DOI (if available)

Example

New research by Jeon, Lee and Park (2018) …

Jeon, I., Lee, K. and Park, J.-H. (2018) 'Ramond-Ramond cohomology and O(D,D) T-duality'. To be published in *Journal of High Energy Physics* [Preprint]. Available at: http://arxiv.org/abs/1206.3478 (Accessed: 24 August 2018).

E8 Published reports, working papers, briefing papers

NB For unpublished internal reports, see Section E25.

Citation order:

♦ Author or organisation
♦ Year of publication (in round brackets)
♦ Title of report, working paper, briefing paper (in italics)
♦ Place of publication: Publisher

If accessed online:

♦ DOI *or* Available at: URL (Accessed: date)

Example

The guidance (NHS England and NHS Improvement, 2016) …

NHS England and NHS Improvement (2016) *NHS Operational Planning and Contracting Guidance 2017–2019*. Available at: https://www.england.nhs.uk/wp-content/uploads/2016/09/NHS-operational-planning-guidance-201617-201819.pdf (Accessed: 17 January 2018).

E8.1 Research reports/working and briefing papers

Citation order:

♦ Author or organisation
♦ Year of publication (in round brackets)
♦ Title of report (in italics)
♦ Place of publication: Publisher

Or if accessed on the internet:

♦ DOI *or* Available at: URL (Accessed: date)

Examples

In-text citations

The minimum cost of living in Britain is £13,400 (Bradshaw *et al.*, 2017, p. 32). Proposals by Basu and Getachew (2017, pp. 23–25) …

Reference list

Basu, P. and Getachew, Y. (2017) *Redistributive innovation policy, inequality and efficiency*. Durham University Business School working paper 2017.2. Available at: https://www.dur.ac.uk/resources/business/working-papers/RD_2017_02.pdf (Accessed: 1 July 2018).

Bradshaw, J. *et al.* (2017) *A minimum income standard for Britain: what people think*. Available at: http://www.jrf.org.uk/sites/files/jrf/2226-income-poverty-standards.pdf (Accessed: 3 July 2018).

E8.2 Company reports

Citation order:

♦ Author or organisation
♦ Year of publication (in round brackets)

♦ Title of report (in italics)
♦ Place of publication: Publisher

Or if accessed on the internet:

♦ DOI *or* Available at: URL (Accessed: date)

Examples

In-text citations

The company's profits expanded (BSkyB Ltd, 2017, p. 23) …

Marks and Spencer Group (2017) addressed concerns about its investments …

Reference list

BSkyB Ltd. (2017) *Annual report 2017*. Available at: http://www.annualreports.co.uk/HostedData/AnnualReports/PDF/LSE_BSY_2017.pdf (Accessed: 8 January 2019).

Marks and Spencer Group PLC (2017) *Our approach to human rights*. Available at: https://corporate.marksandspencer.com/documents/imported-documents/plan-a-our-approach/m-and-s-human-rights-report-june-2017 (Accessed: 8 January 2018).

E8.3 Market research reports from online databases

Citation order:

♦ Publishing organisation
♦ Year of publication/last updated (in round brackets)
♦ Title of extract (in italics)
♦ DOI *or* Available at: URL (Accessed: date)

Example

In-text citation

Mintel Oxygen (2016) noted problems in the market …

Reference list

Mintel Oxygen (2016) *Car insurance UK*. Available at: http://academic.mintel.com (Accessed: 5 January 2018).

E8.4 Financial reports from online databases

Citation order:

- Publishing organisation
- Year of publication/last updated (in round brackets)
- Title of extract (in italics)
- DOI *or* Available at: URL (Accessed: date)

Example

In-text citation

BT's profit margin rose by over 2 per cent in the financial year 2017–2018 (Bureau van Dijk, 2018).

Reference list

Bureau van Dijk (2018) *BT Group plc company report*. Available at: http://fame.bvdep.com (Accessed: 5 October 2018).

E8.5 Financial reports from terminal-based databases

Citation order:

- Publishing organisation
- Year of publication/last updated (in round brackets)

- Title of extract (in italics)
- Available at: Title of database (in italics) (Accessed: date)

Examples

In-text citations

Comparing the company data from Datastream (2018) and Bloomberg (2018) …

Reference list

Bloomberg (2018) *BT share prices 2015–2018*. Available at: *Bloomberg*. (Accessed: 5 October 2018).

Datastream (2018) *BT Group plc company report*. Available at: *Datastream*. (Accessed: 5 October 2018).

E9 Reviews

E9.1 Book reviews

Citation order:

- Name of the reviewer (if indicated)
- Year of publication of the review (in round brackets)
- Title of the review (in single quotation marks)
- Review of … (title of work reviewed – in italics)
- Author/director of work being reviewed
- Publication details (title in italics)

If accessed online:

- DOI *or* Available at: URL (Accessed: date)

Examples

In-text citations

Darden (2007) considered the book …

One online reviewer (Hauck, 2017) …

Reference list

Darden, L. (2007) 'Cell division'. Review of *Discovering cell mechanisms: the creation of modern cell biology*, by W. Bechtel. *Journal of the History of Biology*, 40(1), pp. 185–187.

Hauck, P.G. (2017) 'It is neutron dense'. Review of *Health economics*, by F. Sloan and C-R. Hsieh. Available at: https://www.amazon.co.uk/Health-Economics-Press-Frank-Sloan/dp/0262035111/ (Accessed: 2 March 2018).

E9.2   Drama reviews

Citation order:

- Name of the reviewer (if indicated)
- Year of publication of the review (in round brackets)
- Title of the review (in single quotation marks)
- Review of … (title of work reviewed – in italics)
- Author/director of work being reviewed
- Publication details (title in italics)

If accessed online:

- DOI *or* Available at: URL (Accessed: date)

Example

In-text citation

One reviewer (Billington, 2008, p. 19) wrote …

Reference list

Billington, M. (2008) 'The main event'. Review of *On the rocks*, by D.H. Lawrence. Hampstead Theatre, London. *The Guardian* (Review section), 5 July, p. 19.

E9.3   Film reviews

Citation order:

- Name of the reviewer (if indicated)
- Year of publication of the review (in round brackets)
- Title of the review (in single quotation marks)
- Review of … (title of work reviewed – in italics)
- Author/director of work being reviewed
- Publication details (title in italics)

If accessed online:

- DOI *or* Available at: URL (Accessed: date)

Examples

In-text citations

Barnes (1989) and Parsons (2010) thought it a classic film.

Reference list

Magazine review

Barnes, L. (1989) 'Citizen Kane'. Review of *Citizen Kane*, directed by O. Welles (RKO). *New Vision*, 9 October, pp. 24–25.

Internet review

Parsons, T. (2010) 'A rosebud by any other name'. Review of *Citizen Kane*, directed by O. Welles (RKO). Available at: http://www.imdb.com/title/tt0033467/reviews?start=210 (Accessed: 5 July 2018).

E9.4   Reviews of musical performances

Citation order:

- Name of the reviewer (if indicated)
- Year of publication of the review (in round brackets)
- Title of the review (in single quotation marks)

- Review of ... (title of work reviewed – in italics)
- Author/director of work being reviewed
- Publication details (title in italics)

If accessed online:

- DOI *or* Available at: URL (Accessed: date)

Example

In-text citation

Hickling (2008) thought it was 'a little touch of magic'.

Reference list

Hickling, A. (2008) 'The opera'. Review of *Don Giovanni*, by Mozart. New Vic, Newcastle-under-Lyme. *The Guardian* (Review section), 5 July, p. 19.

E9.5 Author biographical information or cover blurb

Assume that this information is written by the author, unless another person is identified. The location can be given in the in-text citation, as you would a reference to a page within a book.

Citation order:

- Author
- Date (in round brackets)
- Title of book (in italics)
- Place of publication: Publisher

Example

In-text citation

Margaret Atwood won the Booker Prize in 2000 (Atwood, 2009, inside back cover).

Reference list

Atwood, M. (2009) *The year of the flood*. London: Bloomsbury.

E9.6 Second-person review comments on or in a book

If reviewers' comments are published on the book cover or inner covers, indicate the location of these in your text, but give the reference to the author and the book on or in which the comments are published.

Citation order:

- Author
- Date (in round brackets)
- Title of book (in italics)
- Place of publication: Publisher

Examples

In-text citation

Kershaw thought Mann's book (2004, back cover) was 'a brilliant and disturbing analysis'.

Reference list

Mann, M. (2004) *Fascists*. Cambridge: Cambridge University Press.

E9.7 Product reviews

Citation order:

- Name of the reviewer (if indicated)
- Year of publication (in round brackets)
- Title of review (in italics)

If accessed online:

- DOI *or* Available at: URL (Accessed: date)

Example

In-text citation

Described as 'a great entry to the world of photography' (Hall, 2018) …

Reference list

Hall, P. (2018) *Nikon D3500 review*. Available at: https://www.techradar.com/uk/reviews/nikon-d3500-review (Accessed 1 November 2018).

E10 The internet

When referencing information you have retrieved from the internet, you must distinguish what you are referring to. The internet is made up of journal articles, organisation internet sites, personal internet sites, government publications, images, company data, presentations – a vast range of material. Examples of how to reference individual sources, such as journal articles, ebooks and images, are given with the entries for those sources. In this section, you will find examples of how to cite and reference internet sites or **web pages** produced by individuals and organisations.

The nature of what you are referring to will govern how you cite or reference it. You should aim to provide sufficient information for a reader to be able to locate your information source. As material on the internet can be removed or changed, you should also note the date when you accessed/viewed the information – it might not be there in a few months' time.

Remember to evaluate all internet information for accuracy, authority, currency, coverage and objectivity. The ability to publish information on the internet bears no relation to the author's academic abilities.

The defining element in referencing a web page is its uniform resource locator, or URL. This should be included in your reference list, but do not include the URL in your **in-text citation**, unless this is the only piece of information you have.

Generally, web pages do not have page numbers. To help your reader locate where you have quoted or paraphrased from a website, you can number the paragraphs on the page and include the paragraph in your in-text citation.

Example

In-text citation

Lomotey (2018, para. 4) said 'the children remained calm like professionals'.

Reference list

Lomotey, D. (2018) *Behind the scenes of One Girl's Journey*. Available at: https://www.actionaid.org.uk/blog/news/2018/10/22/behind-the-scenes-of-one-girls-journey (Accessed: 27 October 2018).

E10.1 Web pages with individual authors

Citation order:

♦ Author
♦ Year that the site was published/last updated (in round brackets)
♦ Title of web page (in italics)
♦ Available at: URL (Accessed: date)

Example

In-text citation

Burton (2012) provided information for the visit.

Reference list

Burton, P.A. (2012) *Castles of Spain*. Available at: http://www.castlesofspain.co.uk/ (Accessed: 14 October 2018).

E10.2 Web pages with organisations as authors

Example

In-text citation

After identifying symptoms (National Health Service, 2018) …

Reference list

National Health Service (2018) *Check your symptoms*. Available at: http://www.nhsdirect.nhs.uk/checksymptoms (Accessed: 17 October 2018).

E10.3 Web pages with no authors

Use the title of the web page.

Example

In-text citation

Illustrations of the houses can be found online (*Palladio's Italian villas*, 2005).

Reference list

Palladio's Italian villas (2005) Available at: http://www.boglewood.com/palladio/ (Accessed: 23 August 2018).

E10.4 Web pages with no authors or titles

If no author or title can be identified, you should use the web page's URL. It may be possible to shorten a very long URL, as long as the route remains clear, but it may be necessary to give the full URL, even in your citation. If a web page has no author or title, you might question whether or not it is suitable for academic work.

Example

In-text citation

Video files may need to be compressed (http://www.newmediarepublic.com/dvideo/compression.html, 2018).

Reference list

http://www.newmediarepublic.com/dvideo/compression.html (2018) (Accessed: 14 July 2018).

E10.5 Web pages with no dates

If the web page has no obvious date of publication/revision, use the author (no date) and the date you accessed the page. You might question how useful undated information is to your research as it may be out of date.

Example

In-text citation

Compression may be required (New Media Republic, no date).

Reference list

New Media Republic (no date) *Compression*. Available at: http://www.newmediarepublic.com/dvideo/compression.html (Accessed: 16 June 2018).

You should not use web pages for academic work that have no obvious author, title or date.

E10.6 Blogs/vlogs

Blogs (weblogs) and vlogs (video logs) are produced by individuals and organisations to provide updates on issues of interest or concern. Be aware that because blogs/vlogs are someone's opinions, they may not provide objective, reasoned discussion of an issue. Use blogs/vlogs in conjunction with reputable sources. Note that due to the informality of the internet, many authors give first names or aliases. Use the name they have used in your reference.

Citation order:

♦ Author of message
♦ Year that the site was published/last updated (in round brackets)
♦ Title of message (in single quotation marks)
♦ Title of internet site (in italics)
♦ Day/month of posted message
♦ Available at: URL (Accessed: date)

Example

In-text citation
Nick Robinson (2014) had noted the 'Cameron Direct' phenomenon.

Reference list
Robinson, N. (2014) 'Cameron Direct', *Nick Robinson's newslog*, 4 June. Available at: http://www.bbc.co.uk/blogs/nickrobinson/ (Accessed: 11 October 2018).

E10.7   Wikis

Wikis are collaborative websites in which several (usually unidentified) authors can add and edit the information presented. What you read today may have changed by tomorrow. There have also been instances of false information being presented, although wiki editors try to ensure that the information is authentic. If you are going to use information from a wiki, make sure that it is thoroughly referenced. As with other websites, if no authors or references are given, the information is unlikely to be suitable for academic work. Evaluate wiki information against sources of proven academic quality such as books and journal articles.

Citation order:

♦ Title of article (in single quotation marks)
♦ Year that the entry was published/last updated (in round brackets)
♦ Title of wiki site
♦ Available at: URL (Accessed: date)

Example

In-text citation
Telford introduced new techniques of bridge construction ('Thomas Telford', 2018).

Reference list
'Thomas Telford' (2018) Wikipedia. Available at: http://en.wikipedia.org/wiki/Thomas_Telford (Accessed: 11 September 2018).

E10.8   Social networking websites

See also Section E22.5.

Note that because these sites require registration and then acceptance by other members, it is suggested that the main web address be used. You may wish to include a copy of the member-to-member discussion you are referring to as an appendix to your work, so that readers without access to the original can read it.

E10.8a   Instagram posts/stories

See also E20.7c Photographs in online collections.

Citation order:

♦ Author (Instagram account holder/poster)
♦ Year posted (in round brackets)
♦ Title of post (in single quotation marks)
♦ [Instagram]
♦ Day/month of posted message
♦ Available at: URL (Accessed: date)

Example

In-text citation

He offered her a slice of cake (Tusk, 2018) …

Reference list

Tusk, D. (2018) 'A piece of cake perhaps?' [Instagram]. 20 September. Available at: https://www.instagram.com/p/Bn8Luwbjzf9/ (Accessed: 7 February 2019).

E10.8b Facebook

Citation order:

- Author (if available; if not, use title)
- Year that the page was published/last updated (in round brackets)
- Title of page (in italics)
- [Facebook]
- Day/month of posted message
- Available at: URL (Accessed: date)

Example

In-text citation

The campaign had over 7,000 members in less than one week (*Tynemouth outdoor pool*, 2015).

Reference list

Tynemouth outdoor pool (2015) [Facebook] 29 August. Available at: https://www.facebook.com (Accessed: 31 August 2018).

NB For images seen through social networking sites, see Section E20.

E10.8c Facebook Messenger

Citation order:

- Author (if available; if not, use title)
- Year that the page was published/last updated (in round brackets)

- Title of page (in single quotation marks)
- [Facebook Messenger]
- Day/month of posted message
- Available at: URL (Accessed: date)

Example

In-text citation

The image from the class whiteboard (Sanchez, 2018) …

Reference list

Sanchez, F. (2018) 'Physics class notes' [Facebook Messenger] 29 October. Available at: https://www.facebook.com (Accessed: 31 October 2018).

E10.8d Twitter

Citation order:

- Author
- Year tweet posted (in round brackets)
- full text of tweet (unless it is very long, then use ellipsis to shorten)
- [Twitter]
- Day/month tweet posted
- Available at: URL (Accessed: date)

Example

In-text citation

Laura Kuenssberg (2018) tweeted on the party conference.

Reference list

Kuenssberg, L. [@bbclaurak] (2018) anyone might imagine that inside he's a tiny bit pleased [Twitter] 25 September. Available at: https://twitter.com/bbclaurak/status/1044553972277817344 (Accessed: 19 December 2018).

E10.8e   Periscope

Citation order:

♦ Author
♦ Year posted (in round brackets)
♦ Title of video (in single quotation marks)
♦ Title of channel (in italics)
♦ [Periscope]
♦ Day/month posted
♦ Available at: URL (Accessed: date)

Example

In-text citation
The two leaders hugged each other (Siddiqui, 2018, 03:32) …

Reference list
Siddiqui, M. (2018) 'PM @narendramodi at Yamanashi with Japanese PM @AbeShinzo', *CNN-News18* [Periscope] 28 October. Available at: https://www.periscope.tv/w/ 1zqJVOQwDoMxB?channel=news (Accessed: 28 October 2018).

E10.8f   WhatsApp

Citation order:

♦ Author (if available; if not, use title)
♦ Year that the page was published/last updated (in round brackets)
♦ [WhatsApp]
♦ Day/month of posted message

Example

In-text citation
Williams (2018) messaged with the meeting agenda.

Reference list
Williams, J. (2018) [WhatsApp] 4 August.

E10.8g   Snapchat

Citation order:

♦ Author (if available; if not, use title)
♦ Year that the page was published/last updated (in round brackets)
♦ [Snapchat]
♦ Day/month of posted message

Example

In-text citation
The meeting was arranged by Kelvin (2018).

Reference list
Kelvin, D. (2018) [Snapchat] 14 August.

E11   CD-ROMs or DVDs

Citation order:

♦ Title of publication (in italics)
♦ Year of publication (in round brackets)
♦ [CD-ROM] or [DVD]
♦ Producer (where identifiable)
♦ Available: publisher/distributor

Example

In-text citation
The student made extensive use of an authoritative source (*World development indicators*, 2002) …

Reference list
World development indicators (2002) [CD-ROM]. The World Bank Group. Available: SilverPlatter.

E12 Computer/video games, computer programs and mobile apps

E12.1 Computer/video games

These may be physically purchased games (played on platforms such as PlayStation, Xbox and smartphones/tablets), apps, or other programs downloaded directly from the internet.

Citation order:

♦ Company/individual developer
♦ Release year (in round brackets)
♦ Title of game (in italics and capitalise initial letters – include edition if relevant)
♦ [Video game]
♦ Publisher

If accessed online:

♦ DOI *or* Available at: URL (Accessed: date)

Examples

In-text citations
Two of the most popular online games, *FIFA 16* (EA, 2015) and *Halo 5: Guardians* (343 Industries, 2015) …

Reference list
343 Industries (2015) *Halo 5: Guardians – Digital Deluxe Edition* [Video game]. Microsoft Studios. Available at: http://www.xbox.com/en-gb/Search?q=Halo+5 (Accessed: 28 March 2018).

EA (2015) *FIFA 16 – Deluxe Edition* [Video game]. Electronic Arts.

E12.2 Computer programs

Citation order:

♦ Author (if given)
♦ Date – if given (in round brackets)

♦ Title of program (in italics and capitalise initial letters)
♦ Version (in round brackets)
♦ [Computer program]
♦ Availability (that is, distributor, address, order number (if given))

If accessed online:

♦ DOI *or* Available at: URL (Accessed: date)

Example

In-text citation
Camtasia Studio (TechSmith, 2017) can be used to record tutorials.

Reference list
TechSmith Corporation (2017) *Camtasia Studio* (Version 3) [Computer program]. Available at: http://www.techsmith.com/download.html (Accessed: 21 June 2018).

E12.3 Mobile apps

Use the name of the developer of the app if available. If not, use the title of the app as the first element.

Citation order:

♦ Developer
♦ Year of release/update (in round brackets)
♦ Title of app (in italics and capitalise initial letters)
♦ Edition and/or version number (in round brackets)
♦ [Mobile app]
♦ (Accessed: date)

Example

With *Video MP3 Converter* (FunDevs LLC, 2018), you can convert, resize and trim your videos …

FunDevs LLC (2018) *Video MP3 Converter* (Version 1.6.28) [Mobile app]. (Accessed: 26 November 2018).

E13 United Kingdom legal sources using the Harvard (author-date) style

As in the previous tenth edition of *Cite them right*, we give examples for citing legal sources in author-date (Harvard) format. In earlier editions, we employed the referencing systems used in many UK law schools, but many other disciplines use legal sources in their research and do not apply the same conventions for publication abbreviations and punctuation as the law schools. Providing examples for citing legal sources in author-date (Harvard) format will ensure that scholars in other disciplines who already use author-date referencing for non-legal sources, and their readers, can identify legal sources using methods that are familiar to them.

The author-date format uses the elements of references common to other sources as the in-text and reference list documentation: speakers recorded in *Hansard* are treated as authors; law reports are treated as journal articles, with the case name used as the article title.

UK legislation is available on BAILII (http://www.bailii.org/), Legislation.gov.uk (http://www.legislation.gov.uk/) and subscription services, including LexisLibrary and Westlaw.

E13.1 Papers: House of Commons and House of Lords

Citation order:

♦ Parliament. House of …
♦ Year of publication (in round brackets)
♦ Title (in italics)
♦ Paper number (in round brackets) – for House of Lords papers, the paper number is also in round brackets to distinguish it from identical House of Commons paper numbers (see examples below)
♦ Place of publication: Publisher

Examples

Parliamentary reports for the year included the criminal justice system (Parliament. House of Commons, 1999) and renewable energy (Parliament. House of Lords, 1999).

Parliament. House of Commons (1999) *Criminal justice: working together, Session 1999–2000*. (HC 1999–2000 29). London: The Stationery Office.

Parliament. House of Lords (1999) *Electricity from renewables: first report from the Select Committee on the European Union*. (HL 1999–2000 (18)). London: The Stationery Office.

E13.2 House of Commons Library reports

Citation order:

♦ Author or organisation
♦ Year of publication (in round brackets)
♦ Title of report (in italics)

- Title of publication series and number (in round brackets)
- Place of publication: Publisher

If accessed online:

- DOI *or* Available at: URL (Accessed: date)

Example

In-text citation

McGuinness (2017) outlined …

Reference list

McGuinness, F. (2017) *Youth unemployment statistics* (House of Commons Library briefing paper 5871). Available at: http://researchbriefings. files.parliament.uk/documents/ SN05871/SN05871.pdf (Accessed: 17 January 2018).

E13.3 Official records: House of Commons and House of Lords

E13.3a *Hansard*

Hansard is the official record of debates, speeches, oral and written answers/ statements, petitions, and Westminster Hall discussions in the Houses of the UK Parliament. A fully searchable version of *Hansard* from 1988 for the Commons and from 1995 for the Lords is available online at http://www.parliament.uk/business/ publications/hansard/. Historical records for *Hansard* from 1803 to 2005 are available online at https://hansard. parliament.uk/.

Citation order:

- Name of speaker/author
- Year of publication (in round brackets)

- Subject of debate or speech (in single quotation marks)
- Hansard: Name of House of Parliament (in italics)
- Debates/written statement/Westminster Hall or petitions (in italics)
- Day and month
- Volume number, column number or page number
- Available at: URL (Accessed: date)

Example

In-text citation

Hywell Williams MP (2015) questioned the impact of sanctions in Wales.

Reference list

Williams, H. (2015) 'Benefit sanctions', *Hansard: House of Commons debates*, 16 September, 599, c.1032. Available at: http://www. publications.parliament.uk/pa/ cm201516/cmhansrd/chan45.pdf (Accessed: 17 September 2018).

E13.3b *Written questions and answers* and *Written ministerial statements*

Before September 2014, *Written questions and answers* and *Written ministerial statements* were recorded in *Hansard*.

Citation order:

- Name of author
- Year of publication (in round brackets)
- Subject of question, answer or statement (in single quotation marks)
- Hansard: Name of House of Parliament (in italics)
- Debates/written statement/Westminster Hall or petitions (in italics)
- Day and month

- Volume number, column number or page number
- Available at: URL (Accessed: date)

Example

In-text citation

Lansley (2012) welcomed the forum.

Reference list

Lansley, A. (2012) 'NHS future forum', *Hansard: House of Commons written ministerial statements*, 10 January, 7WS. Available at: http://www.publications. parliament.uk/pa/cm201212/cmhansrd/cm120110/wmstext/120110m0001. htm#12011044000132 (Accessed: 23 October 2018).

Since 12 September 2014, *Written questions and answers* have been published in the *Written questions and answers* database (http://www.parliament. uk/business/publications/written-questions-answers-statements/written-questions-answers/) instead of *Hansard*. This means that the column reference is no longer used. Questions and answers in the database are given a number to include in their citation.

Citation order:

- Name of author
- Year of publication (in round brackets)
- Subject of question, answer or statement (in single quotation marks)
- Parliament: written questions and written answers (in italics)
- Day and month
- Question number
- Available at: URL (Accessed: date)

Example

In-text citation

Baroness Lister (2015) wrote to query the number of carers affected.

Reference list

Lister, Baroness (2015) 'Social security benefits: carers', *Parliament: written questions and written answers*, 7 September, HL 1298. Available at: http://www.parliament.uk/business/publications/written-questions-answers-statements/written-questions-answers/ (Accessed: 17 September 2018).

E13.4 Bills: House of Commons and House of Lords

Citation order:

- Title (in italics)
- Year of publication (in round brackets)
- Parliament: House of Commons or Lords
- Bill number
- Place of publication: Publisher

Example

In-text citation

Mr Vaz introduced the *Food Labelling (Sugar Content) Bill* (2013).

Reference list

Food Labelling (Sugar Content) Bill (2013). Parliament: House of Commons. Bill no. 23. London: The Stationery Office.

E13.5 UK statutes (Acts of Parliament)

Before 1963, an Act was cited according to the regnal year (that is, the number of years since the monarch's accession). You may see references to legislation in this format in early publications – for example, *Act of Supremacy 1534* (26 Hen 8 c1). However, for all Acts (including pre-1963), you should use the short title of the Act with the year in which it was enacted. Most Acts and parts of Acts are now available as PDFs or web pages to be viewed online, so reference the website where you located the Act.

NB As the date appears in the title of the Acts, there is no need to repeat the date in round brackets after the title.

If you are referencing documents from more than one country (jurisdiction), include the country (jurisdiction) in round brackets after the title of the documentation (see examples in Section E15).

Citation order:

♦ Title of Act, including year and chapter number (in italics)
♦ Country/jurisdiction (only if referencing more than one country's legislation)
♦ Available at: URL (Accessed: date)

Example: whole Act

In-text citation
Recent social care legislation (*Health and Social Care Act 2012*) …

Reference list
Health and Social Care Act 2012, c. 7. Available at: http://www.legislation.gov. uk/ukpga/2012/7/contents/enacted (Accessed: 17 September 2018).

Or if you use the PDF version:

Available at: http://www.legislation.gov.uk/ ukpga/2012/7/pdfs/ukpga_20120007_ en.pdf (Accessed: 17 September 2018).

Example: section of an Act

In-text citation
As defined in section 10(2) of the Act (*Children Act 2004*) …

Reference list
Children Act 2004, c. 31. Available at: http://www.legislation.gov.uk/ukpga/ 2004/31/contents (Accessed: 17 September 2018).

E13.6 Statutory Instruments (SIs)

Citation order:

♦ Name/title, including year (in italics)
♦ SI year and number (in round brackets)
♦ Available at: URL (Accessed: date)

Example

In-text citation
Referring to the *General Dental Council (Constitution) (Amendment) Order 2012* …

Reference list
General Dental Council (Constitution) (Amendment) Order 2012 (SI 2012/1655). Available at: http://www.legislation.gov. uk/uksi/2012/1655/contents/made (Accessed: 17 September 2018).

E13.7 Legislation from UK devolved legislatures

NB Legislation from UK devolved legislatures is available online at http:// www.legislation.gov.uk.

E13.7a Acts of the Scottish Parliament

For Acts of the post-devolution Scottish Parliament, replace the chapter number with 'asp' (meaning Act of the Scottish Parliament).

Citation order:

- Title of Act, including year (in italics)
- asp number (in round brackets)
- Available at: URL (Accessed: date)

Example

In-text citation

In the legislation (*Budget (Scotland) Act 2015*) …

Reference list

Budget (Scotland) Act 2015 (asp 2). Available at: http://www.legislation.gov. uk/asp/2015/2/contents (Accessed: 17 September 2018).

E13.7b Scottish Statutory Instruments (SSIs)

Citation order:

- Title of SSI, including year (in italics)
- SSI year/number (in round brackets)
- Available at: URL (Accessed: date)

Example

In-text citation

In the SSI of 2005 (*Tuberculosis (Scotland) Order 2005*) …

Reference list

Tuberculosis (Scotland) Order 2005 (SSI 2005/434). Available at: http://www. legislation.gov.uk/ssi/2005/434/ contents/made (Accessed: 17 September 2018).

E13.7c Acts of the Northern Ireland Assembly

Citation order:

- Title of Act (Northern Ireland), including year (in italics)
- Available at: URL (Accessed: date)

Example

In-text citation

… which was discussed in the legislation (*Pensions Act (Northern Ireland) 2015*).

Reference list

Pensions Act (Northern Ireland) 2015. Available at: http://www.legislation.gov. uk/nia/2015/5/contents (Accessed: 17 September 2018).

E13.7d Statutory Rules of Northern Ireland

The Northern Ireland Assembly may pass Statutory Instruments. These are called Statutory Rules of Northern Ireland.

Citation order:

- Title of Rule (Northern Ireland), including year (in italics)
- SR year/number (in round brackets)
- Available at: URL (Accessed: date)

Example

In-text citation

The rules relating to flavourings (*Smoke Flavourings Regulations (Northern Ireland) 2005*).

Reference list

Smoke Flavourings Regulations (Northern Ireland) 2005 (SR 2005/76). Available at: http://www.legislation.gov. uk/nisr/2005/76/contents/made (Accessed: 17 September 2018).

E13.7e National Assembly for Wales legislation

The National Assembly for Wales may pass Assembly Measures (nawm), which are primary legislation but are subordinate to UK statutes.

Citation order:

- Title of Assembly Measure, including year (in italics)
- (nawm number)
- Available at: URL (Accessed: date)

Example

In-text citation

The 2008 Measure (*NHS Redress (Wales) Measure 2008*) …

Reference list

NHS Redress (Wales) Measure 2008 (nawm 1). Available at: http://www.legislation.gov.uk/mwa/2008/1/2008-07-09 (Accessed: 17 September 2018).

The National Assembly for Wales may also pass Statutory Instruments. As well as the SI number and year, Welsh Statutory Instruments have a W. number.

Citation order:

- Title of Wales Statutory Instrument including year (in italics)
- SI year and number (W. number) (all in round brackets)
- Available at: URL (Accessed: date)

Example

In-text citation

The legislation (*The Carbon Accounting (Wales) Regulations 2018*) …

Reference list

The Carbon Accounting (Wales) Regulations 2018 (SI 2018/1301 (W.255)). Available at: http://www.legislation.gov.uk/wsi/2018/1301/contents/made (Accessed: 17 December 2018).

E13.8 Law Commission reports and consultation papers

Citation order:

- Law Commission
- Year of publication (in round brackets)
- Title of report or consultation paper (in italics)
- Number of report or consultation paper, Command Paper number (if given) (in round brackets)
- Place of publication: Publisher

Or, if accessed online:

- DOI *or* Available at: URL (Accessed: date)

Examples

In-text citation

The report (Law Commission, 2001) recommended that retrial after acquittal should be permitted in cases of murder, if new evidence became available.

Reference list

Law Commission (2001) *Double jeopardy and prosecution appeals* (Law Com No 267, Cm 5048). London: The Stationery Office.

Or

Law Commission (2001) *Double jeopardy and prosecution appeals* (Law Com No 267, Cm 5048). Available at: http://lawcommission.justice.gov.uk/areas/doublejeopardy.htm (Accessed: 17 September 2018).

E13.9 Command Papers, including Green and White Papers

Citation order:

- Department
- Year of publication (in round brackets)
- Title of report or consultation paper (in italics)

- ♦ Command Paper number (in round brackets)
- ♦ Place of publication: Publisher

Or, if accessed online:

- ♦ DOI *or* Available at: URL (Accessed: date)

Examples

In-text citations

In her essay she cited proposals on the Minimum Wage (Department for Business, Innovation & Skills, 2015) and Trade Practices (Secretary of State for Prices and Consumer Protection, 1979).

Reference list

Department for Business, Innovation & Skills (2015) *Regulations implementing the National Minimum Wage – a report on the Apprentice Rate* (Cm 9061). Available at: https://www.gov.uk/ government/publications/national-minimum-wage-report-on-the-2015-apprentice-rate (Accessed: 17 September 2018).

Secretary of State for Prices and Consumer Protection (1979) *Review of Restrictive Trade Practices Policy* (Cmnd. 7512). London: HMSO.

E13.10   Law reports

E13.10a   Law reports (cases) before 2002

Citation order:

- ♦ Name of case (in single quotation marks)
- ♦ Year (in round brackets)
- ♦ Title of law report (in italics)
- ♦ Volume number
- ♦ Page numbers

Example

In-text citation

The earlier case ('R v. Edward (John)', 1991) …

Reference list

'R v. Edward (John)' (1991) *Weekly Law Reports*, 1, pp. 207–208.

E13.10b   Law reports (cases) from 2002 with neutral citations

From 2002, cases have been given a neutral citation that identifies the case without referring to the printed law report series in which the case was published. This helps to identify the case online – for example, through the freely available transcripts of the British and Irish Legal Information Institute (www.bailii.org) and databases including Westlaw and LexisLibrary. If you are using the neutral citation, also provide the publication in which the case was reported or the database or website that you used.

Citation order:

- ♦ Name of parties involved in case (in single quotation marks)
- ♦ Year (in round brackets)
- ♦ Court and case no.
- ♦ Database or website (in italics)
- ♦ DOI *or*
- ♦ Available at: URL (Accessed: date)

Example

In-text citation

The case of 'Humphreys v. Revenue and Customs' (2012) …

Reference list

'Humphreys v. Revenue and Customs' (2012) United Kingdom Supreme Court, case 18. *BAILII*. Available at: http://www.bailii.org/uk/cases/UKSC/2012/18.html (Accessed: 17 September 2018).

E13.10c   Case analyses

In addition to law reports, legal chambers or publishers may publish comments or analyses of cases. It is important to be clear that these are opinions by individual or organisation authors, and are different to law reports.

Citation order:

♦ Author or organisation
♦ Year of publication (in round brackets)
♦ Title of case (in single quotation marks)
♦ Title of website (in italics)
♦ DOI *or* Available at: URL (Accessed: date)

Examples

In-text citations

Two analyses of the case (Essex Chambers, 2018; Thomson Reuters, 2018) …

Reference list

Essex Chambers (2018) 'CH v A Metropolitan Council'. *Essex Chambers*. Available at: http://www.39essex.com/cop_cases/ch-v-metropolitan-council (Accessed: 17 August 2018).

Thomson Reuters (2018) 'CH v A Metropolitan Council'. *Westlaw*. Available at: http://www.westlaw.com (Accessed: 17 August 2018).

E13.11   Inquiries

Public and independent inquiries may be published by order of Parliament, and if so are given a Parliamentary or Command Paper number.

Citation order:

♦ Author
♦ Year of publication (in round brackets)
♦ Title of inquiry (in italics)
♦ Parliamentary or Command Paper number (in round brackets)
♦ Place of publication: Publisher

Or, if accessed online:

♦ DOI *or* Available at: URL (Accessed: date)

Examples

In-text citations

The Leveson (2012), Hillsborough (2012) and Francis (2013) inquiries …

Reference list

Francis, R. (2013) *Report of the Mid Staffordshire NHS Foundation Trust public inquiry*. (HC 898). London: The Stationery Office.

Hillsborough. Report of the Hillsborough Independent Panel. (2012) (HC 581). Available at: http://hillsborough.independent.gov.uk/repository/report/HIP_report.pdf (Accessed: 27 October 2018).

Leveson, Lord (2012) *An inquiry into the culture, practices and ethics of the press*. (HC 780). Available at: https://www.gov.uk/government/publications/leveson-inquiry-report-into-the-culture-practices-and-ethics-of-the-press (Accessed: 27 October 2018).

E14 European Union (EU) legal sources

Legal documents from the EU include legislation, directives, decisions and regulations. The most authoritative source is the *Official Journal of the European Union*.

E14.1 EU legislation

Citation order:

♦ Legislation title (in italics)
♦ Year (in round brackets)
♦ Official Journal (in italics)
♦ Series initial issue
♦ Page numbers

Example

In-text citation
All signatories to the Treaty (*Consolidated Version of the Treaty on European Union*, 2008) …

Reference list
Consolidated Version of the Treaty on European Union (2008) *Official Journal* C 115, 9 May, pp. 13–45.

E14.2 EU directives, decisions and regulations

Citation order:

♦ Legislation type (in single quotation marks)
♦ Number and title (in single quotation marks)
♦ Year (in round brackets)
♦ Official Journal (OJ) series (in italics)
♦ Issue
♦ Page numbers

Or

♦ DOI *or* Available at: URL (Accessed: date)

Examples

In-text citations
The minister highlighted the terms of 'Council directive 2008/52/EC' (2008), 'Council regulation (EU) 2015/760' (2015) and 'DS Smith/Duropack' (2015) …

Reference list

Directives
'Council directive 2008/52/EC on certain aspects of mediation in civil and commercial matters' (2008) *Official Journal* L136, p. 3.

Regulations
'Council regulation (EU) 2015/760 on European long-term investment funds' (2015) *Official Journal* L123, p. 98.

Commission decisions are cited as cases
'Case M.7558 – DS Smith/Duropack' (2015) Commission decision. *Eur-Lex*. Available at: http://ec.europa.eu/ competition/mergers/cases/decisions/ m7558_20150521_20310_4308239_ EN.pdf (Accessed: 27 September 2018).

E14.3 Judgements of the European Court of Justice (ECJ) and General Court (GC)

Citation order:

♦ Case name (in single quotation marks)
♦ Year (in round brackets)
♦ Case number
♦ European Case Law Identifier (ECLI, see p. 226)
♦ Publication title (in italics)
♦ Section, page numbers

Example

In-text citation

Consideration of the Swedish view ('Commission of the European Communities v Kingdom of Sweden', 2005) ...

Reference list

'Commission of the European Communities v Kingdom of Sweden' (2005) Case no. C-111/03; ECLI:EU:C:2005:619. *European Court Reports*, I, 08789.

E15 International legal sources

E15.1 United Nations resolutions

For General Assembly resolutions, place A/RES/ before the resolution number (for example, A/RES/62/24).

For Security Council resolutions, place S/RES/ before the resolution number (for example, S/RES/1801).

Citation order:

- ◆ Organisation
- ◆ Year (in round brackets)
- ◆ Title (in italics)
- ◆ Resolution no.
- ◆ DOI *or* Available at: URL (Accessed: date)

Example

In-text citation

The climate change resolution (United Nations General Assembly, 1994) ...

Reference list

United Nations General Assembly (1994) *United Nations framework convention on climate change*. Resolution A/RES/48/189. Available at: http://daccess-dds-ny.un.org/doc/UNDOC/GEN/N94/036/43/PDF/N9403643.pdf?OpenElement (Accessed: 15 September 2018).

E15.2 International treaties, conventions and accords

NB If possible, cite from the United Nations Treaty Series.

Citation order:

- ◆ Title of treaty (in italics)
- ◆ Year (in round brackets)
- ◆ Treaty number
- ◆ Publication title (in italics)
- ◆ Volume and page numbers

If accessed online:

- ◆ DOI *or* Available at: URL (Accessed: date)

Example

In-text citation

The UK supported the *Convention relating to the status of refugees* (1951) ...

Reference list

Convention relating to the status of refugees (1951) Treaty no. 2545. *United Nations Treaty Series*, 189, pp. 137–221. Available at: https://treaties.un.org/doc/Publication/UNTS/Volume%20189/v189.pdf (Accessed: 17 September 2018).

E15.3 International Court of Justice (ICJ) cases

Documentation produced in hearing cases at the ICJ includes merits, written and oral proceedings, orders, judgements, press releases, and correspondence.

Citation order:

- ◆ Case name (in single quotation marks)
- ◆ Year (in round brackets)
- ◆ International Court of Justice cases (in italics)
- ◆ Publication type and date (if required)
- ◆ DOI *or* Available at: URL (Accessed: date)

Examples

In-text citations

The cases of 'East Timor (Portugal v. Australia)' (1991) and 'Maritime Dispute (Peru v. Chile)' (2014) considered ...

Reference list

General reference

'East Timor (Portugal v. Australia)' (1991) *International Court of Justice cases*. Available at: http://www.icj-cij.org/docket/index.php?p1=3&p2=3&code=pa&case=84&k=66&p3=0 (Accessed: 14 September 2018).

Documentation

'Maritime Dispute (Peru v. Chile)' (2014) *International Court of Justice cases*. Judgement of 27 January. Available at: http://www.icj-cij.org/docket/files/137/17930.pdf (Accessed: 14 September 2018).

E16   Government publications

Citation order:

♦ Name of government department
♦ Year of publication (in round brackets)
♦ Title (in italics)
♦ Place of publication: Publisher
♦ Series (in round brackets) – if applicable

If accessed online:

♦ DOI *or* Available at: URL (Accessed: date)

Many UK government publications may be accessed via https://www.gov.uk, but you should use the specific author or department as the author, if given.

Examples

In-text citations

Prison numbers increased last year (Ministry of Justice, 2007) as did the disparity in medical care (Department of Health, 2004; 2008).

Reference list

Department of Health (2004) *Primary medical services allocations 2004/05*. Health Service Circular HSC 2004/003. Available at: http://www.dh.gov.uk/en/Publicationsandstatistics/Lettersandcirculars/Healthservicecirculars/DH_4071269 (Accessed: 21 June 2018).

Department of Health (2008) *Health inequalities: progress and next steps*. Available at: http://www.dh.gov.uk/en/Publicationsandstatistics/Publications/PublicationsPolicyAndGuidance/DH_085307 (Accessed: 18 June 2018).

Ministry of Justice (2007) *Sentencing statistics (annual)*. Available at: http://www.justice.gov.uk/publications/sentencingannual.htm (Accessed: 3 June 2018).

NB If you are referencing government publications from more than one country, include the country of origin (in round brackets) after the department name.

Examples

The UK and Canada oppose the use of landmines (Department for International Development (UK), 2010; Department of Foreign Affairs and International Trade (Canada), 2012).

Department for International Development (UK) (2010) *Creating a safer environment: clearing landmines and other explosive remnants of war*. Available at: https://www.gov.uk/government/publications/demining-strategy-2010-2013 (Accessed: 5 January 2019).

Department of Foreign Affairs and International Trade (Canada) (2012) *Reaffirming the commitment*. Available at: http://www.international.gc.ca/mines/documents/cnd-fund-fond-can/00-01-introduction.aspx?lang=eng&view=d (Accessed: 5 January 2019).

E17 Publications of international organisations

Citation order:

♦ Name of organisation or institution
♦ Year of publication (in round brackets)
♦ Title (in italics)
♦ Place of publication: Publisher

If accessed online:

♦ DOI *or* Available at: URL (Accessed: date)

Examples

Reports by the European Commission (2013), the United Nations (2011) and International Chamber of Commerce, Commission for Air Transport (2015) …

European Commission (2013) *Making globalisation work for everyone*. Luxembourg: Office for Official Publications of the European Communities.

International Chamber of Commerce, Commission for Air Transport (2015) *The need for greater liberalization in international air transport*. Available at: http://www.iccwbo.org/Advocacy-Codes-and-Rules/Document-centre/2015/The-need-forgreater-liberalization-of-international-airtransport/ (Accessed: 9 February 2019).

United Nations (2011) *Yearbook of the United Nations, 2007 vol. 61*. New York: United Nations Department of Public Information.

E18 Scientific and technical information

E18.1 Technical standards

Citation order:

♦ Name of authorising organisation
♦ Year of publication (in round brackets)
♦ Number and title of standard (in italics)
♦ Place of publication: Publisher

If accessed online:

♦ DOI *or* Available at: URL (Accessed: date)

Examples

Loft conversions are subject to strict controls (British Standards Institution, 2004).

British Standards Institution (2004) *BSEN1995-1-2:2004: Design of timber structures*. London: British Standards Institution.

Or

British Standards Institution (2004) *BSEN1995-1-2:2004: Design of timber structures*. Available at: http://www.standardsuk.com/products/BS-EN-1995-1-2-2004.php (Accessed: 30 June 2018).

E18.2 Patents

Citation order:

♦ Inventor(s)
♦ Year of publication (in round brackets)
♦ Title (in italics)
♦ Authorising organisation
♦ Patent number
♦ Available at: URL (Accessed: date)

Example

Padley (2012) proposed a solution.

Padley, S. (2012) *Radiator isolating valve*. UK Intellectual Property Office Patent no. GB2463069. Available at: http://www.ipo.gov.uk/p-find-publication (Accessed: 24 August 2018).

E18.3 Scientific datasets

Reference where you located the data (for example, journal article/book/online).

Citation order:

♦ Author
♦ Date (in round brackets)
♦ Title of data (in single quotation marks)
♦ Available at: URL (Accessed: date)

Example

The data (Ralchenko, 2014) proved ...

Ralchenko, Y. (2014) 'Na levels holdings'. Available at: http://physics.nist.gov/asd3 (Accessed: 2 August 2018).

E18.4 Requests for Comments (RFCs)

Citation order:

♦ Author/editor
♦ Year (in round brackets)
♦ Title (in italics)
♦ Document number
♦ DOI *or* Available at: URL (Accessed: date)

Example

A number of comments were made relating to the document (Hoffman and Harris, 2015).

Hoffman, P. and Harris, S. (2015) *The Tao of IETF: a novice's guide to the Internet Engineering Task Force*. Nos: FYI 17 and RFC 4677. Available at: http://tools.ietf.org/html/rfc4677 (Accessed: 20 October 2018).

E18.5 Mathematical equations

Reference where you located the equation (for example, online journal article).

Citation order:

- Author
- Year of publication (in round brackets)
- Title of article (in single quotation marks)
- Title of journal (in italics – capitalise first letter of each word in title, except for linking words such as and, of, the, for)
- Volume, issue, page numbers
- DOI *or* Available at: URL (Accessed: date)

Example

In-text citation

Fradelizi and Meyer (2008, p. 1449) noted that for $z>0$ $P(K) \geq \dfrac{e^{n+1-z}Z^{n+1}}{(n!)^2}$ …

Reference list

Fradelizi, M. and Meyer, M. (2008) 'Some functional inverse Santaló inequalities', *Advances in Mathematics*, 218(5), pp. 1430–1452. doi:10.1016/j.aim.2008.03.013.

E18.6 Graphs

Reference where you located the graph – for example, graph in a book (give book details).

Citation order:

- Author
- Year of publication (in round brackets)
- Title of book (in italics)
- Place of publication: Publisher
- Page number or figure number for graph
- Graph

Example

In-text citation

The effects of the compounds (Day and Gastel, 2006, p. 95) …

Reference list

Day, R. and Gastel, B. (2006) *How to write and publish a scientific paper*. Cambridge: Cambridge University Press, p. 95, graph.

E19 Maps

E19.1 Ordnance Survey maps

Citation order:

- Ordnance Survey
- Year of publication (in round brackets)
- Title (in italics)
- Sheet number, scale
- Place of publication: Publisher
- Series (in round brackets)

Example

In-text citation

Archaeological sites are italicised (Ordnance Survey, 2002).

Reference list

Ordnance Survey (2002) *Preston and Blackpool*, sheet 102, 1:50,000. Southampton: Ordnance Survey (Landranger series).

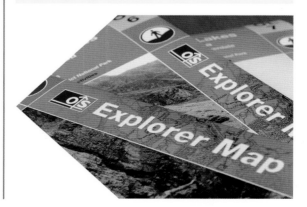

E19.2 Geological Survey maps

Citation order:

♦ Corporate author and publisher
♦ Year of publication (in round brackets)
♦ Title (in italics)
♦ Sheet number, scale
♦ Place of publication: Publisher
♦ Series (in round brackets)

Example

In-text citation

The landscape has undergone profound changes since the map (Ordnance Survey, 1980) was printed.

Reference list

Ordnance Survey (1980) *Bellingham (solid)*, sheet 13, 1:50,000. Southampton: Ordnance Survey. (Geological Survey of Great Britain [England and Wales]).

E19.3 Online maps

Citation order:

♦ Map publisher
♦ Year of publication (in round brackets)
♦ Title of map section (in italics)
♦ Sheet number or tile, scale
♦ DOI *or* Available at: URL (Accessed: date)

Examples

Ordnance Survey

In-text citation

The leisure centre is close to Tiddenfoot Lake (Ordnance Survey, 2018).

Reference list

Ordnance Survey (2018) *Tiddenfoot Lake*, Tile sp92sw, 1:10,000. Available at: http://edina.ac.uk/digimap/ (Accessed: 3 May 2018).

Google Maps

In-text citation

The dock layout and road network can be seen using Google Maps (Google, 2018).

Reference list

Google (2018) *Cardiff Bay*. Available at: http://maps.google.co.uk (Accessed: 5 July 2018).

E19.4 GIS maps

Citation order:

♦ Corporate author and publisher
♦ Year of publication (in round brackets)
♦ Map title (in italics)
♦ Scale
♦ Datafile title (in italics)
♦ Using: software (name in italics)
♦ Place of publication: Publisher

Example

In-text citation

The decline of woodland is evident (Natural England, 2017).

Reference list

Natural England (2017) *Map of deciduous woodland in North Yorkshire.* Scale 1cm = 1km. *Deciduous woodland BAP priority habitat (England) datafile.* Using: *Explorer for ArcGIS.* Redlands, CA: Esri.

E19.5   Map datasets

Citation order:

♦ Corporate author/publisher
♦ Year of publication (in round brackets)
♦ Datafile title (in italics)
♦ Format (in square brackets)
♦ DOI *or* Available at: URL (Accessed: date)

Examples

In-text citations

Examining brownfield use in Birmingham (Ordnance Survey, 2017) and Scotland (Environment Agency, 2016) …

Reference list

Environment Agency (2016) *2m LIDAR composite DSM and DTM for Scotland* [Dataset]. Available at: https://ea.sharefile.com/share/view/s11cd1dd359d4ad18 (Accessed: 21 January 2018).

Ordnance Survey (2017) *Birmingham city centre* [Dataset]. Available at: http://edina.ac.uk/digimap (Accessed: 21 January 2018).

E19.6   Atlases

Citation order:

♦ Author/editor (if available; if not, use title)
♦ Year of publication (in round brackets)
♦ Title (in italics)
♦ Place of publication: Publisher

Example

In-text citation

The Korean border with China (*The Times comprehensive atlas of the world*, 2011, p. 201) …

Reference list

The Times comprehensive atlas of the world (2011) 13th edn. London: Times Books.

E20   Visual and artistic sources

See also Section E22 'Audiovisual material (including broadcasts, streaming/sharing services, DVDs and videos)'.

Visual sources are available in many different formats, and the same image might be viewed in physical form (such as a painting in a gallery), in a printed book or online. The key principle is: cite what you have seen and in the format in which you saw them. If you are looking at an image in a book, it may have been cropped to fit into the page size. If you are looking at the image online, it may have been digitally altered or cropped. This will make it clear to your reader that you may not have seen the original image, and you are relying upon the publisher of the image (in print or online) to reproduce it accurately or to note what changes they may have made.

E20.1 Book and article illustrations, figures, diagrams and tables

If you are citing an illustration, figure, diagram or table, start with the source in which it appeared. In your in-text citation, give the page number and any caption number that will help to identify the illustration, using the terminology in the book or article (for example, illus./fig./diagram/logo/table). The reference list entry will be for the whole article or book.

Citation order:

♦ Author
♦ Year of publication (in round brackets)
♦ Publication information for book or article

Examples

In-text citations
Holbein's painting illustrated the prelate's ornate mitre (Strong, 1990, p. 62, fig. 12).

The GDP data for the UK (James, 2018, p. 12, table 2) …

Reference list
James. T. (2018) 'UK economic forecasts 2017–18', *Business Insider*, 4(2), pp. 9–14.

Strong, R. (1990) *Lost treasures of Britain*. London: Viking.

E20.2 Exhibitions

E20.2a Whole exhibitions

Citation order:

♦ Title of exhibition (in italics)
♦ Year (in round brackets)
♦ [Exhibition]
♦ Location. Date(s) of exhibition

Example

In-text citation
The acclaimed exhibition in London is one of the finest (*Pre-Raphaelites: Victorian Avant-Garde*, 2012).

Reference list
Pre-Raphaelites: Victorian Avant-Garde (2012) [Exhibition]. Tate Britain, London. 12 September 2012–13 January 2013.

E20.2b Installations/exhibits/ artefacts or objects in galleries and museums

If you wish to cite an object (for example, an exhibit or object in a museum or gallery), include the creator if known and a description, as well as the location and any further identification information. If you don't know the creator, use the description as the in-text citation and first element of the reference.

Citation order:

♦ Artist
♦ Year (in round brackets)
♦ Title of installation or exhibit (in italics)
♦ [Installation] or [Exhibit]
♦ Gallery or location
♦ (Viewed: date)

Example

In-text citation
My bed by Tracey Emin (1999) …

Reference list
Emin, T. (1999) *My bed* [Installation]. Tate Gallery, London (Viewed: 31 October 2000).

E20.3   Paintings/drawings

Citation order:

- ♦ Artist
- ♦ Year (if available)
- ♦ Title of the work (in italics)
- ♦ Medium (in square brackets)
- ♦ Institution or collection that houses the work, followed by the city

If accessed online:

- ♦ DOI *or* Available at: URL (Accessed: date)

Examples

In-text citations

Works by Coello (1664) and Dalí (1958) …

Reference list

Coello, C. (1664) *The triumph of St Augustine* [Oil on canvas]. Museo del Prado, Madrid.

Dalí, S. (1958) *Madonna* [Oil on canvas]. Available at: http://www.oxfordartonline.com (Accessed: 9 July 2018).

E20.4   Silhouettes

Citation order:

- ♦ Artist
- ♦ Year (in round brackets)
- ♦ Title of work (in italics)
- ♦ [Silhouette]
- ♦ Location
- ♦ Reference number

If accessed online:

- ♦ DOI *or* Available at: URL (Accessed: date)

Example

In-text citation

The silhouette (Leslie, 1926) captured the 1920s dress.

Reference list

Leslie, H. (1926) *Doreen Graham* [Silhouette]. National Portrait Gallery, London. NPG D46674. Available at: https://www.npg.org.uk/collections/search/portrait/mw269357 (Accessed: 14 June 2018).

E20.5   Collages

A collage is a new artwork created by mixing material from photography, painting, printed text and artefacts. As with any image, cite what you have seen (for example, a photograph on a website or an original piece of work in a gallery).

With digital technology, it is possible to create a digital collage by modifying any image or video to incorporate material from other sources (for example, blending photographs, cartoons and paintings to create a new image).

Citation order:

- ♦ Artist
- ♦ Year (in round brackets)
- ♦ Title (in italics)
- ♦ [Collage]
- ♦ Exhibited at (if required)
- ♦ Location. Date(s) of presentation (if required)

If accessed online:

- ♦ DOI *or* Available at: URL (Accessed: date)

Examples

In-text citations for collages

His blending of newspaper, photos and paint (Schwitter, 1942; 1947) …

Reference list

Schwitter, K. (1942) *The proposal* [Collage]. Available at: https://www.tate.org.uk/art/artworks/schwitters-the-proposal-t12398 (Accessed: 12 June 2018).

Schwitter, K. (1947) *Big fight* [Collage]. Exhibited at Victoria & Albert Museum, London.

Examples

In-text citations for digital collages

The mystical image (Jasmine, no date) …

Triumph (2016) displayed the fears of Brexit.

Reference list

Jasmine (no date) *Wolf girl* [Digital collage]. Available at: https://pixabay.com/en/wolf-girl-large-mystical-fog-mood-2082333/ (Accessed: 21 August 2018).

Triumph (2016) *Brexit* [Digital collage]. Available at: https://www.qutee.com/q/brexit/brexit-satire/ (Accessed: 21 August 2018).

E20.6   Cinemagraphs

These are still images that incorporate short movement within the frame. They are increasingly used in advertising to hold viewers' attention longer than a still image does.

Citation order:

♦ Artist
♦ Year (in round brackets)
♦ Title (in italics)
♦ [Cinemagraph]
♦ DOI *or* Available at: URL (Accessed: date)

Example

In-text citation

mrjonkane (2017) reversed the movement between the hummingbird and its background.

Reference list

mrjonkane (2017) *Summer hummmer in Sonoma, California* [Cinemagraph]. Available at: https://flixel.com/cinemagraph/f1y9e6dsund1ixdnoalm/ (Accessed: 21 August 2018).

E20.7   Photographs/images

Students often become confused when referencing works of art they have photographed. They are unsure whether to reference themselves as the image-maker or to reference the work itself. The answer is clear: you reference what you are referring to (that is, your photograph or the work of art). Thus, if you wish to discuss the way you photographed a sculpture by Rodin, you would reference yourself, following the examples below (omitting, if necessary, place of publication and publisher). If, however, you photographed Rodin's sculpture in a gallery and you are discussing the sculpture itself, you would follow the guidelines in Sections E20.2 or E20.17.

E20.7a   Prints or slides

Citation order:

♦ Photographer
♦ Year (in round brackets)
♦ Title of photograph (in italics)
♦ [Photograph]
♦ Place of publication: Publisher (if available)

Example

In-text citation

The seasonal and architectural changes were captured on film (Thomas, 2017).

Reference list

Thomas, T. (2017) *Redevelopment in Byker* [Photograph]. Newcastle upon Tyne: Then & Now Publishing.

E20.7b   Photographs from the internet

Citation order:

♦ Photographer
♦ Year of publication (in round brackets)
♦ Title of photograph (in italics)
♦ Available at: URL (Accessed: date)

Example: personal website

In-text citation

His beautiful photograph (Kitto, 2013) …

Reference list

Kitto, J. (2013) *Golden sunset*. Available at: http://www.jameskitto.co.uk/ photo_1827786.html (Accessed: 14 June 2018).

E20.7c   Photographs in online collections

On occasions, you may need to reference images that you have found through social media sites such as Snapseed, Pinterest or Tumblr, or that you have viewed directly on Flickr. You may also use sites such as Instagram to view photographs or videos or upload your own. Do not be confused; you simply take the reader to where you viewed or uploaded the image or video.

Citation order:

♦ Photographer
♦ Year of publication (in round brackets)
♦ Title of photograph/video (or collection) (in italics)
♦ Available at: URL (Accessed: date)

Example: Tumblr

In-text citation

Solar ikon's recent work (2014) …

Reference list

Solar ikon (2014) *Green onion*. Available at: http://www.tumblr.com/tagged/food (Accessed: 13 June 2018).

Example: Flickr

In-text citation

Chunyang Lin's (Solar ikon) recent work (2017) …

Reference list

Lin, C. (2017) *Green onion*. Available at: http://www.flickr.com/photos/ chunyang/4004866489/ (Accessed: 13 June 2018).

Example: Instagram

In-text citation

Photographs by Fisher (2016) …

Reference list

Fisher, D. (2016) *deepbody*. Available at: https://instagram.com/deepbody/ (Accessed: 25 April 2018).

Example: Pinterest

In-text citation

The pH scale (Pathak, no date) …

Reference list

Pathak, S. (no date) *Acids, alkalis and the pH scale*. Available at: https:// www.pinterest.co.uk/pin/ 667095763524863148/ (Accessed: 25 April 2018).

E20.7d   Images with no creator

Citation order:

♦ Title (in italics)
♦ Year (in round brackets)
♦ Available at: URL (Accessed: date)

Example

In-text citation

The image of the wonderful installation (*Flow*, 2016) …

Reference list

Flow (2016) Available at: http://www. star2.com/culture/arts/2016/10/30/ public-art-made-of-bamboo-konstruk-in-johor/ (Accessed: 2 November 2018).

E20.7e   Clip art

If using clip art images from online collections, use the details you are given to take the reader to the relevant piece of artwork. Be aware that some of the citation order details may not always be available.

Citation order:

♦ Producer
♦ Year of publication (in round brackets)
♦ Title of clip art (in italics)
♦ Available at: URL (Accessed: date)

Example

In-text citation
The image of the dog (*Dogs*, 2015) …

Reference list
Dogs (2015) Available at: http://www. clipart.co.uk/cgi-bin/icdisplay.pl?1, dog,1 (Accessed: 15 October 2018).

E20.7f   Medical images

Many kinds of medical/anatomical images can be viewed and downloaded from the internet (for example, MRI, PET, CT and ultrasound scans, as well as X-rays) for use in supporting your arguments or demonstrating particular aspects of anatomical or medical information. These would simply be referenced as photographs/images from the internet (see Section E20.7b).

Other images may be found in online databases such as Anatomy TV. For these, use the following format.

Citation order:

♦ Image title (in italics)
♦ Year (in round brackets)
♦ Medium (in square brackets)
♦ DOI *or* Available at: URL (Accessed: date)

Example

In-text citation

The X-ray and scan (*The spine*, 2013) clearly showed …

Reference list

The spine (2013) [X-ray and MRI scan]. Available at: http://www.anatomy.tv/ new_home.aspx (Accessed: 28 July 2018).

However, if you are working on placement in a hospital, there will be occasions when you may want to reference an individual patient's scan, for example. These are confidential sources of information, and as such these images would need to be anonymised (as shown in Section E27), and the patient and hospital's permission obtained if you wanted to use the image in your text/appendices. In these circumstances, use the following format.

Citation order:

♦ Anonymised patient's name (in square brackets)
♦ Year image produced (in round brackets)
♦ Image title (in italics)
♦ Medium (in square brackets)
♦ Location: institution

Example

In-text citation
Patient Y's X-ray (2018) …

Reference list
[Patient Y] (2018) *Left knee joint* [X-ray]. Bradford: Bradford Royal Infirmary.

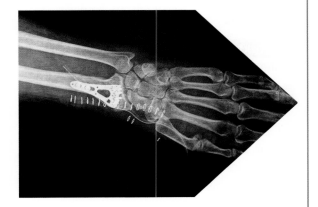

E20.8 Body art, including tattoos and Mehndi (henna)

Tattoos are visible in several formats, and you should use the citation order for the format in which you saw the image.

E20.8a Photograph of body art in a book

Citation order:

♦ Author of book
♦ Year (if available)
♦ Title of the book (in italics)
♦ Place of publication: Publisher

Example

In-text citation
The tattoos of a Marquesan warrior (Kuwuhara, 2005, p. 92) …

Reference list
Kuwuhara, M. (2005) *Tattoo: an anthropology*. Oxford: Berg.

E20.8b Online photograph of body art

Citation order:

♦ Photographer (if known)
♦ Year (if available, in round brackets)
♦ Title of the image (in single quotation marks)
♦ Title of the website (in italics)
♦ DOI *or* Available at: URL (Accessed: date)

Example

In-text citation

The bride's vibrant robes and elaborate Mehndi decoration (NY wedding and events, 2018) …

Reference list

NY wedding and events (2018) 'Flowers', *Latest bridal Mehndi designs*. Available at: https://www.pinterest.co.uk/pin/605874956094393915/ (Accessed: 27 July 2018).

E20.8c   Body art on a person

If you have seen the tattoo in person, put the title in italics as you would for a work of art.

Citation order:

♦ Tattoo artist (if known)
♦ Year (if available, in round brackets)
♦ Title of the image (in italics)
♦ [Tattoo]
♦ On Name of person
♦ Viewed: date (in round brackets)

Example

In-text citation

The image of the eagle (Riley, 2017) …

Reference list

Riley, K. (2017) *Eagle* [Tattoo]. On Kiara James (Viewed: 28 July 2018).

E20.9   Packaging

Citation order:

♦ Manufacturer
♦ Year seen (in round brackets)
♦ Product name (in italics)
♦ Medium (in square brackets)

If accessed online:

♦ DOI *or* Available at: URL (Accessed: date)

Examples

In-text citations

The different forms of packaging (The Premier Foods Group, 2012; Mars Incorporated, 2013) …

Reference list

Mars Incorporated (2013) *Mars Bar* [Wrapper].

The Premier Foods Group (2012) *Loyd Grossman tomato and mushroom sauce* [Jar label]. Available at: www.loydgrossmansauces.co.uk (Accessed: 23 May 2018).

E20.10   Cartoons

Citation order:

♦ Artist
♦ Date (if available)
♦ Title of cartoon (in single quotation marks)
♦ [Cartoon]
♦ Title of publication (in italics)
♦ Day and month

If accessed online:

♦ DOI *or* Available at: URL (Accessed: date)

Example

In-text citation

Steve Bell (2008) warned of the danger …

Reference list

Bell, S. (2008) 'Don't let this happen' [Cartoon]. *The Guardian*, 19 June. Available at: http://www.guardian.co.uk/world/cartoon/2008/jun/19/steve.bell.afghanistan.troops (Accessed: 2 July 2018).

E20.11 Comics

Comic and motion books and graphic novels are referenced as books (see Section E1).

To reference an *entire issue of a comic*, use the following:

Citation order with author:

♦ Author
♦ Year of publication (in round brackets)
♦ Title of comic (in italics)
♦ Other contributors (letterer, artists, painter) – if available
♦ Day, month, issue number (use the elements that are given)

If accessed online (including via app):

♦ Available at: URL or app name (include app version number if available)
♦ (Accessed: date)

Citation order without author:

♦ Title of comic (in italics)
♦ Year of publication (in round brackets)
♦ Other contributors (letterer, artists, painter) – if available
♦ Day, month, issue number (use the elements that are given)

If accessed online (including via app):

♦ Available at: URL or app name (include app version number if available)
♦ (Accessed: date)

Example: print

In-text citation

The latest issue (*Commando*, 2015) …

Reference list

Commando (2015) 12 September, no. 4814.

Example: online

In-text citation

The depiction of the super hero (Jason, 2018) …

Reference list

Jason, A. (2018) *Thor #2*. Letterer J. Sabino and painter M. del Mundo. 27 June. Available at: Marvel Comics app, version 3.10.7 (Accessed: 27 December 2018).

To reference a *comic strip*, use the following.

Citation order with author:

♦ Author
♦ Title of comic strip (in single quotation marks)
♦ Year of publication (in round brackets)
♦ Title of comic (in italics)
♦ Day, month, issue number, page (use the elements that are given)

If accessed online (including via app):

♦ Available at: URL or app name (include app version number if available)
♦ (Accessed: date)

Citation order without author:

♦ Title of comic strip (in single quotation marks)
♦ Year of publication (in round brackets)
♦ Title of comic (in italics)
♦ Day, month, issue number, page (use the elements that are given)
♦ If accessed online (including via app):
♦ Available at: URL or app name (include app version number if available)
♦ (Accessed: date)

Example

In-text citation

Jessica Ennis starred as Ennis the Menace in the hilarious comic strip ('The menace heptathlon', 2018).

Reference list

'The menace heptathlon' (2018) *The Beano*, 25 August, pp. 30–31.

E20.12 Posters

Citation order:

♦ Artist (if known, or use title)
♦ Year (in round brackets)
♦ Title (in italics)
♦ [Poster]
♦ Exhibited at location and date(s) of exhibition
♦ Dimensions (if relevant and available)

Example: poster copy of painting

In-text citation

The image (Chagall, no date) …

Reference list

Chagall, M. (no date) *Le violiniste* [Poster]. 84cm × 48cm/33″ × 19″.

Example: poster for exhibition

In-text citation

Smith's poster (2003) …

Reference list

Smith, K. (2003) *Prints, books and things* [Poster]. Exhibited at New York, Museum of Modern Art. 5 December 2003 to 8 March 2004.

E20.13 Mood boards

Citation order:

♦ Designer (if known)

♦ Year (in round brackets)
♦ Title (in italics)
♦ [Mood board]
♦ Presented at location and date(s) of presentation

If accessed online:

♦ DOI *or* Available at: URL (Accessed: date)

Example

In-text citation

His highly effective mood board (Weitzel, 2018) …

Reference list

Weitzel, L. (2018) *Say cheese* [Mood board]. Available at: http://flickr.com/photos/daisies7/5857970176/ (Accessed: 12 June 2018).

E20.14 Postcards

Citation order:

♦ Artist (if available)
♦ Year (in round brackets if available)
♦ Title (in italics)
♦ [Postcard]
♦ Place of publication: Publisher

Example

In-text citation

The flat sandy beach (Corrance, no date) …

Reference list

Corrance, D. (no date) *Gairloch, Wester Ross* [Postcard]. Scotland: Stirling Gallery.

E20.15 Logos

Citation order:

♦ Artist/organisation
♦ Year (in round brackets) – if available
♦ Title of logo (in italics)
♦ [Logo]

If accessed online:

♦ DOI *or* Available at: URL (Accessed: date)

Example

In-text citation ▶

Controversy surrounded the Olympic logo (London2012, 2010) …

Reference list ▶

London2012 (2010) *London2012* [Logo]. Available at: http://www.london2012.com (Accessed: 23 May 2018).

E20.16   Sewing/knitting patterns

Citation order:

♦ Producer
♦ Year (in round brackets) – if available
♦ Title of the pattern (in italics) with pattern/design number (in round brackets) – if available
♦ Medium (in square brackets)
♦ Place of publication: Publisher

If accessed online:

♦ DOI *or* Available at: URL (Accessed: date)

Examples

In-text citations ▶

The two detailed patterns (Simplicity NewLook, 2017; UK Hand Knitting Association, no date) …

Reference list ▶

Simplicity NewLook (2018) *Toddlers' & child's sportswear* (US1785AA) [Sewing pattern]. Available at: https://www.simplicitynewlook.com/1785 (Accessed: 22 August 2018).

UK Hand Knitting Association (no date) *Double knitting: cardigans, hat and blanket* (UKHKA 110) [Knitting pattern]. Bingley: UK Hand Knitting Association.

E20.17   Sculpture, statues and memorials

E20.17a   Sculpture

Citation order:

♦ Sculptor
♦ Year (in round brackets)
♦ Title (in italics)
♦ [Sculpture]
♦ Gallery or name of collection

If accessed online:

♦ DOI *or* Available at: URL (Accessed: date)

Example

In-text citation ▶

His talents were proven with *The lovers* (Rodin, 1886).

Reference list ▶

Rodin, A. (1886) *The lovers* [Sculpture]. Private collection.

E20.17b   Statues

Citation order:

♦ Sculptor
♦ Year (in round brackets)
♦ Title (in italics)
♦ [Statue]
♦ Location (and/or GPS coordinates, if available) (Viewed: date)

Example

In-text citation

The admiral's statue (Melton, 2000) looks across the Channel to France.

Reference list

Melton, S. (2000) *Admiral Sir Bertram Home Ramsey* [Statue]. Dover Castle, Kent, England, GPS coordinates: 51° 7′ 36.29″ N, 1° 19′ 26.22″ E (Viewed: 8 August 2018).

E20.17c   Memorials

Citation order:

♦ Name of architect (if known; if not, use name of memorial)
♦ Date of construction (in round brackets)
♦ Name of memorial (in italics)
♦ Location (and/or GPS coordinates, if available) (Viewed: date)

Example

In-text citation

The memorial (Leong Swee Lim, 1967) …

Reference list

Lim, L.S. (1967) *Civilian War Memorial*. War Memorial Park, Beach Road, Singapore, GPS coordinates: 1° 17′ 32.91″ N, 103° 51′ 11.11″ E (Viewed: 4 February 2018).

E20.18   Inscriptions

E20.18a   Inscriptions on monuments

Inscriptions on gravestones and memorials are, in many instances, the only detailed record of a person's existence, circumstances and relationships, apart from basic information given in birth, marriage and death certificates and the census.

Referencing this source can be difficult, but (as with printed material) you should aim to provide as much information as possible for another person to locate the gravestone or memorial. In some instances, the plot number of a grave will be obtainable and can be referenced; if not, try to give an indication of the location from a landmark.

Citation order:

♦ Name of deceased (in single quotation marks)
♦ Year of death/event (in round brackets)
♦ [Monument inscription]
♦ Location (Viewed: date)

Examples

In-text citation

The gravestone of the railway engineman ('Oswald Gardiner', 1840) compares him to one of the locomotives he drove: 'My engine now is cold and still. No water does my boiler fill.'

Reference list

'Oswald Gardiner' (1840) [Monument inscription]. St Mary the Virgin Churchyard (5m north-west of church), Whickham, Tyne and Wear (Viewed: 12 August 2018).

In-text citation

Corporal Pears was killed during the retreat to Dunkirk ('Wilfrid Pears', 1940).

Reference list

Where plot number available
'Wilfred Pears' (1940) [Monument inscription]. Plot 13, row E, grave 13, London Cemetery and Extension, Longueval, France (Viewed: 27 July 2018).

E20.18b   Inscriptions on statues

Referencing inscriptions on statues can also be difficult, as the author may not be identified and the wording may be a quotation from an earlier source. Give as much information as you are able to.

Citation order:

♦ Author (if known; if not, use title of statue)
♦ Year of inscription (in round brackets)
♦ Inscription on statue to/of ... (in italics)
♦ Location (Viewed: date)

Example

In-text citation

The inscription by Herbert (2000) ...

Reference list

Herbert, A.P. (2000) *Inscription on statue to Admiral Bertram Home Ramsey*. Dover Castle, Kent, England (Viewed: 8 August 2018).

E20.18c   Inscriptions on buildings

Citation order:

♦ Author (if known; if not, use first three words of inscription)
♦ Year of inscription (in round brackets)
♦ Inscription on ... (in italics)
♦ Location (Viewed: date)

Example

In-text citation

The exterior inscription by Lewis (2004) ...

Reference list

Lewis, G. (2004) *Inscription on Wales Millennium Centre*. Cardiff Bay, Cardiff, Wales (Viewed: 8 August 2018).

E20.19   Graffiti

By its nature, graffiti is anonymous (even when the graffitist includes their signature tag). It is usually short-lived artistic expression (or vandalism, depending on one's perspective). As it may be removed at any time, it is essential to include as much information as possible to describe the content, location and date viewed. Be careful if citing offensive language or imagery in graffiti.

Citation order:

♦ Title or description (with graffitist's tag, if present) (in italics)
♦ Year (in round brackets)
♦ [Graffiti]
♦ Location (Viewed: date)

Example

In-text citation

The graffiti (*Marty u dare!*, 2012) demonstrated ...

Reference list

Marty u dare! (2012) [Graffiti]. 3 Westland Street, Londonderry, Northern Ireland (Viewed: 27 June 2012).

E21   Live performances

E21.1   Concerts

Citation order:

♦ Composer
♦ Year of performance (in round brackets)
♦ Title (in italics)
♦ Performed by ... conducted by ...
♦ [Location. Date seen]

Examples

Classical concert

In-text citation

A wonderful premiere (Lord, 2007) …

Reference list

Lord, J. (2007) *Durham Concerto*. Performed by the Liverpool Philharmonic Orchestra, conducted by M. Damev [Durham Cathedral, Durham. 20 October].

Band concert

In-text citation

The Kings of Leon (2008) wowed the crowd …

Reference list

Kings of Leon (2008) [Glastonbury Festival. 27 June].

E21.2   Dance

Citation order:

♦ Name of choreographer or composer
♦ (chor.) or (comp.)
♦ Year of performance (in round brackets)
♦ Title (in italics)
♦ Directed by (if available)
♦ Produced by (if available)
♦ Performed by (dance company, if available)
♦ [Location. Date seen]

Example

In-text citation

The performance was true to the intentions of its creator (Ashton, 1937).

Reference list

Ashton, F. (chor.) (1937) *A wedding bouquet*. Performed by the Royal Ballet [Royal Opera House, London. 22 October 2004].

E21.3   Plays

Citation order:

♦ Title (in italics)
♦ by Author
♦ Year of performance (in round brackets)
♦ Directed by
♦ [Location. Date seen]

Example

In-text citation

One innovation was the use of Sellotape for the fairies' webs (*A midsummer night's dream*, 1995).

Reference list

A midsummer night's dream by W. Shakespeare (1995) Directed by I. Judge. [Theatre Royal, Newcastle upon Tyne. 26 February].

E21.4 Dances/plays filmed and viewed online

Citation order:

♦ Name of choreographer or composer
♦ (chor.) or (comp.)
♦ Year of performance (in round brackets)
♦ Title (in italics)
♦ Directed by (if available)
♦ Produced by (if available)
♦ Performed by (if available)
♦ Available at: URL (Accessed: date)

Example

In-text citation

The atmospheric dance (Lafeuille, 2014) ...

Reference list

Lafeuille, P. (chor.) (2014) *Alice in China*. Directed by P. Sevastikoglou. Produced by M-P. Bousquet. Performed by National Circus and Acrobats of China. Available at: https://search.alexanderstreet.com/ preview/work/bibliographic_ entity%7Cvideo_work%7C1417232 (Accessed: 25 February 2019).

E21.5   Musicals

Citation order:

♦ Composer
♦ Year of performance (in round brackets)
♦ Title (in italics)
♦ Other attributions (for example, Choreography by ...; Lyrics by ...; Directed by ...)
♦ [Location. Date seen]

Example

In-text citation

Parker and Nicholaw's irreverent comedy (2018) ...

Reference list

Parker, T. and Nicholaw, C. (2018) *The Book of Mormon*. Lyrics and music by T. Parker, R. Lopez and M. Stone; choreography by C. Nicholaw. [Prince of Wales Theatre, London. 4 May].

E21.6   Circuses

Citation order:

♦ Name of circus
♦ Year of performance

♦ Title of circus (if available, in italics)
♦ Presented by (if relevant)
♦ [Location. Date seen]

Example

In-text citation

The spectacular circus (Zippos Circus, 2018) ...

Reference list

Zippos Circus (2018) *Legacy*. Presented by N. Barrett. [London, Gladstone Park. 22 May].

E22   Audiovisual material (including broadcasts, streaming/catch-up/ sharing services, DVDs and videos)

There are now many means to watch or listen to audiovisual material, and you should use the reference format for the media you used. If you wish to refer to a specific time within a video, use a time code in your in-text reference, with the format minutes:seconds. See the examples in Sections E22.1a, E22.4d, E22.4e and E22.11 below.

E22.1   Radio

E22.1a   Radio programmes

Citation order:

♦ Title of programme (in italics)
♦ Year of transmission (in round brackets)
♦ Transmission channel
♦ Date of transmission (day/month), time of transmission

Example

In-text citation

The interview with the minister (*Today*, 2018, 08:10) …

Reference list

Today (2018) BBC Radio 4, 15 August, 06:00.

E22.1b Radio programmes heard online

You may listen to radio programmes live online, or days after the original transmission through radio catch-up services such as the BBC's Sounds. If available, specify the full date of the original broadcast as well as the date you accessed the programme.

Citation order:

♦ Title of programme (in italics)
♦ Year of original transmission (in round brackets)
♦ Transmission channel
♦ Date and time of original transmission (if available)
♦ DOI *or* Available at: URL (Accessed: date)

Examples

In-text citation

Throughout the show, Cryer had the audience in stitches (*I'm Sorry I Haven't a Clue*, 2018) …

Reference list

I'm Sorry I Haven't a Clue (2018) BBC Radio 4, 25 July 18:30. Available at: https://www.bbc.co.uk/radio/play/b0bbp9q9 (Accessed: 8 August 2018).

In-text citation

Football dominated the discussion (*The Alan Brazil Sports Breakfast*, 2018).

Reference list

The Alan Brazil Sports Breakfast (2018) talkSPORT – Listen Again, 31 July 21:00. Available at: https://talksport.com/radio/listen-again/1533013200 (Accessed: 10 August 2018).

E22.2 Television

NB For television programmes viewed via video streaming (catch-up TV or subscription) services (for example, Netflix, Amazon Prime Video, BBC iPlayer, Box of Broadcasts), see Section E22.3.

E22.2a Television programmes

Citation order:

♦ Title of programme (in italics)
♦ Year of transmission (in round brackets)
♦ Transmission channel
♦ Date of transmission (day/month), time of transmission

Example: individual programme

In-text citation

The embarrassing corporate wannabes (*The Apprentice*, 2017) ...

Reference list

The Apprentice (2017) BBC One Television, 23 September, 21:00.

Example: to quote something a character/presenter has said

In-text citation

'You're fired!' (Sugar, 2017) ...

Reference list

Sugar, A. (2017) *The Apprentice*. BBC One Television, 23 June, 21:00.

E22.2b   Episodes of a television series

Citation order:

♦ Title of episode (in single quotation marks) if known; if not, use series title
♦ Year of transmission (in round brackets)
♦ Title of programme (in italics)
♦ Series and episode numbers
♦ Transmission channel
♦ Date of transmission (day/month), time of transmission

Example

In-text citation

Some Daleks were mad and bad ('Asylum of the Daleks', 2012).

Reference list

'Asylum of the Daleks' (2012) *Doctor Who*, Series 33, episode 1. BBC One Television, 1 September, 18:00.

E22.2c   Television programmes/series on DVD/Blu-ray

Citation order:

♦ Title of episode (in single quotation marks)
♦ Year of distribution (in round brackets)
♦ Title of programme/series (in italics)
♦ Series and episode numbers (if known)
♦ Date of original transmission (if known)
♦ [DVD, catalogue number] or [Blu-ray, catalogue number]
♦ Place of distribution: Distributor

Example

In-text citation

The origins of the Doctor's most fearsome foe were revealed in 'Genesis of the Daleks' (2006).

Reference list

'Genesis of the Daleks' (2006) *Doctor Who*, season 12, episode 1. First broadcast 1975 [DVD, VFD 00154]. London: BBC DVD.

E22.2d   Separate episodes from DVD/ Blu-ray box-sets

Citation order:

♦ Title of episode (in single quotation marks)
♦ Year of distribution (in round brackets)
♦ Title of programme/series (in italics)
♦ 'In'
♦ Title of compilation or box-set (in italics)
♦ [DVD, catalogue number] or [Blu-ray, catalogue number]
♦ Place of distribution: Distributor

Example

Close attention was paid to period details ('Episode 8', 2014) …

'Episode 8' (2014) *Downton Abbey*. In *Downton Abbey Series 5* [DVD, VFD 019861]. London: Universal Pictures UK.

E22.3 Programmes viewed via streaming services

These can include catch-up services such as Box of Broadcasts, BBC iPlayer, ITV Hub, All 4, My5 and subscription services such as Netflix, Amazon Prime Video and Now TV. You do not need to refer to the device you have used to view the video; the examples below illustrate the elements required to reference this material correctly and consistently.

E22.3a Programmes

Citation order:

♦ Title of programme (in italics)
♦ Year of original broadcast (in round brackets)
♦ Name of transmitting channel
♦ Date and time of transmission (if available)
♦ Available at: Name of streaming service (Accessed: date)

Example: single programme

Lessons were not learnt from previous disasters (*The Fires That Foretold Grenfell*, 2018).

The Fires That Foretold Grenfell (2018) BBC Two, 30 October, 20:00. Available at: BBC iPlayer (Accessed: 5 October, 20:00 2018).

E22.3b Episode from a series

Citation order:

♦ Title of episode (in single quotation marks) if known; if not, use series title
♦ Year of original broadcast (in round brackets)
♦ Title of series/season (in italics)
♦ Series/Season and episode numbers, or day/month (if available)
♦ Production company
♦ Available at: Name of streaming service (Accessed: date)

Example: Amazon Prime Video

The brilliantly-paced episode ('God sees', 2017) highlighted …

'God sees' (2017) *Bosch*, Series 3, episode 3. Amazon Studios. Available at: Amazon Prime Video (Accessed: 5 October 2018).

Example: Now TV

In-text citation

Moss's heart-breaking performance ('The last ceremony', 2018) ...

Reference list

'The last ceremony' (2018) *The Handmaid's Tale*, Season 2, episode 10. MGM Television. Available at: Now TV (Accessed: 16 August 2018).

Example: Netflix

In-text citation

Princess Margaret's love life was exposed in 'Gloriana' (2016).

Reference list

'Gloriana' (2016) *The Crown*, Season 1, episode 10. Netflix. Available at: http://www.netflix.com/gb/title/80025678 (Accessed: 24 July 2018).

Example: BBC iPlayer

In-text citation

As revealed in 'The lost children' (2018) ...

Reference list

'The lost children' (2018) *Panorama*, 30 September. BBC One. Available at: BBC iPlayer (Accessed: 5 October 2018).

Example: Box of Broadcasts

In-text citation

Simon Schama's exploration of the Renaissance ('The triumph of art', 2018) ...

Reference list

'The triumph of art' (2018) *Civilisations*, episode 5, 1 March. BBC Two. Available at: Box of Broadcasts (Accessed 5 October 2018).

E22.4   Films

E22.4a   Films viewed at the cinema

Citation order:

- Title of film (in italics)
- Year of distribution (in round brackets)
- Directed by
- [Feature film]
- Place of distribution: Distributor

Example

In-text citation

Movies were used to attack President Bush's policies (*Fahrenheit 9/11*, 2004).

Reference list

Fahrenheit 9/11 (2004) Directed by M. Moore. [Feature film]. Santa Monica, CA: Lionsgate Films.

E22.4b   Films viewed via streaming services

Citation order:

- Title of film (in italics)
- Year of distribution (in round brackets)
- Directed by
- DOI *or* Available at: Name of service
- (Accessed: date)

Example

In-text citation

The hero (*Black Panther*, 2018) …

Reference list

Black Panther (2018) Directed by R. Coogler. Available at: Netflix (Accessed: 5 December 2018).

E22.4c   Films on Blu-ray/DVD

Citation order:

◆ Title of film (in italics)
◆ Year of distribution (in round brackets)
◆ Directed by
◆ [Blu-ray, catalogue number] or [DVD, catalogue number]
◆ Place of distribution: Distributor

Example

In-text citation

Special effects can dominate a film, for example *The Matrix Reloaded* (2003).

Reference list

The Matrix Reloaded (2003) Directed by A. Wachowski and L. Wachowski. [DVD, 68058]. Los Angeles, CA: Warner Bros Inc.

For *films that have been reissued*, use the following format.

Citation order:

◆ Title of film (in italics)
◆ Year of original film distribution (in round brackets)
◆ Directed by
◆ [Blu-ray, catalogue number] or [DVD, catalogue number]

◆ Reissued
◆ Place of distribution: Distributor
◆ Year of reissue

Example

In-text citation

… in this breathtaking, poetic film (*Pink Narcissus*, 1971).

Reference list

Pink Narcissus (1971) Directed by J. Bidgood. [DVD, BFIVD620]. Reissued. London: BFI, 2007.

Thus, just the year of the original film distribution is given in-text. The reference list also includes the date of reissue.

Many films on Blu-ray/DVD come with additional material on other discs, such as interviews with actors and directors and outtakes. Sections E22.4d and E22.4e give examples for referencing some of this material.

E22.4d   Directors' commentaries on Blu-ray/DVD

Citation order:

◆ Name of commentator
◆ Year (in round brackets)
◆ Director's commentary (in single quotation marks)
◆ Name of film (in italics)
◆ Directed by
◆ [Blu-ray, catalogue number] or [DVD, catalogue number]
◆ Place of distribution: Distributor

Example

In-text citation

The director thought this was a profitable franchise (Wachowski, 2003, 14:20).

Reference list

Wachowski, A. (2003) 'Director's commentary', *The Matrix Reloaded*. Directed by A. Wachowski and L. Wachowski. [DVD, 68058]. Los Angeles, CA: Warner Bros Inc.

E22.4e   Interviews with film directors

Citation order:

♦ Name of person interviewed
♦ Year of interview (in round brackets)
♦ Title of the interview (if any) (in single quotation marks)
♦ Interviewed by Interviewer's name
♦ Title of film (in italics)
♦ [Blu-ray, catalogue number] or [DVD, catalogue number]
♦ Place of distribution: Distributor

Example

In-text citation

The director thought this was a profitable franchise (Wachowski, 2003, 14:20).

Reference list

Wachowski, A. (2003) 'Interview with A. Wachowski'. Interviewed by L. Jones. *The Matrix Reloaded* [DVD, 68058]. Los Angeles, CA: Warner Bros Inc.

E22.4f   Films on video cassettes

Citation order:

♦ Title of film or programme (in italics)
♦ Year of distribution (in round brackets)
♦ Directed by
♦ [Video cassette, catalogue number]
♦ Place of distribution: Distributor

Example

In-text citation

When the story finally made it to the silver screen (*The Lord of the Rings: The Two Towers*, 2003).

Reference list

The Lord of the Rings: The Two Towers (2003) Directed by P. Jackson. [Video cassette, EDV9179]. New York: New Line Productions Inc.

E22.5   Online video sharing platforms (including YouTube, Vimeo, IGTV, Dailymotion, TED)

If you wish to refer to a specific time within a video, use a time code in your in-text reference, with the format minutes: seconds.

Citation order:

♦ Name of person/organisation posting video
♦ Year video posted (in round brackets)
♦ Title of film or programme (in italics)
♦ Date uploaded (if available)
♦ DOI
♦ OR Available at: URL or Name of streaming service/app (Accessed: date)

Examples

In-text citation for specific part of video

When mixing the plaster (Leponline, 2017, 02:00) …

Reference list

Leponline (2017) *Ask the experts – plastering a wall*. 4 December. Available at: http://www.youtube.com/watch?v=J9wpcellxCU (Accessed: 13 January 2017).

In-text citation for whole video

By making Mars inhabitable (National Geographic, 2018) …

Reference list

National Geographic (2018) *Could we terraform Mars?* 1 November. Available at: https://www.instagram.com/p/BppNEWllmRh/ (Accessed: 21 July 2018).

E22.6 Music streaming/ subscription services

Music streaming/downloads are available from a range of different websites and apps, including Spotify, YouTube Music, Apple Music, SoundCloud, Deezer, Google Play Music and iTunes.

Citation order:

♦ Artist name (individual, band, orchestra, etc.)
♦ Year of release (in round brackets)
♦ Title of song/track title (if required, in single quotation marks)
♦ Title of album (if required, in italics)
♦ Available at: Name of streaming service (Accessed: date)

Example: single song/track

In-text citation

The exceptional track (The Paper Kites, 2015) …

Reference list

The Paper Kites (2015) 'Electric Indigo'. Available at: Spotify (Accessed: 5 October 2018).

Example: track from an album

In-text citation

The haunting track from their second album (The Paper Kites, 2015) …

Reference list

The Paper Kites (2015) 'Too late', *Twelvefour*. Available at: Spotify (Accessed: 8 December 2018).

Example: whole album

In-text citation

… their acclaimed album (The Paper Kites, 2015).

Reference list

The Paper Kites (2015) *Twelvefour*. Available at: Deezer (Accessed: 12 January 2019).

E22.7 Music or spoken word recordings on audio CDs or vinyl

E22.7a Tracks released on CD or vinyl as singles

Citation order:

♦ Artist
♦ Year of release (in round brackets)
♦ Title of track (in italics)
♦ [CD, catalogue number] or [vinyl, catalogue number] (if available)
♦ Place of distribution: Distributor

Example

In-text citation

Her best-selling album (Jessie J, 2012) …

Reference list

Jessie J (2012) *Domino* [CD, 2364]. New York, NY: Universal Republic Records.

E22.7b Classical music tracks released on CD or vinyl

Citation order:

♦ Composer
♦ Year of publication (in round brackets)
♦ Title of composition (in italics)
♦ Format and catalogue number (if available) (in square brackets)
♦ Additional notes if required
♦ Place of distribution: Distributor

Example

In-text citation

The Orchestra's performance of Mahler (1994) …

Reference list

Mahler, G. (1994) *Symphony No. 10* [CD, 286]. BBC National Orchestra of Wales, conducted by M. Wrigglesworth. 26 November 1993. London: BBC.

Or if notes are not required:

Mahler, G. (1994) *Symphony No. 10* [CD]. London: BBC.

E22.7c Tracks on a CD or vinyl album

Citation order:

♦ Artist
♦ Year of release (in round brackets)
♦ Title of track (in single quotation marks)
♦ Title of album (in italics)

♦ [CD, catalogue number] or [vinyl, catalogue number]
♦ Place of distribution: Distributor

Example

In-text citation

The song 'My heaven' (Carpenter, 2004) …

Reference list

Carpenter, M.C. (2004) 'My heaven', *Between here and gone* [CD, 5712]. New York: Columbia Records.

E22.7d Whole albums

Citation order:

♦ Artist
♦ Year of release (in round brackets)
♦ Title of album (in italics)
♦ [CD, catalogue number] or [vinyl, catalogue number]
♦ Place of distribution: Distributor

Example

In-text citation

The band's acclaimed album (Emily Barker & The Red Clay Halo, 2008) …

Reference list

Emily Barker & The Red Clay Halo (2008) *Despite the snow* [CD, E52008]. London: Everyone Sang.

E22.7e Music or spoken word recordings on audio cassettes

Citation order:

♦ Artist (if available; if not, use title in italics first)
♦ Year of release (in round brackets)
♦ Title of recording (in italics)
♦ [Audio cassette, catalogue number]
♦ Place of publication: Publisher

Example

In-text citation

Determination is a key attribute (*It's your choice: selection skills for managers*, 1993).

Reference list

It's your choice: selection skills for managers (1993) [Audio cassette, 626]. London: Video Arts.

E22.8   Liner notes

The liner notes in CD, DVD, vinyl and cassette containers often have information that can be referenced.

Citation order:

- Author
- Year (in round brackets)
- Title of liner notes text (in single quotation marks)
- 'In'
- Title of recording (in italics)
- [CD liner notes]
- Place of distribution: Distributor

Example

In-text citation

Thrills (1997, p. 11) described Weller's lyrics as 'sheer poetry'.

Reference list

Thrills, A. (1997) 'What a catalyst he turned out to be'. In *The very best of The Jam* [CD liner notes]. London: Polydor.

E22.9   Lyrics from songs/hymns

Citation order:

- Lyricist
- Year of release (in round brackets)

- Title of song/hymn (in italics)
- Place of distribution: Distributor

Example

In-text citation

Lennon and McCartney (1966) expressed the frustration of every new author: 'Dear Sir or Madam, will you read my book? It took me years to write, will you take a look?'

Reference list

Lennon, J. and McCartney, P. (1966) *Paperback writer*. Liverpool: Northern Songs Ltd.

E22.10   Musical scores (sheet music)

Citation order:

- Composer
- Year of publication (in round brackets)
- Title of score/sheet music collection (in italics)
- [Musical score]
- Notes (if required)
- Place of publication: Publisher

Example

In-text citation

The composer's evocation of the sea in *The Hebrides* (Mendelssohn, 1999) …

Reference list

Mendelssohn, F. (1999) *The Hebrides* [Musical score]. Edited from composer's notes by J. Wilson. London: Initial Music Publishing.

E22.11   Podcasts

Although podcasts can be downloaded on to portable devices, you should reference where they were published or displayed for download rather than trying to give your electronic device as a source.

Citation order:

♦ Author/presenter
♦ Year that the site was published/last updated (in round brackets)
♦ Title of podcast (in italics)
♦ [Podcast]
♦ Day/month of posted message
♦ DOI *or* Available at: URL (Accessed: date)

Example: with author/presenter

In-text citation

Verity *et al.* (2018) noted that the Olympics had a detrimental effect on sales.

Reference list

Verity, A. *et al.* (2018) *Retail sales figures* [Podcast]. 4 September. Available at: http://www.bbc.co.uk/podcasts/series/money (Accessed: 25 September 2018).

Example: without author

In-text citation

Internal networks are critical (Oracle Business Sense, 2013) …

Reference list

Oracle Business Sense (2013) *Structure* [Podcast]. 12 June. Available at: http://www.guardian.co.uk/podcast/0,,329509709,00.xml (Accessed: 27 June 2018).

E22.12   Phonecasts

Phonecasts are audio or video programmes transmitted to a user's mobile phone. The user dials a number to access the programme. Alternatively, phonecasters can broadcast by using their telephones in place of microphones. Although phone calls are personal communications, it is possible to reference phonecasts if the access details are available in a publication or web page.

Citation order:

♦ Title of phonecast (in italics)
♦ Year of production (in round brackets)
♦ [Phonecast]
♦ DOI *or* Available at: URL (Accessed: date)

Example

In-text citation

Zuckerberg created Facebook in 2004 (*A conversation with Mark Zuckerberg*, 2017).

Reference list

A conversation with Mark Zuckerberg (2017) [Phonecast]. Available at: http://www.phonecasting.com/Channel/ViewChannel.aspx?id=1904 (Accessed: 11 July 2018).

E22.13   Screencasts

Also called 'video screen captures', screencasts are digital recordings of computer screen activity. Screencast videos can provide instructions for using software applications.

Citation order:

♦ Title of screencast (in italics)
♦ Year of production (in round brackets)
♦ [Screencast]
♦ DOI *or* Available at: URL (Accessed: date)

Example

In-text citation

An online video demonstrated functions (*Learning Rails the zombie way*, no date).

Reference list

Learning Rails the zombie way (no date) [Screencast]. Available at: http://www.rubyonrails.org/screencasts (Accessed: 27 January 2018).

E22.14   Screenshots

These save still images of your computer desktop or anything shown on your screen to a static image file.

Citation order:

♦ Title of screenshot (in italics)
♦ Year of production (in round brackets)
♦ [Screenshot]
♦ DOI *or* Available at: URL (Accessed: date)

Example

In-text citation

My screenshot (*Poppy*, 2018) …

Reference list

Poppy (2016) [Screenshot]. Available at: https://www.google.co.uk/trends/hottrends (Accessed: 2 November 2018).

E22.15   Vodcasts/vidcasts

Video podcasts – called vodcasts or vidcasts – can be viewed online or downloaded for later viewing. So that readers can locate the original, cite and reference where you obtained the vodcast.

Citation order:

♦ Author

♦ Year that the site was published/last updated (in round brackets)
♦ Title of vodcast (in italics)
♦ [Vodcast]
♦ DOI *or* Available at: URL (Accessed: date)

Example

In-text citation

The vodcast (Walker and Carruthers, 2008) explained the proposal.

Reference list

Walker, A. and Carruthers, S. (2014) *Storage on your network* [Vodcast]. Available at: http://www.labrats.tv/episodes/ep126.html (Accessed: 19 June 2018).

E22.16   Microform (microfiche and microfilm)

Citation order:

♦ Author
♦ Year of publication (in round brackets)
♦ Title of microform (in italics)
♦ Medium (in square brackets)
♦ Place of publication: Publisher

Example

In-text citation

Data from Fritsch (1987) …

Reference list

Fritsch, F.E. (1987) *The Fritsch collection: algae illustrations on microfiche* [Microfiche]. Ambleside: Freshwater Biological Association.

E23   Interviews

Citation order:

♦ Name of person interviewed
♦ Year of interview (in round brackets)

- Title of the interview (if any) (in single quotation marks)
- Interview with Interviewee
- Interviewed by Interviewer's name
- for Title of publication or broadcast (in italics)
- Day and month of interview, page numbers (if relevant)

If accessed online:

- DOI *or* Available at: URL (Accessed: date)

Example: newspaper interview

In-text citation

Riley (2008) believed that 'imagination has to be captured by reality'.

Reference list

Riley, B. (2008) 'The life of Riley'. Interview with Bridget Riley. Interviewed by J. Jones for *The Guardian*, 5 July, p. 33.

Example: television interview

In-text citation

The prime minister avoided the question (Blair, 2003).

Reference list

Blair, A. (2003) Interviewed by J. Paxman for *Newsnight*, BBC Two Television, 2 February.

Example: internet interview

In-text citation

The President appeared confident in the discussion (Obama, 2015).

Reference list

Obama, B. (2015) Interviewed by J. Sopel for *BBC News*, 24 July. Available at: http://www.bbc.co.uk/news/world-us-canada-33646543 (Accessed: 16 September 2018).

E24   Public communications

These include lectures, seminars, webinars, PowerPoint presentations, video conferences/electronic discussion groups, bulletin boards/press releases, announcements/leaflets, advertisements/ display boards and RSS feeds.

NB For communications in *virtual learning environments*, see Section E6.

E24.1   Live speeches

NB For live and recorded lectures as part of your course, see Sections E6.1–E6.2.

Citation order:

- Author/speaker
- Year (in round brackets)
- Title of speech (in italics)
- Medium (in square brackets)
- Institution or venue
- Day/month

Example

In-text citation

Stanton (2018) illustrated …

Reference list

Stanton, J. (2018) *Wordsworth's imagination* [Speech]. Durham Book Festival, Gala Theatre, Durham. 18 September.

If referencing an *online presentation*, use the following.

Citation order:

- Author
- Year (in round brackets)
- Title of communication (in italics)
- Medium (in square brackets)
- DOI *or* Available at: URL (Accessed: date)

NB If you wish to cite the contents of a specific slide, do this in the in-text citation.

Example

In-text citation

The fifteen endangered species listed by Mahindrakar (2013, slide 22) …

Reference list

Mahindrakar, R. (2013) *Biodiversity of India* [PowerPoint presentation]. Available at: https://www.slideshare.net/RameshMahindrakar/biodiversity-of-india (Accessed: 16 August 2018).

E24.2 Electronic discussion groups and bulletin boards

NB For personal email correspondence, see Section E28.

Citation order:

♦ Author of message
♦ Year of message (in round brackets)
♦ Subject of the message (in single quotation marks)
♦ Discussion group or bulletin board (in italics)
♦ Date posted: day/month
♦ Available email: email address

Example

In-text citation

Debt cancellation was discussed by Peters (2018) …

Reference list

Peters, W.R. (2018) 'International finance questions', *British Business School Librarians Group discussion list*, 11 March. Available email: lisbusiness@jiscmail.com

E24.3 Entire discussion groups or bulletin boards

Citation order:

♦ List name (in italics)
♦ Year of last update (in round brackets)
♦ Available email: email address (Accessed: date)

Example

In-text citation

The *Photography news list* (2018) …

Reference list

Photography news list (2018) Available email: pnl@btinfonet (Accessed: 3 April 2018).

E24.4 Press releases/ announcements

Citation order:

♦ Author/organisation
♦ Year issued (in round brackets)
♦ Title of communication (in italics)
♦ Medium (in square brackets)
♦ Day/month

If accessed online:

♦ DOI *or* Available at: URL (Accessed: date)

Example

In-text citation

This development (Google Inc., 2012) offered …

Reference list

Google Inc. (2012) *Google Maps heads north … way north* [Press release]. 23 August. Available at: http://www.google.com/intl/en/press/ (Accessed: 13 January 2018).

E24.5 Leaflets/flyers

By their nature, leaflets are unlikely to have all the citation/reference elements, so include as much information as possible. It may also be useful to include a copy of the leaflet in an appendix to your assignment.

Citation order:

♦ Author (individual or corporate)
♦ Date (if available – in round brackets)
♦ Title (in italics)
♦ [Leaflet obtained …]
♦ Date obtained

Example

In-text citation

Lloyds (no date) provides insurance for its mortgages.

Reference list

Lloyds (no date) *Mortgages* [Leaflet obtained in Paisley branch]. 4 June 2018.

E24.6 Advertisements

If referencing information in an advertisement, you will need to specify where it was seen. This might be online, in a newspaper, on television or in a location. Advertisements are often short-lived, so it is important to include the date you viewed them.

Citation order:

♦ Cite and reference according to the medium in which the advertisement appeared (see examples)

Examples

In-text citations

Advertisements by BT (2018), Lloyds (2018) and Northern Electric (2018) and that for the WOMAD festival in *The Guardian* (2018) …

Reference list

Television advertisement
BT (2018) *Office relocation gremlins* [Advertisement on ITV1 Television]. 23 November.

Newspaper advertisement
The Guardian (2018) *WOMAD festival* [Advertisement]. 14 January, p. 12.

Internet advertisement
Lloyds TSB Bank plc (2018) *Selling your house?* [Advertisement]. Available at http://www.hotmail.com (Accessed: 13 February 2018).

Billboard advertisement
Northern Electric plc (2018) *Green energy* [Billboard at Ellison Road, Dunston-on-Tyne]. 14 January.

E24.7 Display boards (for example, in museums)

It is very rare for an author to be given for information on display boards, so the example uses the title first.

Citation order:

♦ Title (in italics)
♦ Year of production (if available – in round brackets)
♦ Display board at
♦ Name of venue, city
♦ Date observed

Example

In-text citation

Martin's vivid colours are a noted feature of his work (*Paintings of John Martin*, 2017).

Reference list

Paintings of John Martin (2017) Display board at Laing Art Gallery exhibition, Newcastle upon Tyne, 23 April 2017.

E24.8 RSS feeds

Rich Site Summary (RSS) is a method of notifying subscribers, through 'feeds', when a favourite web page such as a news source has been updated. You should reference the details of the original source (for example, news web page, blog or newly published journal article), not the RSS feed.

Citation order:

♦ Author/organisation
♦ Year issued (in round brackets)
♦ Title of communication (in italics)
♦ [RSS]
♦ Day/month

If accessed online:

♦ DOI *or* Available at: URL (Accessed: date)

Example

In-text citation

The library extension was completed in April 2012 (Durham University Library, 2012).

Reference list

Durham University Library (2012) *Library east wing opens* [RSS]. 23 April. Available at: https://www.dur.ac.uk/feeds/news/?section=14 (Accessed: 25 April 2018).

E25 Unpublished materials (including hard copy, on intranets and files shared online between group members)

NB For published reports, see Section E8.

Unpublished is generally understood as meaning 'not in the public domain'. This section includes a number of the most commonly used unpublished documents. Documents that are available only in hard copy, or held on an organisation's intranet, or distributed only to certain members of a group or organisation in print or online should be treated as unpublished sources as they are inaccessible to anyone outside the organisation (or even within the organisation if they do not have permission to access them). This includes documents such as minutes of meetings that are shared through online services such as Sharepoint, Onedrive, Dropbox and WeTransfer. Although these are online, it would be difficult for anyone outside the organisation or group to read the document. If you have permission from other group members, these sources could be included at the end of your work as an appendix.

Citation order:

♦ Author or organisation
♦ Year produced (in round brackets)
♦ Title of report, document or file (in single quotation marks)
♦ Name of organisation
♦ Unpublished

Examples

In-text citation

Jones (2017, item 3.1) suggested work shadowing.

Reference list

Jones, T. (2017) 'Minutes of staff development committee meeting 23 February 2017'. Western Health Trust, Shrewsbury. Unpublished.

In-text citation

The editor sent the proofs through Dropbox (Fern, 2018).

Reference list

Fern, R.W. (2018) 'Article 10, 2018'. Society of Antiquaries of Newcastle upon Tyne. Unpublished.

E26 Student assignments

You should check with your tutor if it is acceptable to cite your own or other students' assignments. For theses, see Section E4.

Citation order:

♦ Student name
♦ Year of submission (in round brackets)
♦ Title of essay/assignment (in single quotation marks)
♦ Assignment for
♦ Module and degree (in italics)
♦ Institution
♦ Unpublished

Example

In-text citation

The topic of the essay (Sanders, 2018) …

Reference list

Sanders, M. (2018) 'An examination of the factors influencing air routes and the siting of international airports'. Assignment for *GEM1092, BSc. Geography and Environmental Management*, City University. Unpublished.

E27 Confidential information

In many cases, you will need to anonymise the person or institution involved. In medical situations, for example, you may use terms such as 'Subject 1', 'Patient X' or 'Baby J' instead of real names, or 'Placement school', 'Placement hospital' or 'Placement agency' instead of actual institutions. These documents are likely to be unpublished.

Citation order:

♦ Anonymised institution/agency (in square brackets)
♦ Year produced (in round brackets)
♦ Anonymised title (in italics) (use square brackets for the anonymised part)
♦ Location
♦ Anonymised producer (in square brackets)
♦ Unpublished

Example

In-text citation

The records they produced (Placement hospital, 2017) …

Reference list

[Placement hospital] (2017) *[Placement hospital] examination criteria for elderly patients*. London: [Placement hospital]. Unpublished.

If providing the town or city name is likely to identify a specific institution, you can simply insert the county – for example, Lancashire: [Placement hospital].

Note that you may be asked by your tutor to supply them with the agency/employer name if there is any doubt about the authenticity of your reference.

NB See Section E20.7f for information relating to using and referencing medical images.

E28 Personal communications

NB For phonecasts, see Section E22.12.

Personal communications via conversation, phone, Skype, FaceTime, email, text message, letter or fax can be referenced as follows.

Citation order:

♦ Sender/speaker/author
♦ Year of communication (in round brackets)
♦ Medium of communication
♦ Receiver of communication
♦ Day/month of communication

Examples

In-text citation

This was disputed by Walters (2018).

Reference list

Walters, F. (2018) Conversation with John Stephens, 13 August.

Walters, F. (2018) Letter to John Stephens, 23 January.

Walters, F. (2018) Email to John Stephens, 14 August.

Walters, F. (2018) Telephone conversation with John Stephens, 25 December.

Walters, F. (2018) Skype conversation with John Stephens, 21 June.

Walters, F. (2018) FaceTime conversation with John Stephens, 21 June.

Walters, F. (2018) Text message to John Stephens, 14 June.

Walters, F. (2018) Fax to John Stephens, 17 December.

Note that both the in-text citations and references begin with the name of the sender of the communication (for letters, emails, texts or faxes).

NB You may need to seek permission from other parties in the correspondence before quoting them in your work. You might also include a copy of written communications in your appendices, or note where the communication/correspondence can be located (for example, 'library').

E29 Genealogical sources

Use the name of the person(s) and the date of the event as the in-text citation and provide the full details in the reference list.

E29.1 Birth, marriage and death certificates

Citation order:

♦ Name of person (in single quotation marks)
♦ Year of event (in round brackets)
♦ Certified copy of … certificate for … (in italics)
♦ Full name of person (forenames, surname) (in italics)
♦ Day/month/year of event (in italics)
♦ Application number from certificate
♦ Location of register office

If you retrieved the certificate online, after application number from certificate, add:

♦ Year of last update (in round brackets)
♦ DOI *or* Available at: URL (Accessed: date)

Example

In-text citation

Amy was born in Bristol ('Amy Jane Bennett', 1874)

Reference list

'Amy Jane Bennett' (1874) *Certified copy of birth certificate for Amy Jane Bennett, 10 April 1874.* Application number 4001788/C. Bristol Register Office.

E29.2 Wills

Citation order:

♦ Title of document (in italics)
♦ Year of will (in round brackets)
♦ Name of archive or repository
♦ Reference number

Example

In-text citation

Doubleday's nephews inherited his estates (*Will of Michael Doubleday of Alnwick Abbey, Northumberland*, 1797).

Reference list

Will of Michael Doubleday of Alnwick Abbey, Northumberland (1797) The National Archives: Public Record Office. Catalogue reference: PROB/11/1290.

E29.3 Censuses

Citation order:

♦ Name of person (in single quotation marks)
♦ Year of census (in round brackets)
♦ Census return for … (in italics)
♦ Street, place registration subdistrict, county (in italics)
♦ Public Record Office:
♦ Piece number, folio number, page number

If you retrieved the information online, add:

♦ Year of last update (in round brackets)
♦ DOI *or* Available at: URL (Accessed: date)

Example

In-text citation

Thomas Wilson moved to Willington in the 1850s ('Thomas Wilson', 1861).

Reference list

'Thomas Wilson' (1861) *Census return for New Row, Willington, St Oswald subdistrict, County Durham.* Public Record Office: PRO RG9/3739, folio 74, p. 11 (2008). Available at: http://www.ancestry.co.uk (Accessed: 23 July 2018).

E29.4 Parish registers

Citation order:

- Name of person (in single quotation marks)
- Year of event (in round brackets)
- Baptism, marriage or burial of …
- Full name of person (forenames, surname)
- Day/month/year of event
- Title of register (in italics)

If you retrieved the certificate online, add:

- Year of last update (in round brackets)
- DOI *or* Available at: URL (Accessed: date)

Example

In-text citation

Mary and Edward's wedding ('Edward Robson and Mary Slack', 1784) …

Reference list

'Edward Robson and Mary Slack' (1784) Marriage of Edward Robson and Mary Slack, 6 May 1784. *St Augustine's Church Alston, Cumberland marriage register 1784–1812* (2004). Available at: http://www.genuki.org.uk/big/eng/CUL/Alston/MALS1701.html (Accessed: 13 July 2018).

E29.5 Military records

Citation order:

- Name of person (in single quotation marks)
- Year of publication (in round brackets)
- Title of publication (in italics)
- Publication details

If accessed online:

- DOI *or* Available at: URL (Accessed: date)

Example

In-text citation

Private Wakenshaw fought on even after losing his arm ('Adam Herbert Wakenshaw VC', 2008).

Reference list

'Adam Herbert Wakenshaw VC' (2008) *Commonwealth War Graves Commission casualty details*. Available at: http://www.cwgc.org/search/casualty_details.aspx?casualty= 2212745 (Accessed: 21 June 2018).

E30 Manuscripts

E30.1 Individual manuscripts

If the author of a manuscript is known, use the following.

Citation order:
- Author
- Year (in round brackets)
- Title of manuscript (in italics)
- Date (if available)
- Name of collection containing manuscript and reference number
- Location of manuscript in archive or repository

Example

In-text citation

The architect enjoyed a close relationship with his patron (Newton, 1785).

Reference list

Newton, W. (1785) *Letter to William Ord*, 23 June. Ord Manuscripts 324 E11/4, Northumberland Archives, Woodhorn.

Where the author of a manuscript is not known, use the following.

Citation order:

- Title of manuscript (in italics)
- Year (if known, in round brackets)
- Name of collection containing manuscript and reference number
- Location of manuscript in archive or repository

Example

In-text citation

Expenditure was high in this period (*Fenham journal*, 1795).

Reference list

Fenham journal (1795) Ord Manuscripts, 324 E12, Northumberland Archives, Woodhorn.

E30.2 Collections of manuscripts

To refer to a whole collection of manuscripts (MS), use the name of the collection.

Citation order:

- Location of collection in archive or repository
- Name of collection

Example

In-text citation

Consulting the family records (British Library, Lansdowne MS), the author discovered ...

Reference list

British Library, Lansdowne MS.

Note that no date is given for a collection in the text or in the reference list as the collection contains items of various dates.

Section F
American Psychological Association (APA) referencing style

The APA referencing style is used in some social science subjects. Like Harvard, it uses an author-date format to identify the citation in the text. Full details are given in an alphabetical list of references. For more information on using the APA referencing style, see:

American Psychological Association (2009) Publication manual of the American Psychological Association. 6th edn. Washington, DC: American Psychological Association.

Two useful sources of further guidance on APA are the *APA style blog* at http://blog.apastyle.org/ and Purdue University's *Online Writing Lab* (OWL) at https://owl.purdue.edu/owl/research_and_citation/apa_style/apa_style_introduction.html.

Conventions when using the APA referencing style

Reference list layout

♦ All lines after the first line of each reference list entry should be indented half an inch from the left margin. This is called hanging indentation

Example

Harris, P. H. (2016). *The freedom of information and the right to access personal data in Britain*. London: Freedom Press.

Authors/editors

♦ Authors' and editors' names are inverted (last name first). Give the last name (surname/family name) and initials
♦ Full stops are used after each of the author initials and spaces are inserted between initials
♦ Full stops are used after corporate names
♦ For editor or editors, use the abbreviation Ed. or Eds., respectively, in round brackets

Example

Brooks, G. J., & Gibbons, L. (Eds.).

Note the punctuation: ampersand (&) is used for 'and'; full stop after (Eds.).

Multiple authors and et al.

♦ For works with one or two authors, include all names in every **in-text citation**; for works with three, four or five authors, include all names in the first in-text citation and then abbreviate to the first author name plus et al. (not italicised) for subsequent citations; and for works with six or more authors, abbreviate to the first author name plus et al. for all in-text citations
♦ For your **reference list**, give all authors *up to seven*, with the last author name preceded by an ampersand (&). Where you have *more than seven authors*, you should list the *first six* then use an **ellipsis** (…) and list the name of the last author of the work (no ampersand is required)

Example: work with five authors

In-text citation

Games can assist recovery (Weathers et al., 2014) …

Reference list

Weathers, L., Bedell, J. R., Marlowe, H., Gordon, R. E., & Adams, J. (2014). Using psychotherapeutic games to train patients' skills. In R. E. Gordon and K. K. Gordon (Eds.) *Systems of treatment for the mentally ill* (pp. 109–124). New York, NY: Grune & Stratton.

Example: work with more than seven authors

In-text citation

Harris et al. (2015) argue that …

Reference list

Harris, P., Thomas, S. T., Richards, L. R., Winstanley, P., Rubin, L. H., Stamos, A., … Peters, L. P. (2015). *Electromagnetic theory* …

Year of publication

♦ In round brackets, followed by a full stop – for example, (2016)

Titles

♦ The titles of sources are italicised, as are volume numbers of journal articles, but not issue or page numbers
♦ For a book, only the first letter of the first word of the title and subtitle (if there is one) and any **proper nouns** are capitalised
♦ Full stops are inserted after book titles

Example

Psychoanalysis: Its image and its public in China.

♦ Titles of articles within journals, or chapters within books, are not enclosed in quotation marks
♦ For journal titles, each major word of the title is capitalised and followed by a comma

Example

Journal of Comparative and Physiological Psychology,

Editions

♦ Edition is abbreviated to ed. and enclosed in round brackets, with a full stop after the brackets (6th ed.)
♦ With the exception of first editions, edition number is included after the title in round brackets. Note that there is no full stop after the title before the round brackets

Example

Ramage, P. L. (2016). *History in the making* (4th ed.). London: Harvest Press.

Place of publication

♦ For place of publication, you should always list the city and US state, using the two-letter abbreviation without full stops – for example, New York, NY. Spell out the country names if outside the UK or the USA – for example, Melbourne, Australia

Issue information for periodicals

♦ Volume numbers are italicised

Page numbers

♦ APA does not stipulate the addition of page numbers to in-text references for summaries or paraphrases, but we encourage/recommend that they are included when it would help the reader to find the relevant section or information in a long text, section or paragraph. You can also check with your tutors as to their preference in this regard for your assignments
♦ Page numbers for book chapters are given immediately after the title of the book in round brackets and before publication details
♦ Unlike other periodicals (journals and magazines), p. or pp. precedes page numbers for a newspaper reference in APA style

Internet sources

♦ In APA, the word Internet is always capitalised, whereas website is not
♦ Internet sources should be indicated by Retrieved from URL, or doi:

Note that APA style does not include a retrieval date for online sources.

♦ APA also states that it is not necessary to include the name of the database when referencing online journals or ebook collections
♦ No punctuation marks are added after DOIs or URLs in reference list entries

Footnotes and endnotes

♦ APA does not generally recommend the use of footnotes and endnotes. However, if you still need to provide explanatory notes for your work, you should use a **superscript number** following almost any punctuation marks. Footnote numbers should not follow hyphens, and if they appear in a sentence in brackets, the footnote number should be inserted within the brackets

Example

Researchers believe that the occurrence of dementia in England points to a number of highly pertinent facts.[1] (These have now been published separately.[2])

Secondary (indirect) sources

It is always better to read the original or primary sources so that you can reference them fully, but sometimes this is difficult. The APA Publication manual advises that you should 'use secondary sources sparingly, for instance, when the original work is out of print, unavailable through usual sources, or not available in English' (American Psychological Association, 2009, p. 178). In such a case, you would need to cite the original or primary source in the text of your work, the secondary source in round brackets (parentheses) and provide a full reference in the reference list for the secondary source.

Example

Hislop (as cited in Richards, 2013, p. 56) argued that …

Thus, only the details for Richards' work would appear in your reference list (unless you were able to read Hislop's work, then you could also include these details in your reference list).

How to reference common sources

F1 Books

Citation order:

- Author/editor (surname followed by initials)
- Year of publication (in round brackets)
- Title (in italics)
- Edition (only include the edition number if it is not the first edition)
- Place of publication: publisher

Example

In-text citation

Cottrell (2019, p. 54) noted …

Reference list

Cottrell, S. (2019). *The study skills handbook* (5th ed.). London: Red Globe Press.

F2 Chapters/sections of edited books

Citation order:

- Author of the chapter/section (surname followed by initials)
- Year of publication (in round brackets)
- Title of chapter/section
- In
- Name of editor of book (Ed.)
- Title of book (in italics)
- Page numbers of chapter/section (in round brackets)
- Place of publication: publisher

Example

In-text citation

The view proposed by Leites (2013, p. 444) …

Reference list

Leites, N. (2013). Transference interpretations only? In A. H. Esman (Ed.) *Essential papers on transference* (pp. 434–454). New York, NY: New York University Press.

F3 Encyclopedia entries

Citation order:

- Author of entry
- Year (in round brackets)
- Title of entry
- In
- Initial(s) and surname of editor (Ed.)
- Title of encyclopedia (in italics)
- Page span (in round brackets)
- Place of publication: publisher

Example

In-text citation

The process of adaptation is difficult to detect (Rose, 2007, p. 19).

Reference list

Rose, M. R. (2007). Adaptation. In S. A. Levin (Ed.) *Encyclopedia of biodiversity* (pp. 17–23). Amsterdam: Elsevier.

F4 Multi-volume works

Citation order:

- Author/editor
- Year(s) of publication (in round brackets)
- Title of book (in italics)

- Volumes (in round brackets)
- Place of publication: publisher

Example

In-text citation

Butcher's (1961–1963) comprehensive work …

Reference list

Butcher, R. (Ed.). (1961–1963). *A new British flora* (4 vols). London: Leonard Hill.

F5 Anthologies

Whole, edited anthologies should be referenced like any other whole edited book would be. Only the editor appears in the author part of the reference.

Citation order:

- Editor (surname followed by initials) (Ed.)
- Year (in round brackets)
- Title (in italics)
- Place of publication: publisher

If viewed online:

- DOI or Retrieved from URL

Example: print anthology

In-text citation

… in the work (Hollings, 2013).

Reference list

Hollings, P. (Ed.). (2013). *The complete works of Henry Rawlings* (Vol. 3). London: Literary Minds.

Example: online anthology

In-text citation

… in the work (Hollings, 2013).

Reference list

Hollings, P. (Ed.). (2013). *The complete works of Henry Rawlings* (Vol. 3). Retrieved from http://books.google.com/books

To reference multiple volumes in an anthology, include the range of years over which the volumes were published (unless all were published in the same year) and the volume numbers in round brackets after the title.

Example: print

In-text citation

More recent studies (Farrow & Morgan, 2009–2012) …

Reference list

Farrow, P. S., & Morgan, L. (Eds.). (2009–2012). *Homeopathic medicine: A history and study* (Vols 1–4). Lancaster: Pear Tree Books.

Example: online

In-text citation

More recent studies (Farrow & Morgan, 2009–2012) …

Reference list

Farrow, P. S., & Morgan, L. (Eds.). (2009–2012). *Homeopathic medicine: A history and study* (Vols 1–4). Retrieved from http://www.amazon.co.uk/KindleeBooks-books/b?ie=UTF8&node=341689031

F6   Translated works

Citation order:

- Author/editor (surname followed by initials)
- Year of publication (in round brackets)
- Title (in italics)
- Name of translator, Trans. (in round brackets)
- Place of publication: publisher

Example

In-text citation

Zola (1969) …

Reference list

Zola, É. (1969). *The underbelly of Paris* (D. W. Harris, Trans.). London: Grant & Cutler.

F7   Sacred texts

The *APA style guide* (p. 179) states that for classical and religious texts, you need only to provide an in-text reference to the book, chapter and line of the source. Give the version that you have used in your first in-text citation.

Examples

In-text citations

The Beatitudes (Matthew 5: 3–12, New International Version) …

The reply (Shemot 3: 14, Torah) is the most profound …

'And ease for me my task' (Quran 20: 26).

F8   Book reviews

Citation order:

- Reviewer (surname followed by initials)
- Year of publication (in round brackets)
- Title of book review
- [Review of the book *Title of book*, by Author of book, initial(s) and surname]
- Title of serial where the review appears (in italics)
- Volume number (in italics)
- Issue (in round brackets), page numbers

If viewed online:

- Title of website (in italics)
- DOI or Retrieved from URL

Example

In-text citation

The highly critical review by Bradshaw (2015) …

Reference list

Bradshaw, P. (2015). Into a questionable future: reclaiming our heritage [Review of the book *What the future holds*, by S. Hightown]. *New Review of Books*, *53*(3), 347–361. doi:15.1245/newreview.358.8756.8934

If the review is untitled, use the text in square brackets as the title; retain the brackets to indicate that the material is a description of form and content, not a title.

You can use this format for any reviews; simply indicate the medium being reviewed in the brackets (for example, film, DVD, television programme).

If the reviewed item is a film, DVD or other medium, include the year of release after the title of the work, separated by a comma.

F9   Ebooks

Citation order:

- Author/Editor (surname followed by initials)
- Year of publication (in round brackets)

◆ Title (in italics)
◆ DOI or Retrieved from URL

Example

In-text citation

More recent research (Lichtenberg, Lachmann, & Fosshage, 2015, p. 54) ...

Reference list

Lichtenberg, J. D., Lachmann, F. M., & Fosshage, J. L. (2015). *Psychoanalysis and motivational systems: A new look*. Retrieved from http://lib.myilibrary.com/ProductDetail.aspx?id=303727

F9.1   Mobile ebook formats

To reference Kindle or other mobile device ebook formats, you must include the following information: the author, date of publication, title, ebook version and, instead of publisher details, use either the book's **digital object identifier (DOI)** or, if no DOI, the place where you downloaded the book.

Ebooks often lack page numbers (though PDF versions may have them). Kindle books have 'location' numbers and % marks, which are static, but those are of no use to anyone who does not have a Kindle, or is using a different font-size display. So, to cite a quotation or section in-text, follow APA's guidelines for direct quotations of online material, using the major sections (chapter, section and paragraph number – abbreviate if titles are long). In general, provide as much information as the reader needs to locate the material you are using.

Example

In-text citation

One of the main points of his argument (Carmichael, 2014, Chapter 4, Section 3, para. 2) ...

Reference list

Carmichael, B. (2014). *Inheritance* [Kindle version]. Retrieved from http://www.amazon.co.uk

F10   Journal articles

Citation order:

◆ Author (surname followed by initials)
◆ Year of publication (in round brackets)
◆ Title of article
◆ Title of journal (in italics)
◆ Volume number (in italics)
◆ Issue (in round brackets)
◆ Page numbers

Example

In-text citation

Research by Frosch (2012) ...

Reference list

Frosch, A. (2012). Transference: Psychic reality and material reality. *Psychoanalytic Psychology*, *19*(4), 603–633.

F11   Ejournal articles

Citation order:

◆ Author (surname followed by initials)
◆ Year of publication (in round brackets)
◆ Title of article
◆ Title of journal (in italics)
◆ Volume number (in italics)
◆ Issue (in round brackets)
◆ Page numbers
◆ DOI or Retrieved from URL

Example

In-text citation

Violence is a factor in many instances of transference (Shubs, 2014).

Reference list

Shubs, C. H. (2014). Transference issues concerning victims of violent crime and other traumatic incidents of adulthood. *Psychoanalytic Psychology*, 25(1), 122–141. doi:10.1037/0736-9735.25.1.122

F12 Systematic reviews

Citation order:

- Author (surname followed by initials)
- Year of publication (in round brackets)
- Title of review
- Database name (in italics)
- Year of review (in italics) followed by issue number (in round brackets)
- Page numbers
- DOI *or* Retrieved from URL

Example

In-text citation

Following a systematic review (Pasquali et al., 2018) …

Reference list

Pasquali, S., Hadjinicolaou, A. V., Chiarion Sileni, V., Rossi, C. R., & Mocellin, S. (2018) Systemic treatments for metastatic cutaneous melanoma. *Cochrane Database of Systematic Reviews*, 2018(2), 1–338. doi:10.1002/14651858.CD011123. pub2

F13 Magazine/newspaper/ newsletter articles

Dates for magazines, newspapers and newsletters should include the year and the exact date of the publication (month, or month and day). This means that the month should be given for monthlies, and the month and day for weeklies and dailies. If the magazine uses a season with the year, put the year, a comma and the season in parentheses – for example, (2014, Winter).

Citation order:

- Author (surname followed by initials)
- Year and date of publication (in round brackets)
- Title of article
- Title of magazine/newspaper/newsletter (in italics)
- Volume number (in italics) – if available
- Issue (in round brackets) – if available
- Page numbers – if available
- DOI *or* Retrieved from URL – if required

NB APA style requires the use of p. or pp. for specifying pages in a **newspaper reference** (see the example). Their use is not required in other periodicals.

Example: print magazine article

Harrison, L. E. (2014, November 23). The return of the trains. *Cumbria Times*, pp. 54–56.

Example: print newspaper article

Vardy, A. (2014, November 23). New treatments for travel sickness. *The Independent*, pp. 16–17.

F14 Prepublication journal articles

F14.1 Draft manuscripts

A manuscript for an article that is still in draft form can be cited and referenced using the year the draft was written.

Example

In-text citation

… in her latest research (Morgan, 2018).

Reference list

Morgan, P. R. (2018). *Hierarchies in the bee world: A field study*. Manuscript in preparation.

F14.2 Manuscripts submitted for publication

If a manuscript has been submitted for publication, use the year it was written, not the year it was submitted, as the date.

Example

In-text citation

This cutting-edge research (Hastings, 2018) …

Reference list

Hastings, P. L. (2018). *Combined therapy: Medication, talking therapies and self-help in the treatment of anxiety and depression*. Manuscript submitted for publication.

If the article is accepted for publication, the status changes to in press, and the name of the journal can be included in the reference.

Example

In-text citation

This new research (Hastings, in press) …

Reference list

Hastings, P. L. (in press). Combined therapy: Medication, talking therapies and self-help in the treatment of anxiety and depression. *Mental Illness Quarterly*.

F14.3 Advance online publications

Citation order:

◆ Author (surname followed by initials)
◆ Year of posting (in round brackets)
◆ Title of the article
◆ Journal title (in italics)
◆ Advance online publication
◆ DOI of the journal's home page *or* Retrieved from URL

Example

In-text citation

The latest research (Hastings, 2018) …

Reference list

Hastings, P. L. (2018). Combined therapy: Medication, talking therapies and selfhelp in the treatment of anxiety and depression. *Mental Illness Quarterly*. Advance online publication. doi:15.1098/a00045361

F15 Conferences and symposia

F15.1 Full conference proceedings (print or electronic)

Citation order:

♦ Author/editor (surname, followed by initials)
♦ Year of publication (in round brackets)
♦ Title of conference: Subtitle of conference (in italics)
♦ Location, date of conference (in italics)
♦ Place of publication: publisher

If viewed online:

♦ DOI *or* Retrieved from URL

Example

In-text citation

… in the full conference proceedings (Hewlett & Carson, 2015).

Reference list

Hewlett, P., & Carson, L. (Eds.). (2015). *Preparing nurses for the next decade: Proceedings of the National Conference on Education in Nursing, University of Cumbria, 2014.* Lancaster: Greendale Press

F15.2 Conference papers in print proceedings

Citation order:

♦ Author of paper
♦ Year, month, date of paper (in round brackets)
♦ Title of paper
♦ In
♦ Editors (if required)
♦ Title of published proceedings (in italics)
♦ Paper presented at
♦ Title of conference: Subtitle of conference
♦ Location of conference

♦ Page numbers (in round brackets)
♦ Place of publication: publisher

Example

In-text citation

In their expert analysis (Peters & Richards, 2013) …

Reference list

Peters, T., & Richards, K. (2013). Refugees or asylum seekers: How will Europe respond? In M. Dibbs, L. Williams, & S. Hussein (Eds.) *Europe's role in the midst of international crises.* Paper presented at the Proceedings of the 5th International Conference on Human Rights, Geneva, Switzerland (pp. 145–167). Geneva, Switzerland: Jungfrau Press

F15.3 Conference papers from the Internet

Citation order:

♦ Author of paper
♦ Year (in round brackets)
♦ Title of paper (in italics)
♦ Paper presented at
♦ Title of conference: Subtitle of conference
♦ Location of conference
♦ DOI *or* Retrieved from URL

Example

In-text citation

A recent study (Dawson, 2015) …

Reference list

Dawson, H. (2015). *Is Alzheimer's a transmissible disease?* Paper presented at the WHO Symposium on Dementia, Geneva, Switzerland. doi:15.1243/GH.2015.132

F16 Government publications

Citation order:

- Name of government department
- Year of publication (in round brackets)
- Title (in italics)
- Report series and number (in round brackets)
- Place of publication: publisher

Or if viewed online:

- DOI *or* Retrieved from URL

Example

In-text citation

Government policy on energy reduction (Department for Energy & Climate Change, 2014) …

Reference list

Department for Energy & Climate Change. (2014). *Community Energy Strategy* (URN 14D/019). Retrieved from https://www.gov.uk/government/publications/community-energy-strategy

For Command Papers (including Green and White Papers), insert the paper number after the title in round brackets.

Examples

Department for Education. (2015). *Government response to the Education Select Committee report: Extremism in schools – the Trojan Horse affair*. (Cm. 9094). London: Her Majesty's Stationery Office.

Or if viewed online:

Department for Education. (2015). *Government response to the Education Select committee report: Extremism in schools – the Trojan Horse affair*. (Cm. 9094). Retrieved from https://www.gov.uk/government/publications/extremism-in-schools-response-to-education-select-committee

If you are referencing government publications from more than one country, add the country after the department name – for example, Department of Energy (USA) and Department for Education (UK).

F17 Research reports

Research and technical reports form part of the larger body of publications known as grey literature: material that is produced by government, academics, business and industry in print and electronic formats, but which is not controlled by commercial publishers.

Citation order for online reports:

- Author (surname followed by initials)
- Year of publication (in round brackets)
- Title of report (in italics)
- DOI *or* Retrieved from URL

Example

In-text citation

Charnley (2015) highlights the importance …

Reference list

Charnley, S. (2015). *The historical significance of religious iconography*. Retrieved from http://www. religioncounts.govt.nz/data/assets/ pdf_ file/0024/3693.pdf

For printed reports by corporate authors where they are also the publisher, you would substitute 'Author' for the publisher.

Example

In-text citation

… in their report (International Labour Organization, 2014).

Reference list

International Labour Organization. (2014). *Equality at work: Tackling new challenges*. Geneva, Switzerland: Author.

F18   Datasets

Citation order:

♦ Author (surname followed by initials) or name of organisation
♦ Year of publication (in round brackets)
♦ Title (in italics)
♦ Report series and number (in round brackets)
♦ DOI *or* Retrieved from URL

Example

In-text citation

Barley prices fell in January and February 2014 before a sharp increase in early March (Department for Environment, Food & Rural Affairs, 2014).

Reference list

Department for Environment, Food & Rural Affairs. (2014). *Price series for cereals – weekly* (Statistical Data Set Commodity Prices). Retrieved from https://www.gov.uk/government/ statistical-data-sets/commodity-prices

F19   Legal information

F19.1   Legislation

Citation order:

♦ Title of the legislation (including year)
♦ Number (if applicable)

Example

In-text citation

Under Section 7 of the Human Rights Act.

Reference list

Human Rights Act 1998, c42.

F19.2   Cases

The APA style guide does not give examples of UK cases. The citation order below is a modification of examples of US cases, based on APA Style Kitty (2013) 'Citing court decisions in APA style', *APA style blog*, 3 October. Available at: http:// blog.apastyle.org/apastyle/2013/10/citing-court-decisions-in-apa-style.html (Accessed: 13 August 2018). The name of the case report is abbreviated in accordance with the *Cardiff index to legal abbreviations* (2011) Available at: http://www.legalabbrevs.cardiff.ac.uk/ (Accessed: 13 August 2018).

Citation order:

♦ Title of the case (italicised in text but not in reference list)
♦ Year
♦ Neutral citation
♦ Year [in square brackets], volume number, abbreviated name of the case report, first page number of the case.

Example

In-text citation
In the case of *R v. Dunlop* (2006) …

Reference list
R v. Dunlop (2006) EWCA Crim 1354, [2007] 1 All ER 593.

F20   Theses and dissertations

Citation order:

♦ Author (surname followed by initials)
♦ Year of submission (in round brackets)
♦ Title of dissertation/thesis (in italics)
♦ Degree statement (in round brackets)
♦ Degree-awarding body, location

Example

In-text citation
Research by Brodie (2013) …

Reference list
Brodie, L. M. (2013). *Speciality regional foods in the UK: An investigation from the perspectives of marketing and social history* (Unpublished PhD thesis). Newcastle University, Newcastle upon Tyne.

F21   Internet sites

F21.1   Organisation or personal Internet sites

Citation order:

♦ Author
♦ Year the site was published/last updated (in round brackets)
♦ Title of Internet site (with format in square brackets if necessary – for example, for a blog)
♦ DOI *or* Retrieved from URL

Example: organisation

In-text citation
There are several career paths (British Psychological Association, 2012) …

Reference list
British Psychological Association. (2012). How to become a psychologist. Retrieved from https://www.bps.org.uk/public/become-psychologist

Example: personal

In-text citation
As suggested by one website (Black, 2016) …

Reference list
Black, J. B. (2016). Learn to profile people. Retrieved from http://lifehacker.com/346372/learn-to-profile-people

Below are examples of web pages where pieces of information are not available.

Remember, you should always question the validity of sources where crucial elements are missing in order to establish the academic credibility of the source.

F21.2 Web pages with no authors

Use the title of the web page as the first element in the citation and reference.

The in-text citation uses double quotation marks around the title or abbreviated title.

Note that month and date are also given in the reference list.

Example

In-text citation
"Randall's spectacular production" (2015) …

Reference list
Randall's spectacular production has now been running for three years. (2015, February 17). Retrieved from http://www.msnbc.msn.com/id/569876409/ns/arts_news/

F21.3 Web pages with no authors or titles

In the reference list, you should substitute a description of the document inside square brackets.

Example

In-text citation
… the document (Map of the world, 1644).

Reference list
[Map of the world]. (1644). Retrieved from http://www.cartographslibrary/236784/17cent/

F21.4 Web pages with no date

Use the abbreviation n.d. for no date.

Example

In-text citation
… of its history (Rydwell School, n.d.).

Reference list
Rydwell School. (n.d.). History of the school. Retrieved from http://www.educ/about/schoolhistory/index

F22 Blogs

Citation order:

♦ Author (surname followed by initials)
♦ Year and date of post (in round brackets)
♦ Title of post
♦ [Blog post]
♦ Retrieved from URL

Example

In-text citation
The disconcerting comments (Haynes, 2015) …

Reference list
Haynes, R. (2015, March 18). Global warming warnings [Blog post]. Retrieved from http://globalnesslife.blogs.cfg.com/2015/3/18/globalwarming-warnings/

F23 Wikis

Wikis are collaborative sites in which several (usually unidentified) authors can add and edit information. There have been instances of false information being presented, although wiki editors try to ensure that the information is correct. Nevertheless, many tutors specifically prohibit students from citing Wikipedia. Wikipedia is not a scholarly resource, but there are times when it can provide a useful starting point or definition of a topic. In APA, wikis are referenced in the same way as an entry in an online reference work. The retrieval date is always required because the source material may change over time.

Citation order:

♦ Title of article
♦ (n.d.).
♦ In
♦ Title of wiki (in italics)
♦ Retrieved date, from

Example

In-text citation

Homeopathy is a system of alternative medicine (Homeopathy, n.d.).

Reference list

Homeopathy. (n.d.). In *Wikipedia*. Retrieved September 19, 2015, from https://en.wikipedia.org/wiki/Homeopathy

F24   Social media

There are three main ways to cite social media content in the APA style:

♦ Generally with a URL.
♦ As a personal communication.
♦ With a typical APA style in-text citation and reference list entry. If you discuss in a general way any website or page, it is sufficient to give the URL in the text the first time it is mentioned. No reference list entry is needed.

Example

In-text citation

Health agencies such as NICE provide advice and guidance to improve health and social care on their website (https://www.nice.org.uk).

If you paraphrase or quote specific, retrievable information from social media, provide an in-text citation (with the author and date) and a reference list entry (with the author, date, title and source URL).

Specific examples for Twitter and Facebook are given below.

Note that hashtags # are a common sight on Twitter and Facebook and other platforms, but these are not included in your references. You can describe them in your text – for example, 'During the 2015 migrant crisis in Europe, I searched Facebook and Twitter for the hashtags #refugees, #migrants and #asylumseekers appearing between September 1, 2015 and October 15, 2015'.

F24.1   Twitter

On Twitter, provide the author's screen name in square brackets (if only the screen name is known, provide it without brackets).

Note that titles of tweets, status updates or photographs are not italicised: items that stand alone, such as videos and photo albums, are italicised.

Citation order:

♦ Author (surname followed by initials) and/or [screen name]
♦ Year, month, day (in round brackets)
♦ Title of page, or up to first 40 words of tweet
♦ [Tweet]
♦ Retrieved from URL

Example

In-text citation

Laura Kuenssberg (2018) tweeted on the party conference.

Reference list

Kuenssberg, L. [@bbclaurak]. (2018, September 25). anyone might imagine that inside he's a tiny bit pleased … [Tweet]. Retrieved from https://twitter.com/bbclaurak/status/1044553972277817344

F24.2 Facebook

When the author is an individual, as well as providing initials, spell out their given name in square brackets.

Citation order:

♦ Author (surname followed by initials) and [given name in square brackets]
♦ Year, month, day (in round brackets)
♦ Title of page
♦ [Facebook status update]
♦ Retrieved from URL

Example

In-text citation

The use of anti-depressants for new mothers (Sissons, 2018) …

Reference list

Sissons, H. [Hilary]. (2018, April 18). The range of medication prescribed for new mums suffering from postnatal depression … [Facebook status update]. Retrieved from https://www.facebook.com/hilarysissons/posts/103567529148

F25 Film or video recordings

Citation order:

♦ Name of director (surname followed by initials)
♦ (Director) &
♦ Name of producer(s) (surname followed by initials)
♦ (Producer)
♦ Year of distribution (in round brackets)
♦ Title (in italics)
♦ [Medium]
♦ Place of distribution: distributor

Example

In-text citation

Jackson (2014) cleverly demonstrates …

Reference list

Jackson, P. (Director), & Cunningham, C., Weiner, Z., Walsh, F., & Jackson, P. (Producers). (2014). *The Hobbit: The desolation of Smaug* [DVD]. London: Warner Bros. Entertainment UK Ltd.

F26 Online videos (for example, YouTube)

Citation order:

♦ Author (surname followed by initials) and/or [screen name]
♦ Year, month, day (in round brackets)
♦ Title of video (in italics)
♦ [Video file]
♦ DOI *or* Retrieved from URL

Example

In-text citation

He questioned the continuation of life on Earth (Rees, 2012).

Reference list

Rees, M. [TED]. (2012, April 15). *Sir Martin Rees: Earth in its final century?* [Video file]. Retrieved from http://www.youtube.com/watch?v=3qF26MbYgOA

To point the reader to a specific place in an audiovisual source, such as when you cite a **direct quotation**, include a timestamp (hour:minute:seconds) in the in-text citation, just as you would include a page number under similar circumstances for a print source such as a book or journal article.

Example

In-text citation

'The artefact showed all the signs of deliberate vandalism and led us to believe that …' (Harris, Golding, & Bagguley, 2014, 8:25).

Reference list

Harris, G., Golding, P., & Bagguley, L. M. (2014, March 24). *Understanding medieval church architecture in the south-eastern counties of England* [Video file]. Retrieved from http://www.youtube.com/watch?a=5pG34NkYdWQ

F27　Sound/music recordings

Citation order:

- Artist/songwriter (surname followed by initials)
- Copyright year (in round brackets)

- Title of song/recording
- [Recorded by artist if different from songwriter]
- On
- Title of album (in italics)
- [Medium of recording]
- Location: label
- Date of recording (if different from copyright date)

Example

In-text citation

… in his lyrics (Taupin, 1975).

Reference list

Taupin, B. (1975). Someone saved my life tonight [Recorded by Elton John]. On *Captain fantastic and the brown dirt cowboy* [CD]. London: Big Pig Music Limited.

F28　Musical scores (sheet music)

Citation order:

- Name of composer (surname followed by initials)
- (Composer)
- Date (in round brackets)
- Title of work (in italics)
- Place of publication: publisher

You may need to include other relevant information, such as librettist (see example), and you may need to provide more details in square brackets to identify for the reader which score you used.

Example

In-text citation

... Hollins and Simmons (2008).

Reference list

Hollins, J. (Composer), & Simmons, J. D. (Librettist). (2008). *Giselda: An opera in two acts* [Score and parts]. Mainz, Germany: Schott Helicon.

If you are using something like a Dover reprint of an old score, there is no need to include the information about the original publishing company, but do include the original publication date.

NB When you cite a republished work, you should give both dates of publication.

Example

In-text citation

... (Mendelssohn, 1830/1999).

Reference list

Mendelssohn, F. (1999). *The Hebrides.* London: Initial Music Publishing. (Original work published 1830).

F29 Works of art (paintings, sculptures and installations)

There are no specific guidelines in APA for paintings, sculptures or installations, but the *APA style blog* (http://blog.apastyle.org/apastyle/2010/04/theres-an-art-to-it.html) suggests the inclusion of the artist's name, year(s) of production, title of the work, and any other necessary or relevant information, such as the medium and the location of the work.

Citation order:

♦ Artist (surname followed by initials)
♦ Year of production (in round brackets)

♦ Title of work (in italics)
♦ Medium (in square brackets)
♦ Location of the work

Examples

In-text citations

Her favourite pieces were by Gormley (1998), Rodin (1882) and Martin (1817).

Reference list

Gormley, A. (1998). *Angel of the North* [Sculpture]. Low Fell, Gateshead.
Martin, J. (1817). *The Bard* [Painting]. Laing Art Gallery, Newcastle upon Tyne.
Rodin, A. (1882). *The Kiss* [Marble sculpture]. Musée Rodin, Paris, France.

If you want to reference the work as seen on a website, you would use the website as the location element of your reference.

Example

Reference list

Gormley, A. (1998). *Angel of the North* [Sculpture]. Retrieved from http://www.newcastlegateshead.com/things-to-do/the-angel-of-the-north-p26491

F30 Broadcasts

F30.1 Television programmes

Citation order:

♦ Writer (surname followed by initials)
♦ Director (surname followed by initials)
♦ Date of broadcast or copyright (in round brackets)
♦ Title of episode
♦ [Television series episode]
♦ In
♦ Producer (initials followed by surname)
♦ Series title (in italics)
♦ Place of broadcast: broadcaster

Example

… of their intriguing script (Roberts & Moffat, 2014).

Roberts, G., & Moffat, S. (Writers), & Murphy, P. (Director). (2014, September 27). The caretaker [Television series episode]. In N. Wilson (Producer). *Doctor Who.* London: BBC.

F30.2   Radio programmes

Citation order:

- Writer (surname followed by initials)
- (Writer)
- Producer (surname followed by initials)
- (Producer)
- Editor (surname followed by initials)
- (Editor)
- Date of broadcast or copyright (in round brackets)
- Title of radio prgramme (in italics)
- [Radio programme]
- Series title (in italics)
- Place of broadcast: broadcaster

If heard online:

- Retrieved from URL

Example

In-text citation

University vice-chancellors are seeking a ban on essay mills (Brown, 2018) …

Reference list

Brown, E. (Ed.). (2018, September 27). *Today* [Radio programme]. London: BBC Radio 4. Retrieved from https://www.bbc.co.uk/radio/play/b0bkpjnq

F30.3   Podcasts

Citation order:

- Name of producer
- Date that the site was published/last updated (in round brackets)
- Title of podcast (in italics)
- [Podcast]
- Retrieved from URL

Example

In-text citation

Verity (2016) noted that the Olympics had a detrimental effect on sales.

Reference list

Verity, A. (Producer). (2016, 4 September). *Retail sales figures* [Podcast]. Retrieved from http://www.bbc.co.uk/podcasts/series/money

F31 Photographs

Citation order:

- ◆ Photographer
- ◆ Year of production (in round brackets)
- ◆ Title of work (in italics)
- ◆ Medium (in square brackets)
- ◆ Location

If viewed online:

- ◆ Retrieved from URL

Examples

In-text citations

James Kitto's images of a landscape (2018) and a family portrait (2016) …

Reference list

Kitto, J. (2016). *Brothers* [Photograph]. Porthleven Gallery, Cornwall.

Kitto, J. (2018). *October sunset* [Photograph]. Retrieved from http://www.jameskitto.co.uk/photo_1827786.html

If you wish to reference photographs or video files from a social media site such as Instagram (or Tumblr, Flickr or Pinterest), there are distinctions between the media to which you are referring. If you are referencing a photograph, do not italicise the title. However, if you are referencing a photograph collection/album or video file, do italicise the title.

Example: Instagram photograph

In-text citation

… the photograph (Nordeman, 2017).

Reference list

Nordeman, L. (2017). Kentucky Derby [Photograph]. Retrieved from https://instagram.com/tagged/photo_feature

Example: Instagram photograph collection or video file

In-text citation

Fisher's collection of deconstructed photographs (2017) …

Reference list

Fisher, D. (2017). *Deepbody* [Photo album]. Retrieved from https://instagram.com/deepbody

F32 Maps

Citation order:

- ◆ Cartographer
- ◆ Year of publication (in round brackets)
- ◆ Title of map section
- ◆ [Map]
- ◆ Sheet number or tile, scale
- ◆ Publication information (for print)

If viewed online:

- ◆ Retrieved from URL

Examples

In-text citations

The leisure centre is close to Tiddenfoot Lake (Ordnance Survey, 2018), while the access road can be followed on Google Maps (Google, 2018).

Reference list

Google. (2018). Tiddenfoot Lake [Map]. Retrieved from http://maps.google.co.uk

Ordnance Survey. (2018). Tiddenfoot Lake [Map]. Tile sp92sw, 1:10,000. Retrieved from http://edina.ac.uk/digimap

F33   Speeches or lectures

F33.1   Live speeches or lectures

Citation order:

♦ Speaker
♦ Year (in round brackets)
♦ Course/module and title of lecture (in italics)
♦ Medium (in square brackets)
♦ Location and date

Example

In-text citation

Points of interest from the lecture (Brown, 2018) …

Reference list

Brown, T. (2018). *Contemporary design* [Lecture to BSc Design Year 4]. Northumbria University, Newcastle upon Tyne. 21 April.

F33.2   Online lecture notes and presentation slides

If referencing lecture slides or notes, specify the medium in square brackets as above, but add Retrieved from URL.

Examples

In-text citations

The excellent presentation (Schott, 2018) …

Reviewing the notes (Mukwari, 2018) …

Reference list

Mukwari, J. (2018). *LLM module 44415: Takeover regulations* [Lecture notes]. Retrieved from http://duo.dur.ac.uk

Schott, H. (2018). *BSc Biology module 1061: Biodiversity in the UK* [PowerPoint slides]. Retrieved from http://www.biodiverseviews.org.uk/nwales2

F34   Interviews

F34.1 Published interviews

Published interviews should be cited according to the format in which you have used them: if you read the interview in a newspaper or magazine article, or if you watched the interview online (for example, YouTube), use the appropriate citation order for that format.

Example

In-text citation

Riley (2018) related her concerns …

Reference list

Riley, B. (2018, July 5). The life of Riley. Interview with Bridget Riley. Interviewed by Jonathan Jones for *The Guardian*, p. 33.

F34.2   Unpublished interviews

If you interviewed another person as part of your research, and they agreed to be quoted in your work, cite this as a personal communication in your text (see section F35).

Example

In-text citation

The Professor noted the important discoveries she made about memory loss (J. Wilkinson, personal communication, April 27, 2014).

Do not include this in your reference list because there is no copy of the information available for the reader to use.

If interviewees were speaking confidentially, do not include a citation.

Example

In-text citation

Fourteen of the twenty interviewees expressed concerns about steroid use in teenagers.

F35 Personal communications

This includes information in formats that cannot be obtained by a reader, including unrecorded and unpublished interviews, conversations, emails and notes you make during lectures.

No personal communication is included in your reference list; instead, parenthetically cite the communicator's name, the phrase 'personal communication', and the date of the communication in your main text only.

Example

In-text citation

The email stated that the company accepted an error had been made (H. Thomas, personal communication, May 14, 2019).

Sample text

The following sample piece of text illustrates how various in-text sources would be included in APA style in your work.

Homeopathy is a system of alternative medicine (Homeopathy, n.d.) and its history is comprehensively documented in a multi-volume work (Farrow & Morgan, 2009–2012). However, for brief introductory studies of the subject, the recently published articles of Bradley (2015) and Harvey (2016) present excellent starting points and complement the seminal analysis by Carmichael (2014). A more dated government survey sheds light on the issue of evidence relating to the effectiveness of homeopathy (Department of Health, 2010), while one charity's website, promoting and campaigning for access for all, includes a great deal of interesting information, including testimonials (British Homeopathic Association, 2015).

Sample reference list

All sources are listed alphabetically. Note that the first line of the reference is not indented, but subsequent lines are, so that the authors' names are easily identifiable (see 'Reference list layout' at the beginning of Section F).

Bradley, C. H. (2015). Evidential issues concerning patients of homeopathy. *Psychoanalytic Psychology, 28*(4), 122–141. doi:10.1037/0736-9735.25.1.122

British Homeopathic Association. (2015). Homeopathy – a healthcare choice for everyone. Retrieved from http://www.britishhomeopathic.org/

Carmichael, B. (2014). *Homeopathy* [Kindle version]. Retrieved from http://www.amazon.co.uk

Department of Health. (2010). Government response to the Science and Technology Committee report 'Evidence Check 2: Homeopathy'. Retrieved from https://www.gov.uk/government/publications/government-response/

Farrow, P. S., & Morgan, L. (Eds.). (2009–2012). *Homeopathic medicine: A history and study* (Vols 1–4). Lancaster: Greenlife Books.

Harvey, A. (2016). Homeopathy: New evidence for and against. *Medicine Today, 29*(4), 503–543.

Homeopathy. (n.d.). In *Wikipedia*. Retrieved September 19, 2018, from https://en.wikipedia.org/wiki/Homeopathy

Section G
Chicago referencing style

There are two formats within Chicago referencing style: notes and bibliography (NB) and author-date. The Chicago NB format is used in the humanities (see below). The author-date format is used in social sciences (see page 155). This guide focuses upon the notes and bibliography format. For more information on using the Chicago referencing style, see *Chicago manual of style* (2017) 17th edn. Chicago, IL: University of Chicago Press; and *Chicago manual of style online* (2018) Available at: https://www.chicagomanualofstyle.org/home.html (Accessed: 25 August 2018).

Chicago notes and bibliography (NB) format

This format uses footnotes below your text and a **bibliography** at the end of your text.

Instead of naming authors in the text, which can be distracting for the reader, numbers are used to denote **citations**. These numbers in the text are linked to a full **reference** in **footnotes** or **endnotes** and in your bibliography. Word-processing software such as Microsoft Word can create this link between citation number and full reference.

Cited publications are numbered in the order in which they are first referred to in the text. They are usually identified by a **superscript number** – for example, 'Thomas corrected this error'.[1]

Conventions when using the Chicago NB referencing style

Footnotes or endnotes

♦ Check whether footnotes or endnotes are preferred for the work you are producing
♦ All notes end with a full stop

Author names

♦ In the footnotes, author names should be forename followed by surname (for example, Francis Wheen). In the bibliography, author names should be surname followed by forename (for example, Wheen, Francis)
♦ If there are four or more authors, give the name of the first author followed by **et al.** in the footnotes. If there are more than 10 authors, list up to seven in the bibliography followed by et al. The first author's name is given in the bibliography as surname followed by forename, but other authors are written as forename followed by surname

Titles

♦ Italicise the titles of books, journals and websites. Titles of articles, chapters, unpublished sources such as PhDs, and web pages within a website are placed within double quotation marks

Bibliography

♦ List works in alphabetical order by surname of the first author
♦ Names are given as surname followed by forename for the first author, but subsequent authors and editors are given as forename followed by surname (for example, Williams, Edith, Jane Thompson and Claire Hopper)
♦ Sources without an author are listed by title in the alphabetical list

- References in your bibliography end with a full stop
- As well as footnotes or endnotes, you should list all your sources, including those you have read but not cited, in the bibliography

First citation and subsequent short citations

The first time you cite a source, give full details in the footnote or endnote. Subsequent entries of the same source can be abbreviated to author's surname and the first few words of the title, plus a page number if you are citing a specific part of the text, giving you a **short citation**. For example:

Worsley, *Classical Architecture*, 25.

The sample text at the end of this section shows examples of a first citation and subsequent short citation of this book by Worsley.

Ibid.

Ibid. (from Latin *ibidem*) means 'in the same place'. If two (or more) consecutive references are from the same source, then the second (or others) is cited ibid. Capitalise ibid. if used at the beginning of a note. For example:

1. Paulina Grainger, *Imagery in Prose*, London: Dale Press, 2009, 133–81.
2. Ibid., 155.
3. Ibid., 170.

Capitalisation

- Capitalise the first letter of the first word of the title and subtitle and subsequent main words (but not articles such as the, of, and). Capitalise articles if they are the first words of a subtitle after a colon (for example, *Cite Them Right: The Essential Referencing Guide*)

Dates

- For serials such as journals and newspapers, dates should be written as month, day, year

Place of publication: publisher, year of publication

- All in round brackets in footnotes but not in bibliography

Internet addresses (URLs), digital object identifiers (DOIs) and databases

- Whenever possible, use a DOI rather than a URL. The URL is given in full
- If you have obtained the source from a database (such as articles, dissertations or ebooks from JSTOR, EBSCO or Proquest), give the name of the database and omit the URL
- Only include an accessed date if the source does not have a publication date or date of last revision

Page numbers

- Omit p. or pp., but give page numbers for references to information cited, paraphrasing or quotations taken from the original source
- In the footnote, give the specific page number of information you have used in a source after the publication details. In the bibliography, give the span of pages of the whole chapter or section you have used in an edited book before the publication details

Formatting and punctuation

- Chicago referencing style has regulations for formatting your footnotes and references. The first line of footnotes should be indented by ½ inch (1.3cm) and subsequent lines are not indented. For the bibliography, the first line of references is not indented, but the second and subsequent lines have a hanging indent of ½ inch (1.3cm)

♦ Chicago style has different punctuation for entries in your footnotes and in your bibliography. Use commas to separate elements of the reference in the footnote, but use commas or full stops to separate the elements of the reference in the bibliography. In your footnote, the place of publication, publisher and year are enclosed in round brackets, but are unenclosed in the bibliography entry. Editors are referred to as 'ed.' in the footnote, but the phrase 'edited by' is used in the bibliography

Example

Footnote

1. Jane Dickson, "Female Managers in Industry," in *Corporate Leadership*, ed. Janesh Singh (Oxford: Oxford University Press, 2014), 49.

Bibliography

Dickson, Jane. "Female Managers in Industry." In *Corporate Leadership*, edited by Janesh Singh, 48–56. Oxford: Oxford University Press, 2014.

How to reference common sources in footnotes and bibliography

G1 Books

Citation order:

♦ Author
♦ Title (in italics)
♦ Edition (only include the edition number if it is not the first edition)

♦ Place of publication: publisher, year of publication (all in round brackets in footnote but not in bibliography)
♦ Comma then page reference in footnote

Examples

Footnotes

1. Giles Worsley, *Classical Architecture in Britain: The Heroic Age* (London: Published for the Paul Mellon Centre for Studies in British Art by Yale University Press, 1995), 47.

2. Robert Chitham, *The Classical Orders of Architecture*, 2nd ed. (Amsterdam: Elsevier, 2005), 22.

Bibliography

Chitham, Robert. *The Classical Orders of Architecture*. 2nd ed. Amsterdam: Elsevier, 2005.

Worsley, Giles. *Classical Architecture in Britain: The Heroic Age*. London: Published for the Paul Mellon Centre for Studies in British Art by Yale University Press, 1995.

G2 Ebooks

Cite ebooks in the same format as print books, but add details of the medium you used at the end of the reference. If you have read the book online, give the DOI, URL or name of the online collection or database. If you have read the ebook on a personal device, state the format (for example, Kindle). If you are unable to give page numbers for an ebook, give the most accurate information that you can, such as chapter.

Citation order in the footnote:

♦ Author/editor
♦ Title (in italics)
♦ Edition (only include the edition number if it is not the first edition)

- Place of publication: publisher, year of publication (all in round brackets in footnote but not in bibliography)
- Page reference
- DOI, URL, name of database or media

Citation order in the bibliography:

- Author/editor
- Title (in italics)
- Edition (only include the edition number if it is not the first edition)
- Place of publication: publisher, year of publication
- DOI, URL, name of database or media

Examples

Footnotes

1. Anne Cleeve, *White Nights* (London: Pan Books, 2008), chap. 30, Kindle.

2. Robert Adam, *Ruins of the Palace of the Emperor Diocletian at Spalatro in Dalmatia* (London: Printed for the author, 1764), plate 14, Eighteenth Century Collections Online.

3. Richard Adams, *Watership Down* (London: Rex Collings, 1972), epilogue, http://www.mrkingrocks.com/files/watershipdown.pdf.

Bibliography

Adam, Robert. *Ruins of the Palace of the Emperor Diocletian at Spalatro in Dalmatia*. London: Printed for the author, 1764. Eighteenth Century Collections Online.

Adams, Richard. *Watership Down*. London: Rex Collings, 1972, http://www.mrkingrocks.com/files/watershipdown.pdf.

Cleeve, Anne. *White Nights*. London: Pan Books, 2008. Kindle.

G3 Translated books

Citation order:

- Author
- Title (in italics)
- Edition (only include the edition number if it is not the first edition)
- trans. or Translated by
- Forename and surname of translator
- Place of publication: publisher, year of publication (all in round brackets in footnote but not in bibliography)
- Comma then page reference in footnote

Example

Footnote

1. Miguel Delibes, *The Path*, trans. John Haycraft and Rita Haycraft (London: Dolphin Books, 2013), 13.

Bibliography

Delibes, Miguel. *The Path*. Translated by John Haycraft and Rita Haycraft. London: Dolphin Books, 2013.

G4 Sacred texts

G4.1 The Bible

The Chicago manual of style has a list of abbreviations for books of the Bible and published versions (pp. 596–600). Provide references in footnotes; no entry is required in your bibliography.

Citation order:

- Book abbreviation
- Chapter: verse(s)
- Version (written out in first footnote, abbreviated in subsequent notes)

Example

Footnote

1. Eph 6:10–17 (Revised Standard Version).

G4.2   The Quran

Citation order:

♦ Quran
♦ Surah: verse(s)

Example

Footnote

1. Quran, 19:10–11.

G5   Chapters of edited books

Citation order:

♦ Author of the chapter
♦ Title of chapter (in double quotation marks)
♦ in (when used in footnote) / In (when used in bibliography)
♦ Title of book (in italics)
♦ ed. or edited by
♦ Name of editor of book (forename followed by surname)
♦ Page span of chapter or section (only in bibliography)
♦ Place of publication: publisher, year of publication (all in round brackets in footnote but not in bibliography)
♦ Comma then page reference in footnote

Example

Footnote

1. Alexandrina Buchanan, "Interpretations of Medieval Architecture," in *Gothic Architecture and Its Meanings 1550–1830*, ed. Michael Hall (Reading: Spire Books, 2002), 32.

Bibliography

Buchanan, Alexandrina. "Interpretations of Medieval Architecture." In *Gothic Architecture and Its Meanings 1550–1830*, edited by Michael Hall, 27–52. Reading: Spire Books, 2002.

G6   Encyclopedia entry (online)

Citation order:

♦ Author of the entry
♦ Title of entry (in double quotation marks)
♦ in (when used in footnote) / In (when used in bibliography)
♦ Title of encyclopedia (in italics)
♦ ed. or edited by
♦ Name of editor of book (if available)
♦ Place of publication: publisher, year of publication (all in round brackets in footnote but not in bibliography)
♦ online ed., year of update (if different from print details, include in round brackets)
♦ URL *or* DOI.

Example

Footnote

1. Peter Conradi, "Murdoch, Dame (Jean) Iris (1919–1999)," in *Oxford Dictionary of National Biography* (Oxford University Press, 2004; online ed., 2015), https://doi.org/10.1093/ref:odnb/71228.

Bibliography

Conradi, Peter. "Murdoch, Dame (Jean) Iris (1919–1999)." In *Oxford Dictionary of National Biography*. Oxford University Press, 2004; online ed., 2015. https://doi.org/10.1093/ref:odnb/71228.

G7   Anthologies

Citation order:

♦ Author/editor
♦ Title (in italics)
♦ Edition (only include the edition number if it is not the first edition)
♦ Number of volumes
♦ Place of publication: publisher, year of publication (all in round brackets in footnote but not in bibliography)
♦ Comma then page reference in footnote

Example

1. Donald Keane, ed. *Anthology of Japanese Literature*, 3rd ed. (London: Grove, 1955), 42–49.

Keane, Donald, ed. *Anthology of Japanese Literature*. 3rd ed. London: Grove, 1955.

G8   Multi-volume works

Citation order:

♦ Author/editor
♦ Title (in italics)
♦ Edition (only include the edition number if it is not the first edition)
♦ Number of volumes
♦ Place of publication: publisher, year of publication (all in round brackets in footnote but not in bibliography)

Example

1. Damie Stillman, *English Neo-classical Architecture*, 2 vols (London: Zwemmer, 1988).

Stillman, Damie. *English Neo-classical Architecture*. 2 vols. London: Zwemmer, 1988.

G9   Poems

Citation order:

♦ Author
♦ Title of poem (in double quotation marks)
♦ in (when used in footnote) / In (when used in bibliography)
♦ Title of book (in italics)

♦ ed. or edited by
♦ Name of editor of book (forename followed by surname)
♦ Page span of poem (only in bibliography)
♦ Place of publication: publisher, year of publication (all in round brackets in footnote but not in bibliography)
♦ Comma then page reference in footnote

Example

1. William Wordsworth, "Written in Very Early Youth," in *Poetical Works of William Wordsworth*, vol. 1, eds. Ernest De Selincourt and Helen Darbishire (Oxford: Oxford University Press, 2015), 3.

Wordsworth, William. "Written in Very Early Youth." In *Poetical Works of William Wordsworth*. Vol. 1, edited by Ernest De Selincourt and Helen Darbishire, 3. Oxford: Oxford University Press, 2015.

G10   Plays

Citation order:

♦ Author
♦ Title (in italics)
♦ ed. or edited by
♦ Name of editor (forename followed by surname)
♦ Place of publication: publisher, year (all in round brackets in footnotes but not in bibliography)
♦ Reference to cited Act. Scene. Line number, or page number

Example

Footnote

1. William Shakespeare, *Hamlet*, ed. T.J.B. Spencer (London: Penguin, 1980), I.2.177.

Bibliography

Shakespeare, William. *Hamlet*, edited by T.J.B. Spencer. London: Penguin, 1980.

G11   Journal articles

Citation order:

- ◆ Author
- ◆ Title of article (in double quotation marks)
- ◆ Title of journal (in italics)
- ◆ Volume number, issue number (if available)
- ◆ Year of publication (in round brackets)
- ◆ Colon then page reference in footnote or page span in bibliography

Example

Footnote

1. Peter Leach, "James Paine's Design for the South Front of Kedleston Hall: Dating and Sources," *Architectural History* 40 (1997): 160.

Bibliography

Leach, Peter. "James Paine's Design for the South Front of Kedleston Hall: Dating and Sources." *Architectural History* 40 (1997): 159–70.

G12   Ejournal articles

Citation order:

- ◆ Author
- ◆ Title of article (in double quotation marks)
- ◆ Title of journal (in italics)
- ◆ Volume number, issue number

- ◆ Year of publication (in round brackets)
- ◆ Colon then page reference in footnote or page span in bibliography
- ◆ DOI, URL or name of database

Example: footnote with DOI

Footnotes

1. Edwina Thomas Washington, "An Overview of Cyberbullying in Higher Education," *Adult Learning* 26 (2015): 23, https://doi.org/10.1177/1045159514558412.

Example in database

2. Robert T. Teske, "Fifty Years in Folklore," *Journal of American Folklore* 131, no. 531 (Summer 2018): 303, Project MUSE.

Bibliography

Teske, Robert T. "Fifty Years in Folklore." *Journal of American Folklore* 131, no. 531 (Summer 2018): 301–17. Project Muse.

Washington, Edwina Thomas. "An Overview of Cyberbullying in Higher Education." *Adult Learning* 26 (2015): 21–27. https://doi.org/10.1177/1045159514558412.

G13   Newspaper and magazine articles

Citation order:

- ◆ Author
- ◆ Title of article (in double quotation marks)
- ◆ Title of newspaper (in italics)
- ◆ Date
- ◆ Section (if applicable)
- ◆ Page number (in footnote but not in bibliography)
- ◆ If online, add URL or name of database.

NB Omit articles from newspaper titles – for example, write *Times*, not *The Times*. Add a location if this helps to identify it – for example, *Journal* (Newcastle upon Tyne).

Example

Footnotes

1. "Moment Banksy Artwork Shreds Itself," *skynews*, October 6, 2018, https://news.sky.com/video/moment-banksy-artwork-shreds-itself-11519971.

2. Dan Hyde, "Parents Funding Adult Offspring's Holidays," *Daily Telegraph*, September 14, 2015, 7.

3. Benjamin Haas, "Tears Flow as Separated South and North Korean Families Reunite," *Guardian*, August 20, 2018, Factiva.

Bibliography

Haas, Benjamin. "Tears Flow as Separated South and North Korean Families Reunite." *Guardian*, August 20, 2018. Factiva.

Hyde, Dan. "Parents Funding Adult Offspring's Holidays." *Daily Telegraph*, September 14, 2015.

"Moment Banksy Artwork Shreds Itself." skynews, accessed October 6, 2018, https://news.sky.com/video/moment-banksy-artwork-shreds-itself-11519971.

G14 Book reviews

Citation order:

♦ Author of review
♦ Title of review article (in double quotation marks)
♦ Review of
♦ Title of work being reviewed (in italics)
♦ By
♦ Name of author of work being reviewed
♦ Title of publication where review published (in italics)

♦ Date
♦ Page number
♦ DOI or URL

Example

Footnote

1. Willy Maley, "Where No Man Has Gone Before," review of *Samuel Johnson and the Journey into Words*, by Lynda Mugglestone, *Times Higher Education*, September 24, 2015: 24.

Bibliography

Maley, Willy. "Where No Man Has Gone Before." Review of *Samuel Johnson and the Journey into Words*, by Lynda Mugglestone. *Times Higher Education*. September 24, 2015: 24.

G15 Theses and dissertations

Citation order:

♦ Author
♦ Title of thesis (in double quotation marks)
♦ Degree level, university, year (all in round brackets in footnotes but not in bibliography)
♦ Page reference in footnote

NB Chicago style follows the American terminology for Master's thesis and PhD dissertation (rather than Master's dissertation and PhD thesis as in the UK).

Example

Footnote

1. Brian Wragg, "The Life and Works of John Carr of York: Palladian Architect" (PhD diss., University of Sheffield, 1976), 47.

Bibliography

Wragg, Brian. "The Life and Works of John Carr of York: Palladian Architect." PhD diss., University of Sheffield, 1976.

If you have read the thesis or dissertation online, add the name of the database, the DOI or the URL.

Examples in bibliography

Cunningham, Andrew Stewart. "Sympathy in Man and Nature." PhD diss., University of Toronto, 1999. ProQuest Dissertations Publishing (NQ41132).

Johnson, Michael. "Architectural Taste and Patronage in Newcastle upon Tyne, 1870–1914." PhD diss., Northumbria University, 2009. http://nrl.northumbria.ac.uk/id/eprint/2867 (Accessed: 17 December 2018).

G16 Conference proceedings

G16.1 Paper presented at a conference

Citation order:

♦ Author
♦ Title of paper (in double quotation marks)
♦ Paper presented at
♦ Name of conference, location and date
♦ Publication details

Example

Footnote

1. Giorgos Patrolou, "Family and Fortune in Athens," (paper presented at the Biannual Symposium of the Hellenic Studies Institute, University of Bonn, Germany, August 14–16, 2014).

Bibliography

Patrolou, Giorgos. "Family and Fortune in Athens." Paper presented at the Biannual Symposium of the Hellenic Studies Institute, University of Bonn, Germany. August 14–16, 2014.

G16.2 Conference paper available online

Citation order:

♦ Author
♦ Title of paper (in double quotation marks)
♦ Paper presented at
♦ Name of conference, location and date
♦ URL

Example: online conference paper (date and location not in title)

Footnote

1. Balakrishna Hosangadi, "Folktales, Myths and Legends on Sculptors of South India," (paper presented at the Asian Conference on Literature 2017 Official Conference Proceedings, Kobe, March 30–April 2, 2017, Japan. http://papers.iafor.org/submission34635).

Bibliography

Hosangadi, Balakrishna. "Folktales, Myths and Legends on Sculptors of South India." Paper presented at the Asian Conference on Literature 2017 Official Conference Proceedings, Kobe, March 30–April 2, 2017, Japan. http://papers.iafor.org/submission34635.

G16.3 Whole conference proceedings

Citation order:

♦ Title of conference proceedings publication (in italics)
♦ ed.
♦ Name of editor
♦ Place of publication: publisher, year (all in round brackets in footnotes but not in bibliography)

Example

Footnote

1. *Proceedings of the Tenth Conference in Romance Studies, 18 May 2014*, ed. Hilary Jones (Derby: University of Derby Press, 2014).

Bibliography

Proceedings of the Tenth Conference in Romance Studies, 18 May 2014. Edited by Hilary Jones. Derby: University of Derby Press, 2014.

G16.4 Papers in conference proceedings

A paper included in the published proceedings of a conference should be treated like a chapter in a book (see G5), or if the paper is published in a journal, treat it like an article (see G11 or G12).

G17 Official publications

Citation order:

♦ Name of country
♦ Name of committee, department or Royal Commission
♦ Title (in italics)
♦ Volume details and command number, if available
♦ Place of publication: publisher, year (all in round brackets in footnotes but not in bibliography)
♦ Accessed date and URL (if online)

Examples

Footnotes

1. United Kingdom, Department for Business, Innovation & Skills, *Regulations Implementing the National Minimum Wage – a Report on the Apprentice Rate*, Cm 9061 (London: The Stationery Office, 2015), accessed September 17, 2018, https://www.gov.uk/government/publications/national-minimum-wagereport-on-the-2015-apprentice-rate.

2. United Kingdom, Secretary of State for Prices and Consumer Protection, *Review of Restrictive Trade Practices Policy*, Cmnd 7512 (London: HMSO, 1979).

Bibliography

United Kingdom. Department for Business, Innovation & Skills. *Regulations Implementing the National Minimum Wage – a Report on the Apprentice Rate*. Cm 9061. London: The Stationery Office, 2015. Accessed September 17, 2018. https://www.gov.uk/government/publications/national-minimum-wagereport- on-the-2015-apprentice-rate.
United Kingdom. Secretary of State for Prices and Consumer Protection. *Review of Restrictive Trade Practices Policy*. Cmnd 7512. London: HMSO, 1979.

G18 Legal sources

G18.1 Legislation

Citation order:

♦ Title of legislation (including year, in italics)
♦ Country
♦ URL or database

Examples

Footnotes

1. *Human Rights Act 1998*, United Kingdom, accessed April 14, 2018, Westlaw.

2. *Banking Act 2009*, United Kingdom, accessed April 14, 2018, http://www.bailii.org/uk/legis/num_act/2009/ukpga_20090001_en_1.html.

Bibliography

Banking Act 2009. United Kingdom. Accessed April 14, 2018. http://www.bailii.org/uk/legis/num_act/2009/ukpga_20090001_en_1.html.

Human Rights Act 1998. United Kingdom. Accessed April 14, 2018. Westlaw.

G18.2 Cases

Citation order:

♦ Party names (A v B, in italics)
♦ Year
♦ Citation

Example

Footnote

1. *R. v Antoine*, 2000, UKHL 20; [2000] 2 All ER 208.

Bibliography

R. v Antoine. 2000. UKHL 20; [2000] 2 All ER 208.

G19 Music scores

Citation order:

♦ Composer
♦ Title of work (in italics)

♦ Place of publication: publisher, year (all in round brackets in footnotes but not in bibliography)

Example

Footnote

1. Peter Maxwell Davies, *An Orkney Wedding, with Sunrise* (London: Boosey and Hawkes, 1985).

Bibliography

Davies, Peter Maxwell. *An Orkney Wedding, with Sunrise*. London: Boosey and Hawkes, 1985.

G20 Organisation or personal internet sites

If the details of the website can be given in your text, you do not need to add a footnote and bibliography entry – for example: "The text was published on the Auden Society website on August 4, 2015." If you are providing footnote and bibliography entries, use the following.

Citation order in footnote:

♦ Title of internet site (in double quotation marks)
♦ Author/organisation
♦ Accessed date *or* date last modified
♦ URL

Citation order in bibliography:

♦ Author/organisation
♦ Title of internet site (in double quotation marks)
♦ Accessed date *or* date last modified
♦ URL

Examples

Footnotes

   1. "Quote Library," Trollope Society, accessed December 21, 2018, https://trollopesociety.org/works/quotes/.

   2. "The Old Stones of Cornwall," James Kitto, accessed August 23, 2018, http://jameskitto.co.uk/gallery_635813.html.

Bibliography

Kitto, James. "The Old Stones of Cornwall." Accessed August 23, 2018. http://jameskitto.co.uk/gallery_635813.html.

Trollope Society. "Quote Library," Accessed December 21, 2018. https://trollopesociety.org/works/quotes/.

G21   Blogs

Citation order:

◆ Author
◆ Title of post (in double quotation marks)
◆ Title of blog (in italics)
◆ blog
◆ Date
◆ URL

Example

Footnote

   1. Rik Hijmans, "Going Dutch," *Continental Cuisine* (blog), February 22, 2017, https://continentalcuisine.wordpress.com.

Bibliography

Hijmans, Rik. "Going Dutch." *Continental Cuisine* (blog). February 22, 2017. https://continentalcuisine.wordpress.com.

G22   Social media

G22.1   Facebook

Citation order:

◆ Author
◆ Title of post (in double quotation marks)
◆ Facebook
◆ Date of post
◆ URL

Example

Footnote

   1. Durham University Library, "Durham Priory Library Recreated," Facebook, July 29, 2018, https://www.facebook.com/dulib/videos/10153270708178099.

Bibliography

Durham University Library. "Durham Priory Library Recreated." Facebook, July 29, 2018. https://www.facebook.com/dulib/videos/10153270708178099.

G22.2   Twitter

You can include the details of a tweet in a sentence – for example: "In her Twitter post of November 14, 2018, Jane March (@jmarch) stated, 'University entry grades rose by an average of four points in 2018'." If you wish to give footnote and bibliography entries, use the following.

Citation order:

◆ Author or organisation (real name)
◆ Screen name (in round brackets)
◆ Text of post (in double quotation marks)
◆ Social media service
◆ Date and time
◆ URL

Example

Footnote

1. Jane March (@JMarch), "University entry grades rose by an average of four points in 2018," Twitter, November 14, 2018, 1.20 p.m., http://twitter.com/JMarch/status/151509635204723087.

Bibliography

Jane March (@JMarch). "University entry grades rose by an average of four points in 2018." Twitter, November 14, 2018, 1.20 p.m. http://twitter.com/JMarch/status/151509635204723087.

G22.3 Instagram

Citation order:

♦ Author
♦ Title (in double quotation marks)
♦ Instagram photo
♦ Date
♦ URL

Example

Footnote

1. harrypottercast, "Lego Quidditch Pitch," Instagram photo, August 30, 2018, https://www.instagram.com/p/BnHOn1rnhg4/?taken-by=harrypottercast.

Bibliography

harrypottercast. "Lego Quidditch Pitch." Instagram photo, August 30, 2018. https://www.instagram.com/p/BnHOn1rnhg4/?taken-by=harrypottercast.

G23 Personal communications (emails, text messages and telephone calls)

Personal communications can be cited in your text rather than in a footnote or bibliography – for example: "In her email to the author on December 1, 2018 Amanda Hollis listed …" If you wish to cite a personal communication, do so in a footnote.

Example

Footnote

1. Amanda Hollis, email message to the author, December 1, 2018.

G24 Manuscripts in archives

When citing archive sources in your footnote, begin with the item you are citing rather than the full collection. If you are citing only one item from a collection, give full details of the item, beginning with its title, in the bibliography, but if citing two or more items, you need provide only one reference to the collection in the bibliography.

Citation order for single item:

♦ Description of document
♦ Reference number
♦ Name of archive
♦ Location

Citation order for collection (if citing more than one item):

♦ Title of collection
♦ Name of archive
♦ Location

Examples

Footnotes

    1. Howick Hall, south elevation May 1925, Photograph 20248/2, Sir Herbert Baker Collection, Royal Institute of British Architects Library, London.

    2. Howick Hall in 1926 showing fire damage, Photographs 20248/6-8, Sir Herbert Baker Collection, Royal Institute of British Architects Library, London.

Bibliography (for whole collection if citing more than one item)

Sir Herbert Baker Collection. Royal Institute of British Architects Library, London.

G25   Photographs

G25.1   Photographic slides or prints

Citation order:

- Photographer
- Title of photograph (in italics)
- Year
- Medium
- Location

Example

Footnote

    1. Jane Thorn, *Redevelopment in Byker*, 1977, colour print, Side Gallery, Newcastle upon Tyne.

Bibliography

Thorn, Jane. *Redevelopment in Byker*. 1977. Colour print. Side Gallery, Newcastle upon Tyne.

G25.2   Photographs from the internet

Citation order:

- Photographer
- Title of photograph (in italics)
- Year
- Medium
- Accessed date (if required)
- URL

Example

Footnote

    1. James Kitto, *Porthleven Harbour*, 2017, digital photograph, accessed June 13, 2018, http://jameskitto.co.uk/photo-14690012.html.

Bibliography

Kitto, James. *Porthleven Harbour*. 2017. Digital photograph. Accessed June 13, 2018. http://jameskitto.co.uk/photo-14690012.html.

G25.3   Photographs in online databases

Citation order:

- Photographer
- Title of photograph/video (in italics)
- Year
- Name of online database

Example

Footnote

    1. Marie Besson, *Green 2CV*, 2004, ARTstor.

Bibliography

Besson, Marie. *Green 2CV*. 2004. ARTstor.

G26 Films

Citation order:

- ◆ Film title (in italics)
- ◆ Directed by
- ◆ Year released; place: distributor, year (in round brackets in footnote but not in bibliography)
- ◆ Medium

Example

Footnote

1. *Brief Encounter*, directed by David Lean (1945; London: ITV Studios Home Entertainment, 2009), DVD.

Bibliography

Lean, David, dir. *Brief Encounter*. 1945; London: ITV Studios Home Entertainment, 2009. DVD.

G27 Television or radio broadcasts

Citation order:

- ◆ Episode title (if applicable, in double quotation marks)
- ◆ Programme/series title (in italics)
- ◆ Name of broadcaster/channel
- ◆ Month, day, year

Example

Footnote

1. "Scarlet Macaw," *Tweet of the Day*, BBC Radio 4, February 2, 2018.

Bibliography

"Scarlet Macaw." *Tweet of the Day*. BBC Radio 4. February 2, 2018.

G28 Podcasts/videos on the internet

Citation order:

- ◆ Creator
- ◆ Title of recording (in double quotation marks)
- ◆ Date of posting
- ◆ in Title of series (if available, in italics)
- ◆ Format
- ◆ Length of recording
- ◆ URL

Examples

Footnotes

1. Joshua Cuerdo, "Baroque and Rococo Architecture," February 21, 2017, video, 30:51, https://www.youtube.com/watch?v=eqFGq4fLel0.

2. Andrea Verity, "Galleries of Washington, DC," in *ArtAmerica*, March 14, 2018, podcast, 17:32, http://www.newsamerica.com/20180314.

Bibliography

Cuerdo, Joshua. "Baroque and Rococo Architecture." February 21, 2017. Video, 30:51. https://www.youtube.com/watch?v=eqFGq4fLel0.

Verity, Andrea. "Galleries of Washington, DC." *ArtAmerica*. March 14, 2018. Podcast, 17:32. http://www.newsamerica.com/20180314.

G29 Audio recordings

Citation order:

- ◆ Name of composer or performer
- ◆ Title (in italics)
- ◆ Other contributors
- ◆ Date of recording
- ◆ Publication details
- ◆ Medium

Example

1. Gustav Mahler, *Symphony no. 10*, performed by BBC National Orchestra of Wales, conductor Mark Wigglesworth, recorded March 14, 2016, BBC, compact disc.

Mahler, Gustav. *Symphony no. 10*. Performed by BBC National Orchestra of Wales, conductor Mark Wigglesworth. Recorded March 14, 2016. BBC. Compact disc.

G30   Works of art

Citation order:

♦ Artist
♦ Title of work (in italics)
♦ Date
♦ Medium
♦ Dimensions
♦ Location

Examples

1. Auguste Rodin, *The Kiss*, 1882, marble, Musée Rodin, Paris.

2. John Martin, *The Bard*, 1817, oil on canvas, 215 × 157 cm, Laing Art Gallery, Newcastle upon Tyne.

3. Anthony Gormley, *Angel of the North*, 1998, sculpture, Low Fell, Gateshead.

Gormley, Anthony. *Angel of the North*. 1998. Sculpture. Low Fell, Gateshead.
Martin, John. *The Bard*. 1817. Oil on canvas. 215 × 157 cm. Laing Art Gallery, Newcastle upon Tyne.
Rodin, Auguste. *The Kiss*. 1882. Marble. Musée Rodin, Paris, France.

G31   Lectures

Citation order:

♦ Author
♦ Title of lecture (in double quotation marks)
♦ Lecture
♦ Name of event, location, date (all in round brackets in footnotes but not in bibliography)
♦ If viewed online add Accessed date. URL.

Examples

1. Jane Stanton, "Wordsworth's Imagination" (lecture, Durham Book Festival, Gala Theatre, Durham, 18 September 2018).

2. Clare Willard, "Wordsworth in Context" (lecture, MA Literature course, Durham University, 19 October 2018), accessed 25 October 2018, http://duo.dur.ac.uk.

Stanton, Jane. "Wordsworth's Imagination." Lecture to Durham Book Festival. Gala Theatre, Durham. September 18, 2018.

Willard, Clare. "Wordsworth in Context." Lecture to MA Literature course. Durham University. October 19, 2018. Accessed October 25, 2018. http://duo.dur.ac.uk.

G32 Interviews

G32.1 Personal interviews

If you want to cite an interview you have conducted but not published, use the following.

Citation order:

♦ Name of interviewee
♦ Interview by
♦ Date of interview

Example

1. Claire Johnson, interview by Danielle Roberts, October 14, 2018.

Johnson, Claire. Interviewed by Danielle Roberts. October 14, 2018.

G32.2 Published interviews (print or online)

Citation order:

♦ Name of interviewee
♦ Title of interview (in double quotation marks, if available)
♦ Interview by
♦ Name of interviewer (forename followed by surname)
♦ Publication details

Examples

1. Bridget Riley, "The Life of Riley," interview by Jonathan Jones, *Guardian*, July 5, 2008, p. 23.

2. Jessica Staton, "Sometimes I Feel Like a Jack of All Trades," interview by Giverny Masso, *Stage*, September 25, 2018, https://www.thestage.co.uk/features/interviews.

Riley, Bridget. "The Life of Riley." Interview by Jonathan Jones. *Guardian*, July 5, 2008.

Staton, Jessica. "Sometimes I Feel Like a Jack of All Trades." Interview by Giverny Masso. *Stage*, September 25, 2018. https://www.thestage.co.uk/features/interviews.

Sample text

This sample piece of text shows how various sources would be included as in-text citations:

Worsley's *Classical Architecture* highlighted the variety of styles that eighteenth-century architects employed in their buildings.[1] Rich patrons wanted designs in the latest fashion and among those to profit from this demand was Robert Adam, who published his studies of Roman buildings.[2] With this first-hand knowledge he designed many country houses and public buildings, and was even able to take over projects begun by other architects, as at Kedleston in Derbyshire.[3] His work was not always as revolutionary as he claimed,[4] but it certainly impressed clients and was copied by other architects including John Carr.[5] Although most patrons favoured classical styles, Horace Walpole suggested that the Gothic style was 'our architecture', the national style of England.[6] Later authors have suggested that Gothic style signified ancient lineage and the British Constitution.[7]

Sample footnotes

NB The first line of each footnote is indented by 1.3cm (½ inch). Text should be double-spaced.

1. Giles Worsley, *Classical Architecture in Britain: The Heroic Age* (London: Published for the Paul Mellon Centre for Studies in British Art by Yale University Press, 1995), 47.

2. Robert Adam, *Ruins of the Palace of the Emperor Diocletian at Spalatro in Dalmatia* (London: Printed for the author, 1764), Eighteenth Century Collections Online.

3. Peter Leach, "James Paine's Design for the South Front of Kedleston Hall: Dating and Sources," *Architectural History* 40 (1997): 160.

4. Worsley, *Classical Architecture*, 265.

5. Brian Wragg, "The Life and Works of John Carr of York: Palladian Architect" (PhD diss., University of Sheffield, 1976).

6. Horace Walpole, cited in S. Lang, "The Principles of the Gothic Revival in England," *Journal of the Society of Architectural Historians* 25, no. 4 (1966): 244, accessed December 21, 2018, http://www.jstor.org/stable/988353.

7. Alexandrina Buchanan, "Interpretations of Medieval Architecture," in *Gothic Architecture and Its Meanings 1550–1830*, ed. Michael Hall (Reading: Spire Books, 2002): 27–52.

NB Footnote 4 is an example of a **short citation**, and footnote 6 is a **secondary reference**.

Sample bibliography

NB Sources listed in your bibliography should have a hanging indent of 1.3cm (½ inch) and text should be double-spaced.

Adam, Robert. *Ruins of the Palace of the Emperor Diocletian at Spalatro in Dalmatia*. London: Printed for the author, 1764. Eighteenth Century Collections Online.

Buchanan, Alexandrina. "Interpretations of Medieval Architecture." In *Gothic Architecture and Its Meanings 1550–1830*, edited by Michael Hall, 27–52. Reading: Spire Books, 2002.

Lang, S. "The Principles of the Gothic Revival in England." *Journal of the Society of Architectural Historians* 25, no. 4 (1966):240–67. Accessed December 21, 2018, http://www.jstor.org/stable/988353.

Leach, Peter. "James Paine's Design for the South Front of Kedleston Hall: Dating and Sources." *Architectural History* 40 (1997):159–70.

Worsley, Giles. *Classical Architecture in Britain: The Heroic Age*. London: Published for the Paul Mellon Centre for Studies in British Art by Yale University Press, 1995.

Wragg, Brian. "The Life and Works of John Carr of York: Palladian Architect." PhD diss., University of Sheffield, 1976.

Chicago author-date format

As with APA and Harvard styles, the Chicago author-date format uses in-text citations comprising the author's name and year of publication (and specific page reference if required).

Example: in-text citation

Washington (2018, 27) concurred with an earlier assessment (Dickson 2016) …

A reference list (rather than a bibliography) at the end of the work provides full bibliographical details for sources used. These sources are listed in alphabetical order by authors' names.

The major difference in the form of the references is the position of the year of publication. In the notes and bibliography format, the year comes towards the end of the reference, but in author-date format it is moved to second place in the reference, after the author's name, or, if this is unavailable, the title of the source.

Examples

Bibliography in NB format

Dickson, Jane. "Female Managers in Industry." In *Corporate Leadership*, edited by Javid Singh, 48–56. Oxford: Oxford University Press, 2014.

Washington, Edwina Thomas. "An Overview of Cyberbullying in Higher Education." *Adult Learning* 26 (2015): 21–27. https://doi.org/10.1177/1045159514558412.

Reference list in author-date format

Dickson, Jane. 2014. "Female Managers in Industry." In *Corporate Leadership*, edited by Javid Singh, 48–56. Oxford: Oxford University Press.

Washington, Edwina Thomas. 2015. "An Overview of Cyberbullying in Higher Education." *Adult Learning* 26: 21–27. https://doi.org/10.1177/1045159514558412.

Note how the date now comes after the author's name and that the date is also without round brackets in author-date format. Other details and punctuation in author-date format match the examples for the notes and bibliography format.

Footnotes in author-date format

Unlike APA and Harvard, Chicago author-date format allows the use of footnotes to elaborate on something you have mentioned in the text. Footnotes are *not* used to give full bibliographic details, which are given in the reference list.

Example: in-text citation with footnote

In-text citation

Washington (2018, 27) concurred with an earlier assessment.[1]

Footnote

1. Dickson (2016, 50) had examined bullying in male-dominated occupations.

Sample reference list in Chicago author-date format

Adam, Robert. 1764. *Ruins of the Palace of the Emperor Diocletian at Spalatro in Dalmatia*. London: Printed for the author, 1764. Eighteenth Century Collections Online.

Buchanan, Alexandrina. 2002. "Interpretations of Medieval Architecture." In *Gothic Architecture and Its Meanings 1550–1830*, edited by Michael Hall, 27–52. Reading: Spire Books.

Lang, S. 1966. "The Principles of the Gothic Revival in England." *Journal of the Society of Architectural Historians* 25, no. 4: 240–67. Accessed December 21, 2018, http://www.jstor.org/stable/988353.

Leach, Peter. 1997. "James Paine's Design for the South Front of Kedleston Hall: Dating and Sources." *Architectural History* 40: 159–70.

Worsley, Giles. 1995. *Classical Architecture in Britain: The Heroic Age.* London: Published for the Paul Mellon Centre for Studies in British Art by Yale University Press.

Wragg, Brian. 1976. "The Life and Works of John Carr of York: Palladian Architect." PhD diss., University of Sheffield.

Section H
Institute of Electrical and Electronics Engineers (IEEE) referencing style

The IEEE referencing style is a numeric citation system used in engineering, electronics, computer science and information technology publications. This section is based on IEEE (2018) *IEEE reference guide*. Available at: http://ieeeauthorcenter.ieee.org/wp-content/uploads/IEEE-Reference-Guide.pdf (Accessed: 20 January 2019). Our examples below have applied the principles of IEEE style to a fuller range of sources than are covered by the *IEEE reference guide*.

Conventions when using the IEEE referencing style

♦ IEEE uses numeric references in the text, with numbers in square brackets [1]
♦ Each source has its own in-text number
♦ The same citation number is used whenever a source is cited in your text
♦ These in-text numbers are matched to full, numbered **references** for each publication in a list of References
♦ Sources are listed in References in the order that they appear in the text, not alphabetically
♦ In the References, the reference numbers in square brackets are aligned flush left as if in a separate column, while the source information is indented
♦ Months with more than four letters are abbreviated: Jan. Feb. Mar. Apr. Aug. Sep. Oct. Nov. Dec., but May, June and July are written in full

♦ There are well-established abbreviations for titles of journals and conference proceedings
♦ Places of publication include US state abbreviation and country
♦ Dates are given as Abbreviated month, day, year
♦ For online sources, give a doi if available. No accessed date is needed with a doi. If there is no doi, use Accessed: date. [Online]. URL

Author names

♦ You do not need to include an author name in your in-text citation, unless you wish to do so

Examples

Collins [4] tested the theory …

A recent test of the theory [4] …

♦ Authors should be cited in the references by initial(s) of their given name

Example

[4] G. S. Collins

Multiple authors

♦ Many publications are the result of collaborative work, resulting in multiple authors. If there are two to five authors, list each in the order that they appear in the source, with 'and' between the fourth and fifth authors' names

Example

[5] K. Leonis, F. Johnson, M. Willis, P. Chakraborty, and S. Asturias.

♦ If there are six or more authors, use *et al.* after the first author. *Et al.* should be in italics

Example

[6] D. Bourne, P. Davis, E. Fuller, A. J. Hanson, K. N. Price, P. Singh, C. A. Thompson, S. Kim, and J. T. Vaughan.

would appear in the References as

[6] D. Bourne *et al.*

Organisations as authors

♦ Names of organisations are spelt out, not abbreviated

Example

Microsoft Corporation

No authors identified

♦ If no authors or editors are listed, use the title of the source

Example

3D Printing Manual. Birmingham, U.K.: Innovations Ltd, 2018.

Multiple citations

♦ If you have written a section of text based upon several references, these are indicated by listing each source in its own square brackets

Example

Implementations of the new software [2], [3], [5] revealed …

♦ If you are citing consecutive sources, you can link these with a dash

Example

Foster's bridge designs [6]–[9] …

Quoting or paraphrasing

If you quote or paraphrase from a source, or wish to highlight part of it, include the page, paragraph or section numbers after the reference number.

Example

Wind power contributes around 4% of UK energy supply [4, p. 21] …

Secondary referencing

If you want to cite work by an author quoted in another publication, but you have not read the original author's own work, you must indicate that you read it in the second publication. This is because you are relying upon the second author who you have read to give an accurate representation of the first author's work, and to have used the first author's work in the correct context. You should not give a reference to the first author unless you have read their work yourself.

Examples

In-text citation

Data mining analysis by Chen [1, p. 45]

Or

Data mining by Chen, cited in Thompson [1, p. 45].

References

[1] R. Thompson, *Advanced data analysis*. London, U.K.: IT Publ. Ltd, 2018.

Note that in the references, there is no mention of Chen, because you have not read her work. You are relying on Thompson to have represented her work correctly.

Note: Publishing is abbreviated to Publ.

How to reference common sources in the references list

H1   Books

Citation order:

♦ Reference number (in square brackets)
♦ Author's initial(s) followed by surname
♦ Title (in italics – capitalise all major words)
♦ Edition, abbreviated to ed. (only include the edition number if it is not the first edition)
♦ Place of publication: abbreviated name of publisher
♦ Year of publication

Example: single author

References

[1] A. R. Hambley, *Electrical Engineering: Principles and Applications*, 7th ed. Upper Saddle River, NJ, USA: Pearson, 2018.

Example: fewer than six authors

References

[2] N. Mohan, T. M. Undeland, and W. P. Robbins, *Power Electronics: Converters, Applications, and Design*, 3rd ed. New York, NY, USA: Wiley, 2003.

Example: six or more authors

References

[3] D. Bourne *et al.*, *AI Futures*, Piscataway, NJ, USA IEEE Publ., 2018.

H2   Ebooks

Citation order:

♦ Reference number (in square brackets)
♦ Author's initial(s) followed by surname
♦ Title (in italics – capitalise all major words)
♦ Edition, abbreviated to ed. (only include the edition number if it is not the first edition)
♦ Place of publication: publisher, year
♦ DOI *or*
♦ Accessed: date. [Online]. Available: URL

Example

References

[4] J. F. Manwell, J. G. McGowan, and A. Rogers, *Wind Energy Explained: Theory, Design and Application*, 2nd ed. Chichester, U.K.: Wiley, 2009. Accessed: Apr. 20, 2018. [Online]. Available: http://library.dur.ac.uk/record=b2722155~S1

H3   Chapters/sections of edited books

Citation order:

♦ Reference number (in square brackets)
♦ Author's initial(s) followed by surname
♦ Title of chapter in book (in double quotation marks)
♦ in
♦ Title of book (in italics – capitalise all major words)
♦ Series and number (if given, in round brackets)
♦ Editor's initial(s) followed by surname
♦ Ed. or Eds.
♦ Place of publication: publisher, year
♦ Page numbers (preceded by pp.)

Example

References

[5] M. Akrich, "The de-scription of technical objects," in *Shaping Technology/Building Society: Studies in Sociotechnical Change* (Inside Technology), W. E. Bijker and J. Law, Eds., Cambridge, MA, USA: MIT Press, 1994, pp. 205–224.

H4 Handbooks/manuals

Citation order:

♦ Reference number (in square brackets)
♦ Author's initial(s) followed by surname (if available, or use title)
♦ Title of handbook/manual (in italics)
♦ Edition
♦ Initial and surname of editors followed by Eds., *or* name of company
♦ Location of organisation/company
♦ Year

If viewed online, add:

♦ DOI *or*
♦ Accessed: date. [Online]. Available: URL

Examples

References

[6] *Electric Power Engineering Handbook*, 2nd ed., L. L. Grigsby and J. H. Harlow, Eds., Boca Raton, FL, USA: CRC Press, 2007.

[7] *Raspberry Pi: The Complete Manual*, Bournemouth, U.K.: Image Publ. Ltd, 2016. Accessed: Aug. 29, 2018. [Online]. Available: https://archive.org/stream/Raspberry_Pi_The_Complete_Manual_7th_Edition#page/n3/mode/2up

H5 Technical/scientific reports/working papers

Citation order:

♦ Reference number (in square brackets)
♦ Author's initial(s) followed by surname
♦ Title of report (in double quotation marks)
♦ Name of organisation/company
♦ Location of organisation/company
♦ Report number
♦ Year

If viewed online, add:

♦ DOI *or*
♦ Accessed: date. [Online]. Available: URL

Example

References

[8] K. Serkh, "A Note of the Use of the Spectra of Multiplication Operators as a Numerical Tool," Dep. Comp. Sci., Yale Univ., New Haven, CT, USA, Tech. Rep. YALEU/DCS/TR1541, Mar. 2018. Accessed: Nov. 18, 2018. [Online]. Available: https://cpsc.yale.edu/sites/default/files/files/tr1541.pdf

H6 Journal articles

H6.1 Published journal articles

Citation order:

♦ Reference number (in square brackets)
♦ Author's initial(s) followed by surname
♦ Title of article (in double quotation marks)
♦ Abbreviated title of journal (in italics)
♦ Volume, issue number
♦ Pages (preceded by pp.)
♦ Abbreviated month day, year of publication

If viewed online, add:

♦ DOI *or*
♦ Accessed: date. [Online]. Available: URL

Notes for the examples below

The full titles of the journals are *IEEE Transactions on Communications Systems* and *IEEE Transactions on Information Forensics and Security*; they have been abbreviated using the titles listed in *IEEE editorial style manual* (2016) (https://www.ieee.org/documents/style_manual.pdf). Note that *Proceedings of the IEEE* is not abbreviated.

The article by Majumdar has seven authors, but following the IEEE guidance only the first named author of the article is given followed by *et al.*

The article by Strogatz does not have volume, issue or page numbers, so these are omitted.

Example for print journals

References

[9] J. Hopson, "Harmonic structure of modulated light beams," *IEEE Trans. Commun. Syst.*, vol. 11, no. 4, pp. 464–469, Dec. 1963.

Example for electronic journals with DOI

References

[10] S. Majumdar *et al.*, "User-level runtime security auditing for the Cloud," *IEEE Trans. Inf. Forensics Security*, vol. 13, no. 5, pp. 1185–1199, May 2018. doi: 10.1109/TIFS.2017.2779444.

Example for electronic journals with URL but no DOI

References

[11] S. Strogatz, "Explaining why the Millennium Bridge wobbled," *ScienceDaily*, Nov. 3, 2005. Accessed: July 14, 2018. [Online]. Available: http://www.sciencedaily.com/releases/2005/11/051103080801.htm

H6.2 Prepublication journal articles

Citation order

♦ Reference number (in square brackets)
♦ Author's initial(s) followed by surname
♦ Title of article (in double quotation marks)
♦ Abbreviated title of journal in which article will be published (in italics)
♦ To be published.

If viewed online, add:

♦ DOI *or*
♦ Accessed: date. [Online]. Available: URL

Example

References

[12] G. Zhong, A. Dubey, T. Cheng, and T. Mitra, "Synergy: A HW/SW Framework for High Throughput CNNs on Embedded Heterogeneous SoC," *ACM Trans. Embedded Comput. Syst.*, to be published. Accessed: Dec. 1, 2018. [Online]. Available: https://arxiv.org/abs/1804.00706

H7 Magazine articles

Citation order:

- Reference number (in square brackets)
- Author's initial(s) followed by surname
- Title of article (in double quotation marks)
- Abbreviated title of journal (in italics)
- Volume, issue number
- Pages (preceded by pp.)
- Abbreviated month day, year of publication.

If viewed online, add:

- DOI *or*
- Accessed: date. [Online]. Available: URL

NB If no author is identified, use the title of the article as the first part of the reference.

Example for print magazines

References

[13] "The Undervalued Wasp," *The Week*, p. 23, Sep. 29, 2018.

Example for online magazines

References

[14] T. Bajarin, "Is Silicon Valley Over? Not by a Long Shot," *PC Magazine*, Apr. 16, 2018. Accessed: Nov. 21, 2018. [Online]. Available: http://uk.pcmag.com/opinion/94387/is-silicon-valley-over-not-by-a-long-shot

H8 Newspaper articles

Citation order:

- Reference number (in square brackets)
- Author's initial(s) followed by surname
- Title of article (in double quotation marks)
- Title of newspaper (in italics)
- Pages (preceded by p. or pp.)
- Abbreviated month day, year of publication

Example for print newspaper articles

References

[15] D. Murray, "Thousands facing chaos in DLR strike," *Evening Standard*, p. 6, Mar. 27, 2018.

H8.1 Newspaper articles accessed online

There are many means to access news sources online, including news companies' own websites, library subscription databases (such as Nexis, Infotrac and Gale), online-only news providers and mobile phone apps. Include the means through which you accessed the article.

Citation order:

- Reference number (in square brackets)
- Author's initial(s) followed by surname
- Title of article (in double quotation marks)
- Title of newspaper (in italics)
- Pages (preceded by p. or pp.), if available
- Abbreviated month day, year of publication
- Accessed: date. [Online]. Available: URL

Example of articles in online newspapers

References

[16] A. Hern, "Is Spotify really worth $20 billion?" *The Guardian*, p. 32, Mar. 2, 2018. Accessed: Apr. 4, 2018. [Online]. Available: https://www.theguardian.com/technology/2018/mar/02/is-spotify-really-worth-20bn

Example of articles in online subscription newspaper databases

References

[17] "Guidelines issued to boost 'big science,'" *Shenzen Daily*, Apr. 3, 2018. [Online]. Nexis UK, Available: https://library.dur.ac.uk/record=b2045034~S1

Example of online news website articles

References

[18] R. Cellan-Jones, "Microsoft gambles on a quantum leap in computing," *BBC News*, Mar. 31, 2018. Accessed: Apr. 4, 2019. [Online]. Available: http://www.bbc.co.uk/news/technology-43580972

Example of articles in mobile news apps

References

[19] M. Gurman, "Apple is said to work on touchless control, curved iPhones screen," *Bloomberg*, Apr. 4, 2018. Accessed: Apr. 4, 2018. [Online]. Mobile news app.

H9 Conferences

H9.1 Unpublished papers presented at a conference

Citation order:

- Reference number (in square brackets)
- Author's initial(s) followed by surname
- Title of paper (in double quotation marks)
- Presented at
- Name of the conference (use abbreviations for words but not initials, in italics)
- City of conference, US state abbreviation *or* country if not USA
- Year when conference was held if not included in conference title

NB Country is also included after city if the conference was held outside the USA.

Example

References

[20] B. Leigh, "Google Analytics Applications for Websites," presented at *9th Int. Blackboard Conf.*, York, UK, Nov. 1–2, 2017.

H9.2 Papers published in conference proceedings

Citation order:

♦ Reference number (in square brackets)
♦ Author's initial(s) followed by surname
♦ Title of paper (in double quotation marks)
♦ in
♦ Name of conference (in italics – use abbreviations for words but not initials)
♦ City of conference, US state abbreviation *or* country if not USA
♦ Year
♦ Page numbers

If viewed online, add:

♦ DOI *or*
♦ Accessed: date. [Online]. Available: URL

Example

References

[21] C. Wen and Q. Liu, "Mobile Remote Medical Monitoring System," in *Proc. of the 2016 IEEE Int. Conf. on Consumer Electronics-China*, Guangzhou, China, 2016, pp. 1–6. doi: http://10.1109/ICCE-China.2016.7849727.

H9.3 Full conference proceedings

Citation order:

♦ Reference number (in square brackets)
♦ Editor's initial(s) followed by surname
♦ Name of conference (in italics)
♦ City of conference, US state abbreviation *or* country if not USA
♦ Month, day(s), year
♦ Place of publication: publisher, year

If viewed online, add:

♦ DOI *or*
♦ Accessed: date. [Online]. Available: URL

Example

References

[22] A. Bilgin, M. W. Marcellin, J. Serra-Sagrista, and J. A. Storer, Eds. *Data Compression Conf.* Snowbird, UT, Apr. 4–7, 2017. Accessed: Nov. 29, 2018. [Online]. Available: http://ieeexplore.ieee.org.ezphost.dur.ac.uk/xpl/mostRecentIssue.jsp?punumber=7921793

H10 Theses/dissertations

Citation order:

♦ Reference number (in square brackets)
♦ Author's initial(s) followed by surname
♦ Title of thesis (in double quotation marks)
♦ Degree level
♦ Abbreviated names of university department, university
♦ City and US state abbreviation (if relevant)
♦ Year

If viewed online, add:

♦ DOI *or*
♦ [Online]. Available: URL

Example

References

[23] C. M. Wastell, "Communication patterns for randomized algorithms," Ph.D. thesis, Dept. Eng. Comp. Sci., Durham Univ., Durham, UK, 2017. [Online]. Available: http://etheses.dur.ac.uk/12525/

H11 Datasets

Citation order:

- Reference number (in square brackets)
- Author's initial(s) followed by surname
- Title of dataset (in double quotation marks)
- Version or edition
- Title of repository/collection (in italics)
- Year.

If viewed online, add:

- DOI *or*
- Accessed on: abbreviated month, day, year. Accessed: date. [Online]. Available: URL

Example

References

[24] C. Bambra *et al.*, "Brownfield land dataset," *Durham Research Online DATAsets Archive*, 2015. doi: 10.15128/ba0f9472-7587-4393-989a-8f729ef20103.

H12 Standards

Citation order:

- Reference number (in square brackets)
- Title of standard (in italics)
- Standard number
- Date

Example

References

[25] *Methodology for determining the energy efficiency class of electrical accessories*, BS EN 63172, 2018.

H13 Patents

Citation order:

- Reference number (in square brackets)
- Author's initial(s) followed by surname
- Title of patent (in double quotation marks)
- Country abbreviation
- Patent followed by number
- Abbreviated month, day, year.

Example

References

[26] A. J. Ciniglio, "Soldering nozzle," U.K. Patent GB2483265, Feb. 27, 2018.

H14 Government documents

Citation order:

- Reference number (in square brackets)
- Author's initial(s) followed by surname *or* country followed by government department
- Title (in italics)
- Document number (if available)
- Place of publication: publisher, year.

If online, add:

- DOI *or*
- Accessed: date. [Online]. Available: URL

Examples

References

[27] United Kingdom. Dept. for Education and Skills, *21st Century Skills: Realising our potential*. Cm5810. London, U.K.: The Stationery Office, 2003.

[28] United Kingdom. Dept. for Business, Energy and Industrial Strategy, *What is a Heat Network?* 2018. Accessed: Jan. 18, 2019. [Online]. Available: https://www.gov.uk/government/publications/what-is-a-heat-network

H15   Web pages

Citation order:

♦ Reference number (in square brackets)
♦ Author's initial(s) followed by surname, if available
♦ Title of web page (in double quotation marks)
♦ Title of website
♦ URL
♦ (accessed date).

Example

References

[29] "Canadian Honeynet Chapter," Canadian Institute of Cyber Security, http://www.unb.ca/cic/research/honeynet.html (accessed July 9, 2018).

H16   Blogs

Citation order:

♦ Reference number (in square brackets)
♦ Author's initial(s) followed by surname, if available
♦ Title of blog post (in double quotation marks)
♦ Title of website
♦ URL
♦ (accessed date).

Example

References

[30] S. Bhartiya, "Good compliance practices are good engineering practices," TheLinuxFoundation, https://www.linuxfoundation.org/blog/good-compliance-practices-good-engineering/ (accessed July 2, 2018).

H17   Social media (Facebook, Twitter, Instagram)

Citation order:

♦ Reference number (in square brackets)
♦ Author's initial(s) followed by surname, *or* username, *or* organisation
♦ Title of post (in double quotation marks)
♦ Title of site
♦ URL
♦ (accessed date).

Examples

References

[31] IEEE. "What do you know about Green Technology?" IEEE. https://www.facebook.com/IEEE.org/ (accessed Apr. 23, 2018).

[32] IEEE. "Ethernet was named after a 19th century theory." ieeeorg. https://www.instagram.com/p/BgBmaM_HSso/?hl=en&taken-by=ieeeorg (accessed Apr. 23, 2018).

[33] @IEEEorg. "Self-healing metal oxides could protect against corrosion." IEEE. https://twitter.com/IEEEorg (accessed Apr. 23, 2018).

H18 Images

H18.1 Images in physical form (photographic print or slide, drawing, painting)

Citation order:

- Reference number (in square brackets)
- Creator's initial(s) followed by surname, *or* organisation
- Title of image (in italics)
- Year of production
- Medium (in square brackets)
- Collection reference, if available
- Location

Examples

References

[34] H. N. King, *London Bridge, seen from Southwark*, 1872. [Photographic print]. Ref. RIBA7357, RIBA Library, London, U.K.

[35] G. Arnald, *Menai Bridge*, 1828. [Painting]. Plas Newydd, Anglesey, U.K.

[36] J. Green and B. Green, *High Level Tyne Bridge: Plan and section*, 1839. [Architectural drawing]. Ref. D.NCP/4/36, Tyne and Wear Archives, Newcastle upon Tyne, U.K.

H18.2 Images in publications (graphs, tables, figures, plates, equations)

Images in publications may be created by the author of the publication or by other artists. You are relying upon the publisher to represent the image correctly, but bear in mind that the original image may be cropped or converted from colour to black and white for publication. The general principle of referencing is to cite what you have seen. Use the citation order for that source (for example, a book or a journal article), ending with the page number or the figure/illustration number after the in-text reference number.

Examples

In-text citations

The table of laser power ratings [34, p. 98, table 4.2] and the schematic of an LD driver [35, p. 58, figure 7.1] …

References

[37] P. Wilkins, *Measuring lasers*. London, U.K.: Engineering Solutions, 2018.

[38] G. A. Trestman, *Powering laser diode systems*. Washington, DC, USA: SPIE Press, 2017.

You may wish to mention the artist of the image in your text, but your reference will be to the publication in which it appeared.

Example

In-text citation

Leonardo's designs for flying machines [36, p. 211] …

References

[39] C. Nichol, *Leonardo Da Vinci: The flights of the mind*. London, U.K.: Penguin, 2007, p. 211.

H18.3 Images available online

Citation order:

- Reference number (in square brackets)
- Author's initial(s) followed by surname, *or* organisation
- Title of image (in italics)
- Accessed: date.
- [Online]. Available: URL

Example

References

[40] Gettyimages, *AWACS aircraft midair refuelling*. Accessed: Apr. 23, 2018. [Online]. Available: https://www.gettyimages.co.uk/detail/photo/aircraft-midair-refueling-royalty-free-image/506217256/

H19 Software/computer programs/computer code

Citation order:

♦ Reference number (in square brackets)
♦ Author's initial(s) followed by surname, *or* company
♦ Title of software (in italics)
♦ Version or edition (if not part of the title)
♦ Medium (in square brackets)
♦ Place of production: producer, year

If viewed online, add:

♦ Accessed: date.
♦ [Online]. Available: URL

Examples

References

[41] Clarivate Analytics. *EndNote X8.2 for Windows*. [DVD]. Philadelphia, PA: Clarivate Analytics, 2018.

[42] Clarivate Analytics. *EndNote X8.2 for Windows*. Accessed: Feb. 13, 2019. [Online]. Philadelphia, PA: Clarivate Analytics, 2018. Available: http://www.endnote.com

H20 Podcasts

Citation order:

♦ Reference number (in square brackets)
♦ Author's initial(s) followed by surname, if available
♦ Title of podcast (in italics)
♦ Abbreviated month, day, year of web page or last update
♦ Accessed: date. [Online]. Available: URL
♦ Accessed on: abbreviated month, day, year

Example

References

[43] RNIB. *Driverless Cars: The Future is Here*, Mar. 13, 2018. Accessed: Apr. 18, 2018. [Online]. Available: https://audioboom.com/posts/6720652-driverless-cars-the-future-is-here

H21 Online broadcasts (for example, YouTube/Vimeo)

Citation order:

♦ Reference number (in square brackets)
♦ Creator's initial(s) followed by surname, *or* username
♦ Title of broadcast (in italics)
♦ Abbreviated month, day, year of broadcast (in round brackets)
♦ Accessed: date.
♦ [Online Video]. Available: URL

Example

References

[44] EngineeringYeah. *Why Study Engineering?*, (Mar. 1, 2013). [Online Video]. Available: https://www.youtube.com/watch?v=zoHm5AXeYYQ

H22 Programmes viewed on streaming services (for example, Kanopy, Amazon Prime Video, Netflix)

Citation order:

♦ Reference number (in square brackets)
♦ Creator's name or organisation
♦ Title of broadcast (in italics)
♦ Abbreviated month, day, year of broadcast (in round brackets)
♦ Accessed: date
♦ [Online Video]. Available: URL

Example

References

[45] Phoenix Learning Group. *Clean Energy – Solar Power*, (Feb. 11, 2010). Accessed: Apr. 18, 2018. [Online Video]. Available: https://www.kanopy.com/wayf/product/clean-energy-solar-power

H23 Radio or television broadcasts

Citation order:

♦ Reference number (in square brackets)
♦ Presenter's initial(s) followed by surname
♦ Episode of television broadcast if relevant (in double quotation marks)
♦ Name of television programme (in italics)
♦ Abbreviated month, day, year of broadcast

♦ [Television broadcast]
♦ Place of broadcast: broadcaster

Example

References

[46] K. McCloud, "Herefordshire," *Grand Designs*. June 8, 2017. [Television broadcast]. London: Channel Four Television Corporation.

H24 DVDs

Citation order:

♦ Reference number (in square brackets)
♦ Director's initial(s) followed by surname, if available
♦ Director
♦ Title of DVD (in italics)
♦ [DVD]
♦ Place of distribution: distributor, year

Example

References

[47] M. Akdogan, S. Everett, and M. Ibeji, Directors, *Engineering the impossible*. [DVD]. Burbank, CA: Warner Home Video for National Geographic Channel, 2007.

H25 Lectures

H25.1 Unpublished lectures

Citation order:

♦ Reference number (in square brackets)
♦ Author's initial(s) followed by surname
♦ Title of lecture (in double quotation marks)
♦ Presented at
♦ Title of course (in italics)
♦ Location
♦ Abbreviated month, day, year of lecture

Example

References

[48] A. M. Chan, "Forces on structures," presented at *ENGI2231 Mathematics for engineers*, Southampton University, May 8, 2018.

H25.2 Lecture slides or tutor's notes in online learning environment

Citation order:

♦ Reference number (in square brackets)
♦ Author's initial(s) followed by surname
♦ Presentation slides for, *or* tutor's notes for
♦ Title of lecture (in double quotation marks)
♦ Title of course (in italics)
♦ Location
♦ Abbreviated month, day, year of lecture
♦ [Online]. Available: URL
♦ Accessed on: abbreviated month, day, year

Examples

References

[49] A. M. Chan, Presentation slides for "Forces on structures," ENGI2231 Mathematics for engineers, Durham University, May 8, 2018. [Online]. Available: https://duo.dur.ac.uk

[50] A. M. Chan, Tutor's notes for "Forces on structures," ENGI2231 Mathematics for engineers, Durham University, May 8, 2018. [Online]. Available: https://duo.dur.ac.uk

H26 Emails

Email is a form of personal communication, but it is recorded and can be forwarded as a form of documentation.

Citation order:

♦ Reference number (in square brackets)
♦ Author's initial(s) followed by surname
♦ Title (in double quotation marks), if available
♦ Email
♦ Abbreviated month, day, year

Example

References

[51] S. Burywood, "Launch of new edition," email, Apr. 6, 2018.

H27 Unpublished sources, including personal communications (conversations, unrecorded interviews, telephone, letters)

The *IEEE editorial style manual* (2016) provides two options for unpublished sources. These are sources that are unavailable to your readers.

Citation order 1:

- Reference number (in square brackets)
- Author's initial(s) followed by surname
- Title (in double quotation marks), if available
- Unpublished

Citation order 2:

- Reference number (in square brackets)
- Author's initial(s) followed by surname
- Private communication
- Abbreviated month, day, year

Examples

References

[52] S. Burywood, "Launch of new website," unpublished.
[53] R. Wong, private communication, Apr. 6, 2018.

Sample text

Around the world, governments and the private sector are seeking alternatives to fossil fuels [1]. The UK Government has launched an 'ambitious' strategy for renewable energy [2]. This aims to combat greenhouse gas emissions whilst increasing national income [2, p. 5]. However, the UK is unlikely to meet its targets for renewable energy production by 2020 [3]. Caroline Lucas of the Green Party condemned a 56% fall in investment in green technologies in 2017 [4, p. 17].

A KPMG report gave grounds for optimism in 2018 [5]. Statistics showed that in the fourth quarter of 2017, renewable energy capacity was 40 GW, of which wind energy produced 15 GW [6, p. 63, chart 6.3]. New technology is increasing wind power output, but public opposition to the installation of wind turbines continues [7]–[9]. This makes the achievement of green energy targets difficult [3].

References for sample text

[1] IEEE. "What do you know about Green Technology?" IEEE. https://www.facebook.com/IEEE.org/ (accessed Apr. 23, 2018).

[2] Great Britain. HM Government, *The Clean Growth Strategy: Leading the way to a low carbon future*, Oct. 2017. Accessed: Apr. 23, 2018. [Online]. Available: https://assets.publishing.service.gov.uk/government/uploads/system/uploads/attachment_data/file/651916/BEIS_The_Clean_Growth_online_12.10.17.pdf

[3] R. Harrabin, "Renewable energy: UK expected to miss 2020 targets," *BBC News*, July 5, 2016. Accessed: Apr. 14, 2018. [Online]. Available: http://www.bbc.co.uk/news/science-environment-36710290

[4] A. Vaughan, "UK green energy investment halves after policy changes," *The Guardian*, p. 17, Jan. 16, 2018. Accessed: Apr. 14, 2018. [Online]. Available: https://www.theguardian.com/business/2018/jan/16/uk-green-energy-investment-plunges-after-policy-changes

[5] KPMG, *2018 – A Turning Point for UK retail energy?* 2018. Accessed: Apr. 21, 2018. [Online]. Available: https://assets.kpmg.com/content/dam/kpmg/uk/pdf/2018/01/a-turning-point-for-uk-retail-energy.pdf

[6] Great Britain. Department for Business, Energy & Industrial Strategy, *Renewable energy capacity and generation*, Apr. 2018. Accessed: Apr. 21, 2018. [Online].

Available: https://www.gov.uk/ government/statistics/energy-trends- section-6-renewables

[7] F. Blaabjerg and K. Ma, "Wind energy systems," *Proceedings of the IEEE*, vol. 105, no. 11, pp. 2116–2131, Nov. 2017, doi: 10.1109/JPROC.2017.2695485.

[8] J. F. Manwell, J. G. McGowan, and A. Rogers, *Wind Energy Explained: Theory, Design and Application*, 2nd ed. Chichester, U.K.: Wiley, 2009.

Accessed: Apr. 20, 2018. [Online]. Available: http://library.dur.ac.uk/ record=b2722155~S1

[9] M. Hyland and V. Bertsch, "The Role of Community Involvement Mechanisms in Reducing Resistance to Energy Infrastructure Development," *Ecological Economics*, vol. 146, pp. 447–474, Apr. 2018, doi: 10.1016/j.ecolecon. 2017.11.016.

All references end with a full stop except those that end with a URL. References ending with a doi should finish with a full stop.

Section I
Modern Humanities Research Association (MHRA) referencing style

The MHRA referencing style is used in some arts and humanities publications.

Conventions when using the MHRA referencing style

Citing sources in your text

♦ Instead of naming authors in the text, which can be distracting for the reader, numbers are used to denote **citations**. These numbers in the text are linked to a full **reference** in **footnotes** or **endnotes** and in your **bibliography**. Word-processing software such as Microsoft Word can create this link between citation number and full reference

♦ Cited publications are numbered in the order in which they are first referred to in the text. They are usually identified by a **superscript number** – for example, 'Thomas corrected this error.[1]'

♦ Superscript numbers can be created in Microsoft Word by selecting 'References' from the menu bar, then 'Insert Footnote'

Footnotes and endnotes

♦ Check whether footnotes or endnotes are preferred for the work you are producing

♦ All footnotes or endnotes end with a full stop

Author names

♦ Note that in the footnotes, author names should be forename followed by surname – for example, Francis Wheen. In the bibliography, author names should be surname followed by forename – for example, Wheen, Francis

♦ If there are up to three authors of a source, give their names in your bibliography, in the order they are shown in the source. If there are four or more authors, give the name of the first author, followed by 'and others'

Bibliography

♦ List works in alphabetical order by surname of the first author

♦ Names are given as surname followed by forename for the first author, but subsequent authors and editors are given as forename followed by surname – for example, Williams, Edith, Jane Thompson and Claire Hopper

♦ Sources without an author are listed by title in the alphabetical list

♦ References in your bibliography do not end with a full stop

♦ Indent the second and subsequent lines of each reference in the bibliography, but not in footnotes

♦ As well as footnotes or endnotes, you should list all your sources, including those you have read but not cited, in the bibliography

First citation and subsequent short citations

Note that the first time you cite a source, you should give full details in the footnote or endnote. Subsequent entries to the same source can be abbreviated to author's surname and the first few words of the title, plus a page number if you are citing a specific part of the text, giving you a **short citation**. For example:

Worsley, *Classical Architecture*, p. 25.

The sample text at the end of this section shows examples of a first citation and a subsequent short citation of this book by Worsley.

Note that the use of short citations, which are more precise, replaces **op. cit.**, which was previously used.

Ibid.

♦ Ibid. (from Latin *ibidem*) means 'in the same place'. If two (or more) consecutive references are from the same source, then the second (or others) is cited ibid. Capitalise ibid. if used at the beginning of a note. For example:

1. Paulina Grainger, *Imagery in Prose* (London: Dale Press, 2009), pp. 133–81.
2. Ibid., p. 155.
3. Ibid., p. 170.

Capitalisation

♦ Capitalise the first letter of the first word, all nouns, verbs and adjectives. Also capitalise articles if they are the first words of a subtitle after a colon – for example, *Cite Them Right: The Essential Referencing Guide*.

Internet addresses (URLs) and digital object identifiers (DOIs)

♦ The internet address is given in full, but with < in front and > after the address – for example, <http://news.bbc.co.uk> – then [accessed date]
♦ DOIs should be used if they are available as these are a permanent locator. If using a DOI, you do not need to give the accessed date

Commas

♦ Use commas to separate the elements of the reference

Page numbers

♦ Use p. or pp. for books but not for journal articles

How to reference common sources in footnotes and bibliography

I1 Books

Citation order:

♦ Author/editor
♦ Title (in italics)
♦ Edition (only include the edition number if it is not the first edition)
♦ Place of publication: publisher, year of publication (all in round brackets)

Example

Footnote
1. Giles Worsley, *Classical Architecture in Britain: The Heroic Age* (London: Published for the Paul Mellon Centre for Studies in British Art by Yale University Press, 1995), p. 47.

Bibliography
Worsley, Giles, *Classical Architecture in Britain: The Heroic Age* (London: Published for the Paul Mellon Centre for Studies in British Art by Yale University Press, 1995)

I2 Ebooks

Citation order:

♦ Author/editor
♦ Title (in italics)
♦ Edition (only include the edition number if it is not the first edition)
♦ Place of publication: publisher, year of publication (all in round brackets)
♦ in
♦ Title of online collection (in italics)
♦ <URL of collection> [accessed date]

Example

Footnote

1. Robert Adam, *Ruins of the Palace of the Emperor Diocletian at Spalatro in Dalmatia* (London: Printed for the author, 1764), in *Eighteenth Century Collections Online* <https://library.dur.ac.uk/record=b2274207~S1> [accessed 21 December 2018], plate 14.

Bibliography

Adam, Robert, *Ruins of the Palace of the Emperor Diocletian at Spalatro in Dalmatia* (London: Printed for the author, 1764), in *Eighteenth Century Collections Online* <https://library.dur.ac.uk/record=b2274207~S1> [accessed 21 December 2018]

I3 Chapters/sections of edited books

I3.1 Whole book with an editor

Citation order:

♦ Name of editor
♦ ed.
♦ Title of book (in italics)
♦ Place of publication: publisher, year of publication (all in round brackets)

Example

Footnote

1. Michael Hall, ed., *Gothic Architecture and Its Meanings 1550–1830* (Reading: Spire Books, 2002).

Bibliography

Hall, Michael, ed., *Gothic Architecture and Its Meanings 1550–1830* (Reading: Spire Books, 2002)

I3.2 Chapter in an edited book

Citation order:

♦ Author of the chapter/section
♦ Title of chapter/section (in single quotation marks)
♦ in
♦ Title of book (in italics)
♦ ed. by
♦ Name of editor of book
♦ Place of publication: publisher, year of publication (all in round brackets)
♦ Page numbers of chapter/section (preceded by pp.)

Note: footnote reference also has (p.).

Example

Footnote

1. Alexandrina Buchanan, 'Interpretations of Medieval Architecture', in *Gothic Architecture and Its Meanings 1550–1830*, ed. by Michael Hall (Reading: Spire Books, 2002), pp. 27–52 (p. 47).

Bibliography

Buchanan, Alexandrina, 'Interpretations of Medieval Architecture', in *Gothic Architecture and Its Meanings 1550–1830*, ed. by Michael Hall (Reading: Spire Books, 2002), pp. 27–52

I3.3 Poem in an anthology

Citation order:

♦ Author of the poem
♦ Title of poem (in single quotation marks)
♦ in
♦ Title of book (in italics)
♦ ed. by
♦ Name of editor of book
♦ Place of publication: publisher, year of publication (all in round brackets)
♦ Page numbers of chapter/section (preceded by pp.)

Example

Footnote

1. John Masefield, 'Sea-Fever', in *Poetry Please*, ed. by Charles Causley (London: J.M. Dent, 1996), pp. 74–75.

Bibliography

Masefield, John, 'Sea-Fever', in *Poetry Please*, ed. by Charles Causley (London: J.M. Dent, 1996), pp. 74–75

I4 Translated works

Citation order:

♦ Author of original work
♦ Title (in italics)
♦ trans. by name of translator (forename followed by surname)
♦ Place of publication: publisher, year of publication (all in round brackets)

Example

Footnote

1. Ignazio Silone, *Fontamara*, trans. by Gwenda David and Eric Mosbacher (London: Redwords, 1994).

Bibliography

Silone, Ignazio, *Fontamara*, trans. by Gwenda David and Eric Mosbacher (London: Redwords, 1994)

I5 Multi-volume works

Citation order:

♦ Author
♦ Title (in italics)
♦ Number of volumes
♦ Place of publication: publisher, year of publication (all in round brackets)

Example

Footnote

1. Roger Butcher, *New Illustrated British Flora*, 2 vols (London: Leonard Hill, 1961).

Bibliography

Butcher, Roger, *New Illustrated British Flora*, 2 vols (London: Leonard Hill, 1961)

If citing part of a volume, include the volume number (in capital Roman numerals) and the page number(s).

Example

Footnote

1. Roger Butcher, *New Illustrated British Flora*, 2 vols (London: Leonard Hill, 1961), II, 96–98.

Bibliography

Butcher, Roger, *New Illustrated British Flora*, 2 vols (London: Leonard Hill, 1961)

I6 Comic books

Comic books are the work of authors and illustrators. Both of these creators should be recorded in your reference.

Citation order:

♦ Author
♦ Title (in italics)
♦ illust. by (forename followed by surname)
♦ Place of publication: publisher, year (in round brackets)

Example

Footnote

1. Robert Kirkman, *The Walking Dead. Volume 1: Days Gone Bye*, illust. by Tony Moore (Portland, OR: Image Comics, 2013).

Bibliography

Kirkman, Robert, *The Walking Dead. Volume 1: Days Gone Bye*, illust. by Tony Moore (Portland, OR: Image Comics, 2013)

I7   Plays

Citation order:

♦ Author
♦ Title
♦ ed. by (forename followed by surname)
♦ Place of publication: publisher, year (in round brackets)
♦ Reference to cited act/scene/line number, or page number

Example

Footnote

1. William Shakespeare, *Hamlet*, ed. by T. J. B. Spencer (London: Penguin, 1980), I.2.177.

Bibliography

Shakespeare, William, *Hamlet*, ed. by T. J. B. Spencer (London: Penguin, 1980)

I8   Journal articles

Citation order:

♦ Author
♦ Title of article (in single quotation marks)
♦ Title of journal (in italics – capitalise first letter of each word in title, except for linking words such as and, of, the, for)
♦ Volume number, issue number (if available)
♦ Year of publication (in round brackets)
♦ Page numbers of article (not preceded by pp.)

Note: footnote reference also has (p.).

Example

Footnote

1. Peter Leach, 'James Paine's Design for the South Front of Kedleston Hall: Dating and Sources', *Architectural History*, 40 (1997), 159–70 (p. 160).

Bibliography

Leach, Peter, 'James Paine's Design for the South Front of Kedleston Hall: Dating and Sources', *Architectural History*, 40 (1997), 159–70

I9   Ejournal articles

Citation order:

♦ Author
♦ Title of article (in single quotation marks)
♦ Title of journal (in italics – capitalise first letter of each word in title, except for linking words such as and, of, the, for)
♦ Volume number, issue number (if available)
♦ Year of publication (in round brackets)
♦ Page numbers of article
♦ <URL> or <DOI>
♦ [accessed date] if required

Example

1. S. Lang, 'The Principles of the Gothic Revival in England', *Journal of the Society of Architectural Historians*, 25.4 (1966), 240–67 (p. 244) <http://www.jstor.org/ stable/988353> [accessed 21 December 2018].

Footnote with DOI ▸
1. Edwina Thomas Washington, 'An Overview of Cyberbullying in Higher Education', *Adult Learning*, 26 (2015), 21–27 (p. 26) <https://doi.org/10.117 7%2F1045159514558412>.

Bibliography ▸

Lang, S., 'The Principles of the Gothic Revival in England', *Journal of the Society of Architectural Historians*, 25.4 (1966), 240–67 <http://www. jstor.org/ stable/988353> [accessed 21 December 2018]

Washington, Edwina Thomas, 'An Overview of Cyberbullying in Higher Education', *Adult Learning*, 26 (2015), 21–27 <https://doi.org/ 10.1177%2F1045159514558412>

I10 Newspaper and magazine articles

Citation order:

♦ Author
♦ Title of article (in single quotation marks)
♦ Title of newspaper (in italics – capitalise first letter of each word in title, except for linking words such as and, of, the, for)
♦ Date
♦ Section (if applicable)
♦ Page number, preceded by p.

Example

Footnote ▸
1. Dan Hyde, 'Parents Funding Adult Offspring's Holidays', *Daily Telegraph*, 14 September 2015, p. 2.

Bibliography ▸
Hyde, Dan, 'Parents Funding Adult Offspring's Holidays', *Daily Telegraph*, 14 September 2015, p. 2

I11 Book reviews

Citation order:

♦ Author
♦ review of
♦ Author, title (in italics), publication year of work being reviewed
♦ Publication information for work in which review is published

Examples: reviews in journals and newspapers

Footnotes ▸
1. [Anon.], review of Lisa Brennan-Jobs, *Small Fry* (2018), *The Week*, 22 September 2018, 31.

2. Rachel Haworth, review of David Looseley, *Édith Piaf: A Cultural History* (2015), *Journal of European Studies*, 47.2 (2017), 228–29.

Bibliography ▸
[Anon.], review of Lisa Brennan-Jobs, *Small Fry* (2018), *The Week*, 22 September 2018, 31
Haworth, Rachel, review of David Looseley, *Édith Piaf: A Cultural History* (2015), *Journal of European Studies*, 47.2 (2017), 228–29

I12 Theses and dissertations

Citation order:

- Author
- Title of thesis (in single quotation marks)
- Degree level, university, year (in round brackets)

Example

Footnote

1. Adrian Green, 'Houses and Households in County Durham and Newcastle c.1570–1730' (unpublished doctoral thesis, Durham University, 2000).

Bibliography

Green, Adrian, 'Houses and Households in County Durham and Newcastle c.1570–1730' (unpublished doctoral thesis, Durham University, 2000)

I13 Conference sources

I13.1 Published proceedings of a conference

Citation order:

- Title of conference proceedings publication (in italics)
- ed. by
- Name of editor
- Place of publication: publisher, year (in round brackets)
- Page numbers

Example

Footnote

1. *Proceedings of the Tenth Conference in Romance Studies, 18 May 2014*, ed. by Hilary Jones (Derby: University of Derby Press, 2014), pp. 27–39.

Bibliography

Proceedings of the Tenth Conference in Romance Studies, 18 May 2014, ed. by Hilary Jones (Derby: University of Derby Press, 2014), pp. 27–39

I13.2 Papers in published proceedings of a conference

Citation order:

- Author
- Title of paper (in single quotation marks)
- Title of conference proceedings publication (in italics)
- ed. by
- Name of editor
- Place of publication: publisher, year (in round brackets)
- Page numbers

Example

Footnote

1. Mary Stephens, 'Wordsworth's Inspiration', *Proceedings of the Tenth Conference in Romance Studies, 18 May 2014*, ed. by Hilary Jones (Derby: University of Derby Press, 2014), pp. 27–39.

Bibliography

Stephens, Mary, 'Wordsworth's Inspiration', *Proceedings of the Tenth Conference in Romance Studies, 18 May 2014*, ed. by Hilary Jones (Derby: University of Derby Press, 2014), pp.27–39

I13.3 Poster presentations

Citation order:

♦ Author
♦ Title of poster presentation (in single quotation marks)
♦ Poster presentation at
♦ Title of conference (in italics)
♦ City: venue, date (in round brackets)

Example

Footnote
1. Frances Macintosh, 'Wordsworth's Inspiration', poster presentation at *Tenth Conference in Romance Studies* (Derby: University of Derby, 18 May 2014).

Bibliography
Macintosh, Frances, 'Wordsworth's Inspiration', poster presentation at *Tenth Conference in Romance Studies* (Derby: University of Derby, 18 May 2014)

I14 Organisation or personal internet sites

Citation order:

♦ Author
♦ Title of internet site (in italics)
♦ Year that the site was published/last updated (in round brackets)
♦ <URL> [accessed date]

Examples

Footnotes
1. Salvatore Ciro Nappo, *Pompeii: Its Discovery and Preservation* (2012) <http://www.bbc.co.uk/history/ancient/romans/pompeii_rediscovery_01.shtml> [accessed 21 December 2018].

2. UNESCO, *Pompeii* (2018) <http://whc.unesco.org/en/list/829/video> [accessed 21 December 2018].

Bibliography
Nappo, Salvatore Ciro, *Pompeii: Its Discovery and Preservation* (2012) <http://www.bbc.co.uk/history/ancient/romans/pompeii_rediscovery_01.shtml> [accessed 21 December 2018]
UNESCO, *Pompeii* (2018) <http://whc.unesco.org/en/list/829/video> [accessed 21 December 2018]

For **web pages** where no author can be identified, you should use the web page's title.

Example

Footnote
1. *Palladio's Italian Villas* (2005) <http://www.boglewood.com/palladio/> [accessed 21 December 2018].

Bibliography
Palladio's Italian Villas (2005) <http://www.boglewood.com/palladio/> [accessed 21 December 2018]

I15 Blogs

Citation order:

♦ Author
♦ Title of post (in single quotation marks)
♦ Date
♦ Title of blog (in italics)
♦ <URL> [accessed date]

Example

1. Rik Hijmans, 'Going Dutch', 22 February 2017, *Continental Cuisine* <https://continentalcuisine.wordpress.com/> [accessed 17 October 2018].

Hijmans, Rik, 'Going Dutch', 22 February 2017, *Continental Cuisine* <https://continentalcuisine.wordpress.com/> [accessed 17 October 2018]

I16 Social media

I16.1 Facebook

Give the full text of the Facebook post in your footnote and bibliography.

Citation order:

- ◆ Author
- ◆ Title of post (in single quotation marks)
- ◆ Medium (in square brackets)
- ◆ <URL>
- ◆ Date
- ◆ [accessed date]

Example

1. Durham University Library, '20,000th visitor to "Scottish Soldiers" exhibition' [Facebook] <http://www.facebook.com/pages/Durham-University-Library> 26 July 2018 [accessed 29 July 2018].

Durham University Library, '20,000th visitor to "Scottish Soldiers" exhibition' [Facebook] <http://www.facebook.com/pages/Durham-University-Library> 26 July 2018 [accessed 29 July 2018]

I16.2 Twitter

The full text of tweets should be given, either in your text or in a footnote, retaining hashtags # and @handles.

Citation order:

- ◆ Author
- ◆ Title of post (in single quotation marks)
- ◆ Medium (in square brackets)
- ◆ hashtags # and @handle, date (in round brackets)

Example

Chris Cook tweeted that 'Theresa May says unis should "develop sustainable funding models that are not so dependent on international students"' (@xtophercook, 16 July 2015).[1]

1. Chris Cook, 'Theresa May says unis should "develop sustainable funding models that are not so dependent on international students"' [Twitter post] (@xtophercook, 16 July 2015).

Cook, Chris, 'Theresa May says unis should "develop sustainable funding models that are not so dependent on international students"' [Twitter post] (@xtophercook, 16 July 2015)

I16.3 Instagram

Citation order:

- ◆ Author
- ◆ Title (in single quotation marks)
- ◆ Instagram photo (in square brackets)
- ◆ Date
- ◆ <URL> [accessed date]

Example

In-text

The design brings together Lego and Quidditch.[1]

Footnote

1. harrypottercast, 'Lego Quidditch pitch' [Instagram photo] 30 August 2018 <https://www.instagram.com/p/BnHOn1rnhg4/?taken-by=harrypottercast> [accessed 19 December 2018].

Bibliography

harrypottercast, 'Lego Quidditch pitch' [Instagram photo] 30 August 2018, <https://www.instagram.com/p/BnHOn1rnhg4/?taken-by=harrypottercast> [accessed 19 December 2018]

I17 Emails

Citation order:

♦ Author
♦ Title of message (in single quotation marks)
♦ Email to recipient, date (in round brackets)

Example

Footnote

1. Maria Guevara, 'New Spanish Publications' (email to Carlos Pererra, 16 July 2018).

Bibliography

Guevara, Maria, 'New Spanish Publications' (email to Carlos Pererra, 16 July 2018)

I18 Manuscripts in archives

Citation order:

♦ Place
♦ Name of archive
♦ Reference number
♦ Description of document
♦ Date

Example

Footnote

1. London, The National Archives, Public Record Office, PROB 3/42/93 Inventory of Elizabeth Bennett of Deptford, 10 November 1743.

Bibliography

London, The National Archives, Public Record Office, PROB 3/42/93 Inventory of Elizabeth Bennett of Deptford, 10 November 1743

I19 Films

I19.1 Film at cinema

Citation order:

♦ Film title (in italics)
♦ dir. by (forename followed by surname)
♦ Distributor, year (in round brackets)
♦ [Motion picture]

Example

Footnote

1. *Children of Men*, dir. by Alfonso Cuarón (Universal Studios, 2006) [Motion picture].

Bibliography

Children of Men, dir. by Alfonso Cuarón (Universal Studios, 2006) [Motion picture]

I19.2 Films on DVD

Citation order:

♦ Film title (in italics)
♦ dir. by (forename followed by surname)
♦ Distributor, year (in round brackets)
♦ [on DVD]

Example

Footnote

1. *Brief Encounter*, dir. by David Lean (Eagle-Lion Distributors Ltd, 1945) [on DVD].

Bibliography

Brief Encounter, dir. by David Lean (Eagle-Lion Distributors Ltd, 1945) [on DVD]

I19.3 YouTube

Citation order:

♦ Author
♦ Title (in italics)
♦ Type of source
♦ Title of website (not in italics)
♦ Date of publication
♦ <URL> [accessed date]

Example

Footnote

1. Joshua Cuerdo, *Baroque and Rococo Architecture*, online video recording, YouTube, 21 February 2017, <https://www.youtube.com/watch?v=eqFGq4fLel0> [accessed 23 August 2018].

Bibliography

Cuerdo, Joshua, *Baroque and Rococo Architecture*, online video recording, YouTube, 21 February 2017, <https://www.youtube.com/watch?v= eqFGq4fLel0> [accessed 23 August 2018]

I19.4 Streaming video

Citation order:

♦ Title (in italics)
♦ dir. by (forename followed by surname)
♦ Type of source
♦ Title of website (not in italics)
♦ Date of publication
♦ <URL> [accessed date]

Example

Footnote

1. *Chasing Coral*, dir. by Jeff Orlowski, online streaming video, Netflix, 2017, <https://www.netflix.com/gb/title/80168188> [accessed 1 August 2018].

Bibliography

Chasing Coral, dir. by Jeff Orlowski, online streaming video, Netflix, 2017, <https://www.netflix.com/gb/title/80168188> [accessed 1 August 2018]

I20　Television or radio broadcasts

Citation order:

◆ Episode title (if applicable, in single quotation marks)
◆ Broadcast/programme/series title (in italics)
◆ Channel name
◆ Date (day month year)
◆ Time of broadcast

Example

Footnote

1. 'Scarlet Macaw', *Tweet of the Day*, BBC Radio 4, 2 February 2015, 05.58.

Bibliography

'Scarlet Macaw', *Tweet of the Day*, BBC Radio 4, 2 February 2015, 05.58

I21　Sound recordings

Citation order:

◆ Composer
◆ Title (in italics)
◆ Artist, orchestra or conductor (as relevant)
◆ Recording company, CD reference, date (in round brackets)
◆ [on CD]

Example

Footnote

1. Gustav Mahler, *Symphony no. 10*, BBC National Orchestra of Wales, cond. by Mark Wigglesworth (BBC, MM124, 1994) [on CD].

Bibliography

Mahler, Gustav, *Symphony no. 10*, BBC National Orchestra of Wales, cond. by Mark Wigglesworth (BBC, MM124, 1994) [on CD]

I22　Music scores

Citation order:

◆ Composer
◆ Title of work (in italics)
◆ Catalogue number (if available)
◆ Place of publication: publisher, year (in round brackets)

Example

Footnote

1. Wolfgang Amadeus Mozart, *Don Giovanni: Overture to the Opera*, K 527 (New York: Dover, 1964).

Bibliography

Mozart, Wolfgang Amadeus, *Don Giovanni: Overture to the Opera*, K 527 (New York: Dover, 1964)

I23　Works of art

Citation order:

◆ Artist
◆ Title of work (in italics)
◆ Date
◆ Medium
◆ Location

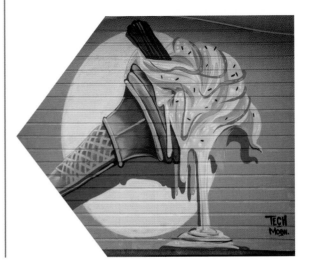

Examples

Footnotes

1. Anthony Gormley, *Angel of the North*, 1998, sculpture, Low Fell, Gateshead.

2. John Martin, *The Bard*, 1817, oil on canvas, Laing Art Gallery, Newcastle upon Tyne.

3. Auguste Rodin, *The Kiss*, 1882, marble, Musée Rodin, Paris, France.

Bibliography

Gormley, Anthony, *Angel of the North*, 1998, sculpture, Low Fell, Gateshead

Martin, John, *The Bard*, 1817, oil on canvas, Laing Art Gallery, Newcastle upon Tyne

Rodin, Auguste, *The Kiss*, 1882, marble, Musée Rodin, Paris, France

I24   Photographs

Citation order:

♦ Artist
♦ Title of work (in italics)
♦ Date (if different from publication date)
♦ Photograph
♦ Location details

Examples

Footnotes

1. Malcolm Collins, *Tumour Section*, 1974, black-and-white photograph, Wellcome Institute, London, Surgery collection, image no. B/473A/1.

2. Angela Vane, *Boxers*, 2016, photograph, from *Sporting Lives* (Cardiff: Virtue Press, 2017), Figure 14.

3. Will Pryce, *Interior of Theatre Royal, Bury St Edmunds*, 2008, online photograph, *Country Life Picture Library*, image no. 553952 <http://www.countrylifeimages.co.uk/553952.jpg> [accessed 25 August 2018].

Bibliography

Collins, Malcolm, *Tumour Section*, 1974, black-and-white photograph, Wellcome Institute, London, Surgery collection, image no. B/473A/1

Pryce, Will, *Interior of Theatre Royal, Bury St Edmunds*, 2008, online photograph, *Country Life Picture Library*, image no. 553952 <http://www.countrylifeimages.co.uk/553952.jpg> [accessed 25 August 2018]

Vane, Angela, *Boxers*, 2016, photograph, from *Sporting Lives* (Cardiff: Virtue Press, 2017), Figure 14

I25   Speeches or lectures

Citation order:

♦ Author/speaker
♦ Title (in single quotation marks)
♦ Lecture to
♦ Venue or course details
♦ Location, date (in round brackets)

If viewed online, add:

♦ <URL> [accessed date]

Examples

Footnotes

1. Jane Stanton, 'Wordsworth's imagination', lecture to Durham Book Festival (Gala Theatre, Durham, 18 September 2018).

2. Clare Willard, 'Wordsworth in context', lecture to MA Literature module (Durham University, 19 October 2018) <http://duo.dur.ac.uk> [accessed 25 October 2018].

Bibliography

Stanton, Jane, 'Wordsworth's imagination', lecture to Durham Book Festival (Gala Theatre, Durham, 18 September 2018)

Willard, Clare, 'Wordsworth in context', lecture to MA Literature module (Durham University, 19 October 2018) <http://duo.dur.ac.uk> [accessed 25 October 2018]

I26 Interviews

Citation order:

♦ Name of interviewee
♦ Interviewed by (forename followed by surname)
♦ Date

Example

Footnote

1. Claire Johnson, interviewed by Danielle Roberts, 14 October 2018.

Bibliography

Johnson, Claire, interviewed by Danielle Roberts, 14 October 2018

Sample text

This sample piece of text shows how various sources would be included as in-text citations.

Worsley's *Classical Architecture* highlighted the variety of styles that eighteenth-century architects employed in their buildings.[1] Initially British architects relied upon the designs of Andrea Palladio, a sixteenth-century Italian architect, who was believed to have studied ancient Roman buildings.[2] As the century progressed, however, more authentic Roman examples were studied, particularly after the discovery of Pompeii.[3] Rich patrons wanted designs in the latest fashion and among those to profit from this demand was Robert Adam, who published his studies of Roman architecture.[4] With this first-hand knowledge he designed many country houses and public buildings.[5] His work was not always as revolutionary as he claimed,[6] but it impressed clients. Adam was even able to take over projects begun by other architects, as at Kedleston in Derbyshire.[7]

Although most patrons favoured classical styles, Horace Walpole suggested that the Gothic style was 'our architecture', the national style of England.[8] Later authors have suggested that Gothic style signified ancient lineage and the British Constitution.[9]

Sample footnotes

1. Giles Worsley, *Classical Architecture in Britain: The Heroic Age* (London: Published for the Paul Mellon Centre for Studies in British Art by Yale University Press, 1995).

2. *Palladio's Italian Villas* (2005) <http://www.boglewood.com/palladio/> [accessed 21 December 2018].

3. Salvatore Ciro Nappo, *Pompeii: Its Discovery and Preservation* (2012) <http://www.bbc.co.uk/history/ancient/romans/pompeii_rediscovery_01.shtml> [accessed 21 December 2018].

4. Robert Adam, *Ruins of the Palace of the Emperor Diocletian at Spalatro in Dalmatia* (London: Printed for the author, 1764), in *Eighteenth Century Collections Online* <https://library.dur.ac.uk/record=b2274207~S1> [accessed 21 December 2018].

5. *Treasures of Britain and Treasures of Ireland* (London: Reader's Digest Association Ltd, 1990).

6. Worsley, *Classical Architecture*, p. 265.

7. Peter Leach, 'James Paine's Design for the South Front of Kedleston Hall: Dating and Sources', *Architectural History*, 40 (1997),159–70.

8. Horace Walpole, cited in S. Lang, 'The Principles of the Gothic Revival in England', *Journal of the Society of Architectural Historians*, 25.4 (1966), 240–67 <http://www.jstor.org/stable/988353> [accessed 21 December 2018].

9. Alexandrina Buchanan, 'Interpretations of Medieval Architecture', in *Gothic Architecture and Its Meanings 1550–1830*, ed. by Michael Hall (Reading: Spire Books, 2002), pp. 27–52.

NB Footnote 6 is an example of a **short citation**, and footnote 8 is a **secondary reference**.

Sample bibliography

Adam, Robert, *Ruins of the Palace of the Emperor Diocletian at Spalatro in Dalmatia* (London: Printed for the author, 1764), in *Eighteenth Century Collections Online* <https://library.dur.ac.uk/record=b2274207~S1> [accessed 21 December 2018]

Buchanan, Alexandrina, 'Interpretations of Medieval Architecture', in *Gothic Architecture and Its Meanings 1550–1830*, ed. by Michael Hall (Reading: Spire Books, 2002), pp. 27–52

Lang, S., 'The Principles of the Gothic Revival in England', *Journal of the Society of Architectural Historians*, 25.4 (1966), 240–67 <http://www.jstor.org/stable/988353> [accessed 21 December 2018]

Leach, Peter, 'James Paine's Design for the South Front of Kedleston Hall: Dating and Sources', *Architectural History*, 40 (1997), 159–70

Nappo, Salvatore Ciro, *Pompeii: Its Discovery and Preservation* (2012) <http://www.bbc.co.uk/history/ancient/romans/pompeii_rediscovery_01.shtml> [accessed 21 December 2018]

Palladio's Italian Villas (2005) <http://www.boglewood.com/palladio/> [accessed 21 December 2018]

Treasures of Britain and Treasures of Ireland (London: Reader's Digest Association Ltd, 1990)

Worsley, Giles, *Classical Architecture in Britain: The Heroic Age* (London: Published for the Paul Mellon Centre for Studies in British Art by Yale University Press, 1995)

NB For more information on using the MHRA referencing style, see MHRA (2013) *MHRA style guide*. 3rd edn. London: Modern Humanities Research Association. Available at: http://www.mhra.org.uk/publications/MHRA-Style-Guide (Accessed: 26 September 2018).

Section J
Modern Language Association (MLA) referencing style

The MLA referencing style is often used in humanities subjects, including languages and literature. It is an author-page style: sources are identified in your text by the author's surname (or, if not available, the title of the source), and a page number if you are quoting or paraphrasing a specific part of the author's work. These **in-text citations** using author names are related to a list of **Works Cited** at the end of your work. To find the full details of the source being cited, the reader must refer to the list of Works Cited.

Conventions when using the MLA referencing style

This section is based upon Modern Language Association (2016) *MLA Handbook for Writers of Research Papers*. 8th edn. New York, NY: Modern Language Association of America. Updates on citations for sources are available online at *MLA Style Center* (2018) https://style.mla.org/. (Accessed: 13 September 2018).

The 8th edition of the *MLA handbook* (2016) introduced several important changes in the use of MLA style. The most important change is a move away from rigid rules for citing specific sources to a set of core principles for documenting the sources you are using. When citing a source, you should look for the following elements in this order:

1. Author or creator.
2. Title of the source.
3. Title of the container, if the source is part of a greater collection (for example, a chapter in a book, an article in a journal, a page or post within a website, or an online journal in a collection such as JSTOR),
4. Other contributors (for example, editors, translators, illustrators),
5. The version or edition of the source that you have used,
6. Any numbers that denote the source (for example, volume, issue and page numbers of a journal article, or document reference),
7. Publisher,
8. Publication date,
9. Location.

If any of these elements are missing from your source (for example, a book is a stand-alone work so does not have a container, and may not have editors or translators), these are omitted in your Works Cited reference. If a source does not have an author, use the next available element in the list above for your in-text citation.

> **Example of in-text citation with an author**
>
> According to Jones (51) …
>
> **Example of in-text citation without an author, using title of source**
>
> The *Oxford Dictionary of Abbreviations* (42) …

Compiling your list of Works Cited

♦ Sources are listed in alphabetical order by author (or source title if there is no author)

- Second and subsequent lines of the reference should be indented by ½ inch (1.3cm)
- Each element of your reference in the Works Cited should end with the punctuation shown at the end of each point above (for example, a full stop after the title of the source)
- MLA uses abbreviations in the list of Works Cited for time periods, organisation names, countries, counties and US states. A full list of abbreviations is given in section 1.6 of the 8th edition of the *MLA handbook*

Author's name

- The authors' full names, as written on the title pages, should be used
- End the author's name with a full stop. If the source has more than one author, see 'Multiple authors' below
- For in-text citations and footnotes, give the author's name as forename(s) or initials followed by surname – for example, Martin Roberts. For the list of Works Cited, give the author's name as surname followed by forename(s) or initials – for example, Roberts, Martin
- If you have two authors with the same surname, use their forename initials in your in-text citations – for example, A. Jones and C. Jones

Several sources by the same author

If you are citing more than one publication by the same author, include a short version of the title of each work in the in-text citation. In the list of Works Cited, give the author's name for the first entry only, and for subsequent references use three hyphens and a full stop ---. to replace the author's name.

Example

In-text citation

Thornberry's research (*Labour Pains* and "Political spin") …

Works Cited

Thornberry, Jane. *Labour Pains: Politics in the Blair Era*. New Vantage, 2017.
---. "Political Spin in the 21st Century", *New Political Thought*, vol. 14, no. 1, 2015, pp. 45–48.

Multiple authors

For a source with two authors, refer to them by their surnames in your in-text citation, but in the list of Works Cited the first author is written as surname followed by forename, and the subsequent authors are written as forename followed by surname.

Example

In-text citation (including a page reference)

A new review (Willis and Singh 14) …

Works Cited

Willis, Anne, and Avjeet Singh. *Digital Music*. SoundMachine, 2019.

If there are three or more authors of a single work, write the name of the first author then use **et al.** instead of the names of the other authors. Note that et al. is not italicised.

Example

In-text citation

This new monograph (Lefevre et al.) …

Works Cited

Lefevre, Michelle, et al. *Contemporary Dance*. Springer, 2018.

Multiple citations in your text

If referring to more than one source to reinforce a point in your text, include them in parentheses in your in-text citation separated by a semicolon.

Example

In-text citation ▶

This point has been made by several authors (Bowey 12; Liu 32; Singh 4) …

Titles of sources

♦ Capitalise the first word, and all nouns, verbs and adjectives. Capitalise articles if they are the first words of a subtitle after a colon – for example, *Cite Them Right: The Essential Referencing Guide*

♦ The title of the source should be in italics if it is a stand-alone item (such as a book), or in double quotation marks if it is within a container (such as an article in a journal or newspaper, or a song on an album)

♦ Some sources may not have a title (for example, tweets, advertisements or graffiti). In these instances, provide a description in normal font as the first element of the citation

♦ For non-English titles, give the title in the original language (unless you are using a translation), but you may include a short translated title after the original, in square brackets – for example, *I Quattro Libri Dell'Archittetura* [*The Four Books of Architecture*]

Containers

The 8th edition of the *MLA handbook* introduced the concept of a container, where a source may be accessed. This can be a journal, containing articles, a book containing chapters by different authors, a website containing different pages, or a social media site containing different posts. The title of the container should be in italics.

It is possible for a source to have more than one container – for example, an article in a journal accessed within a database such as *JSTOR*. In the example below, the titles of both containers are italicised.

Example

Gapinski, James H. "The Economics of Performing Shakespeare." *The American Economic Review*, vol. 74, no. 3, 1984, pp. 458–466. *JSTOR*, www.jstor.org/stable/1804020.

Other contributors

The exact nature of work by other contributors is indicated by phrases before their names (for example, edited by, translated by, illustrated by, directed by).

Examples

Buchanan, Alexandrina. "Interpretations of Medieval Architecture." *Gothic Architecture and Its Meanings 1550–1830*, edited by Michael Hall, Spire, 2002, pp. 27–52.

Silone, Ignazio. *Fontamara*, translated by Gwenda David and Eric Mosbacher. Redwords, 1994.

Version

As sources such as books and software may be altered and updated, it is important to clarify which version you have used. Use abbreviated words to indicate edition (ed.), volume (vol.) and number (no.), but do not abbreviate 'version'.

Publisher

In the Works Cited list, omit business words (Limited, Corporation, Incorporated) from the name of the company – for example, instead of Pergamon Ltd, use Pergamon. If the publisher is a university press, abbreviate this to UP – for example, Cambridge UP.

Date

Spell out the names of months and days in your text, but abbreviate them in the list of Works Cited – for example, Jan., Feb., Mar., Apr., Aug., Sept., Oct., Nov. and Dec., and Mon., Tues., Wed., Thu., Fri., Sat. and Sun.

NB May, June and July do not need to be abbreviated.

Location

The location may be the page numbers of a journal article or book chapter, or the specific pages that you are quoting. For online sources, the location will be the URL or DOI. For a physical object such as a work of art, the location will be the museum or gallery in which you viewed it.

Page numbers

Provide a page number in your in-text citation if you are quoting or paraphrasing. The in-text citation does not include p. before the page number, but in your list of Works Cited page references for book chapters or journal articles include pp. Do not elide page ranges.

Example

In-text citation

The costs of the theatre production (Gapinski 461) …

Works Cited

Gapinski, James H. "The Economics of Performing Shakespeare." *The American Economic Review*, vol. 74, no. 3, 1984, pp. 458–466. *JSTOR*, www.jstor.org/stable/1804020.

You can include page numbers (in parentheses) in your in-text citation after the author's name, in parentheses with the author's name if referring to the source indirectly, or put the page number in parentheses at the end of the sentence if this is more convenient for the flow of your text.

Example

The performance divided critics' opinions: one thought it was 'moving' (Ali 12), and Blanche (34) called it 'captivating'. However, Williams was unimpressed by the leading actor's delivery (41).

URLs and DOIs

One of the significant changes in the 8th edition of the *MLA handbook* was the reinstatement of full URLs or DOIs (instead of the word Web) when documenting online sources. This is because search engine algorithms, new content, and commercial practices (such as boosting some websites) can result in different search results: what was easy to locate one day may be more difficult on another occasion. The ability to modify or even delete internet content also makes it essential that you state where and when you accessed online sources.

If the source has a DOI or a stable URL (sometimes called a permalink), this should be used in preference to a URL. If using an online source that does not have a DOI or stable URL, include the date that you accessed it as well as the URL.

When using a URL, copy it from the browser but omit the http:// or https://. Do not use shortened URLs such as bit.ly.

Optional elements of citations

Place of publication

With most sources, you do not need to list a place of publication. However, if a work was published before 1900, works were associated with the city of publication or may have been produced by a printer. For more recent works, it may be useful to include a place of publication if a publisher has produced editions with different spellings and vocabulary (for example, a British and an American edition of a book).

Date of original publication

If an older source has been republished, you may give the original date of publication immediately after the title to help your reader distinguish between the original and the new versions. The new version may have additional information, such as an editor's introduction.

Footnotes or endnotes

MLA discourages the use of long footnotes or endnotes, but they can be used for supplementary information or where a digression might otherwise disturb the flow of your main text. Use a superscript number for the footnote or endnote.

Example

In-text citation

Schultz has disputed the traditional method (67).[1]

Note

1. As have Weike 42–53 and Thomas 12–17.

Sources cited in footnotes or endnotes should also be included in the Works Cited list.

Secondary references

Only provide references to sources that you have read. If you read a summary of other works, you are relying upon the author of the summary to accurately represent the words and meaning of the other works. You should cite the source information for the summary in your in-text citations and Works Cited.

How to reference common sources

The following are given as examples of frequently used sources in academic work. If the source you wish to cite is not included, use the core principles and list of elements at the beginning of this chapter to produce your reference.

J1 Books

Citation order:

♦ Author (surname, forenames).
♦ Title (in italics).
♦ Publisher, year of publication.
♦ Series title (if available, in italics)

Example

In-text citation

Worsley's study of the period …

Works Cited

Worsley, Giles. *Classical Architecture in Britain: The Heroic Age*. Yale UP, 1995.

J2   Ebooks in online collections

Citation order:

♦ Author (surname, forenames).
♦ Title (in italics).
♦ Version,
♦ Publisher, year of publication.
♦ Title of container (in italics),
♦ DOI *or* URL and Accessed date.

Example

In-text citation

Volutes are the principal feature of the Ionic order (Chitham 43).

Works Cited

Chitham, Robert. *The Classical Orders of Architecture*. 2nd ed., Elsevier, 2005. *Internet Archive*, archive.org/details/TheClassicalOrdersOf Architecture. Accessed 29 Nov. 2018.

J3   Translated books

Citation order:

♦ Author (surname, forenames).
♦ Title (in italics).
♦ Translated by forename surname.
♦ Publisher, year of publication.

Example

In-text citation

Homer's description of the fall of Troy (22–27) …

Works Cited

Homer. *The Iliad*. Translated by David Green. U of California P, 2015.

In some instances, you may wish to highlight the role of the translator of a source (for example, if you need to discuss differences between editions of the source). You can do this by placing their name and their role as the first element of your reference. The original author may not be known, or if they are they can be identified after the title of the source.

Example

In-text citation

Green's translation places emphasis upon …

Works Cited

Green, David, translator. *The Iliad*. By Homer. U of California P, 2015.

J4   Books with an editor

Some sources will be the combination of work by several authors, brought together and often given an introduction by an editor (for example, collections of essays). In these instances, use the name of the editor in place of the author, but include the description of their role.

Citation order:

♦ Editor's surname, followed by forename,
♦ editor.
♦ Title (in italics).
♦ Publisher, year of publication.
♦ Series title (if available, in italics)

Example

In-text citation

A new collection of essays (Rollason) …

Works Cited

Rollason, David, editor. *Princes of the Church: Bishops and their Palaces*. Routledge, 2017. Society for Medieval Archaeology Monograph 39.

J5 Chapters in edited books

Citation order:

- Author of the chapter/section (surname, forename).
- Title of chapter/section (in double quotation marks).
- Title of book (in italics),
- edited by forename surname of editor,
- Publisher, year of publication,
- Page numbers of chapter/section.

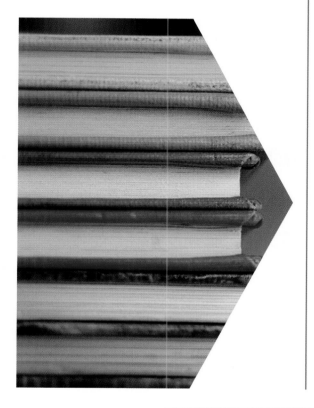

Example

In-text citation

As argued by Buchanan (29–30) …

Works Cited

Buchanan, Alexandrina. "Interpretations of Medieval Architecture." *Gothic Architecture and Its Meanings 1550–1830*, edited by Michael Hall, Spire, 2002, pp. 27–52.

J6 Books with no authors

Citation order:

- Title of book (in italics).
- Publisher, year of publication.

Example

In-text citation

As defined in the *Oxford Dictionary of Abbreviations* (42) …

Works Cited

Oxford Dictionary of Abbreviations. Clarendon P, 1992.

J7 Anthologies

Citation order:

- Author/editor (surname, forename),
- editor (if not the author).
- Title (in italics).
- Edition (only include the edition number if it is not the first edition).
- Publisher, year of publication.

Example

In-text citation

An older collection of Japanese fiction (Keane) …

Works Cited

Keane, Donald, editor. *Anthology of Japanese Literature*. 3rd ed. Grove, 1955.

J8 Multi-volume works

Citation order:

- Author/editor (surname, forename).
- Title (in italics).
- Edition (only include the edition number if it is not the first edition),
- Publisher, year of publication.
- Number of volumes.

Example

In-text citation

Stillman's comprehensive work …

Works Cited

Stillman, Damie. *English Neo-classical Architecture*. Zwemmer, 1988. 2 vols.

If citing from only one volume, specify the volume in the Works Cited entry.

Example

In-text citation

Classical details on public buildings (Stillman 290) …

Works Cited

Stillman, Damie. *English Neo-classical Architecture*. Vol. 2, Zwemmer, 1988. 2 vols.

If citing from several volumes, include the volume number and page number in the in-text citation.

Example

In-text citation

Exterior details on public buildings (Stillman 2: 47) were more restrained than those in private houses (1: 27–93).

Works Cited

Stillman, Damie. *English Neo-classical Architecture*. Zwemmer, 1988. 2 vols.

J9 Sacred texts

When referring generally to sacred texts, they are not italicised, but when citing specific editions these should be italicised. In the Works Cited, give any information required to identify the specific edition or translation that you have used.

Citation order:

- Title (in italics).
- Version (if required).
- Editor (if available),
- Publisher,
- Year.

Example

In-text citation

The Bible, Talmud and Quran are read by millions of people. Reading the *NIV First-Century Study Bible* …

Works Cited

NIV First-Century Study Bible. Editor, Kent Dobson, Hodder and Stoughton, 2015.

J10 Book reviews

Citation order:

- ◆ Reviewer (surname, forename).
- ◆ Review of
- ◆ Title of book being reviewed (in italics),
- ◆ by
- ◆ Author of book being reviewed (forename, surname).
- ◆ Publication title (in italics),
- ◆ Volume and issue numbers (if available),
- ◆ Date,
- ◆ Page numbers.

Example

In-text citation

A favourable review of Tomb's book (Ward) …

Works Cited

Ward, Paul. Review of *The English and Their History*, by Robert Tombs. *History Today*, Mar. 2015, pp. 60–61.

J11 Journal articles

Citation order:

- ◆ Author (surname, forename).
- ◆ Title of article (in double quotation marks).
- ◆ Title of journal (in italics),
- ◆ Volume number, issue number (if available),
- ◆ Year of publication,
- ◆ Page numbers.

Example

In-text citation

Leach's assessment of the design …

Works Cited

Leach, Peter. "James Paine's Design for the South Front of Kedleston Hall: Dating and Sources." *Architectural History*, vol. 40, 1997, pp. 159–170.

J12 Ejournal articles

Citation order:

- ◆ Author (surname, forename or initial).
- ◆ Title of article (in double quotation marks).
- ◆ Title of journal (in italics),
- ◆ Volume number, issue number,
- ◆ Year,
- ◆ Page numbers of article.
- ◆ Name of collection (in italics),
- ◆ DOI *or* URL and Accessed date.

Example

In-text citation

Strawberry Hill House was a key building in the Revival (Lang 251).

Works Cited

Lang, S. "The Principles of the Gothic Revival in England." *Journal of the Society of Architectural Historians*, vol. 25, no. 4, 1966, pp. 240–267. *JSTOR*, www.jstor.org. stable/988353.

NB This is a stable URL so no access date is required.

J13 Magazine articles

Citation order:

- ◆ Author (surname, forename).
- ◆ Title of article (in double quotation marks).
- ◆ Title of magazine (in italics),
- ◆ Date,
- ◆ Page numbers of printed magazine article.

If viewed online, add:

- ◆ DOI *or* URL and Accessed date.

Example: print article

In-text citation

Bletcher noted several useful exercises (10).

Works Cited

Bletcher, Katherine. "Matters of the Heart." *Heart Matters*, Aug.–Sept. 2012, pp. 9–11.

Example: online article

In-text citation

Reisz took a central European view.

Works Cited

Reisz, Matthew. "History: From a Different Perspective." *Times Higher Education*, 16 Aug. 2018, www. timeshighereducation.com/features/ history-different-perspective. Accessed 29 Nov. 2018.

J14   Newspaper articles

Citation order:

♦ Author (surname, forename).
♦ Title of article (in double quotation marks).
♦ Title of newspaper (in italics),
♦ Date,
♦ Page numbers of newspaper article.

If viewed online, add:

♦ Title of the collection (in italics, if applicable),
♦ DOI *or* URL and Accessed date.

Example: print article

In-text citation

Attempts to recruit more science graduates (Mansell and Bloom) …

Works Cited

Mansell, William, and Anne Bloom. "£10,000 Carrot to Tempt Physics Experts." *The Guardian*, 20 June 2012, p. 5.

Example: newspaper article from website

In-text citation

Roberts and Ackerman reported …

Works Cited

Roberts, Dan, and Sue Ackerman. "US draft resolution allows Obama 90 days for military action against Syria." *The Guardian*, 4 Sept. 2013, www. theguardian.com/world/2013/ sep/04/syria-strikes-draftresolution- 90- days. Accessed 17 Oct. 2018.

Example: newspaper article from an online database

In-text citation

There was positive news from Korea (Haas).

Works Cited

Haas, Benjamin. "Tears flow as separated South and North Korean Families Reunite." *The Guardian*, 20 Aug. 2018. *Factiva*, www.global. factiva.com. Accessed 17 Oct. 2018.

J15 Theses and dissertations

Citation order:

♦ Author (surname, forename).
♦ Title of thesis or dissertation (in italics).
♦ Year of award.
♦ Awarding institution,
♦ Level of qualification.

If accessed online, add:

♦ Repository name (in italics),
♦ URL and Accessed date.

Examples

In-text citations

Theses can be available in hardcopy (Baines) and online (Fordham).

Works Cited

Baines, John. *Musical Composition*. 2007. Durham U, PhD dissertation.
Fordham, Douglas. *Raising Standards: Art and Imperial Politics in London, 1745–1776*. 2003. Yale U, PhD dissertation. *ProQuest,* search-proquest-com /docview/305298249? accountid=14533. Accessed 17 Oct. 2018.

J16 Published proceedings of a conference

J16.1 Full published proceedings

Citation order:

♦ Name of editor (surname, forename),
♦ editor.
♦ Conference title (in italics),
♦ Conference date and location (if not part of the conference title).
♦ Publisher, year of publication.

Example (date and location in title of conference)

In-text citation

The conference papers covered a range of research (Jones).

Works Cited

Jones, Hilary, editor. *Proceedings of the Tenth Conference in Romance Studies, Derby 18 May 2014*. U of Derby P, 2014.

J16.2 Papers in published proceedings of a conference

Citation order:

♦ Author (surname, forename).
♦ Title of paper (in double quotation marks).
♦ Conference title (in italics),
♦ Conference date and location (if not part of the conference title).
♦ Edited by
♦ Name of editor(s),
♦ Publisher, year of publication.

If accessed online, add:

♦ DOI *or* URL and Accessed date.

Example

In-text citation

Some similarities were noted by Worsley (42–47).

Works Cited

Worsley, Giles. "Adam as a Palladian." *Adam in Context: Papers Given at the Georgian Group Symposium, London 1992*. Edited by Giles Worsley, Georgian Group, 1993.

Example: online conference paper (date and location not in title)

In-text citation

Hosangadi gave a paper on Indian folklore.

Works Cited

Hosangadi, Balakrishna B. M. "Folktales, Myths and Legends on Sculptors of South India." *Asian Conference on Literature 2017 Official Conference Proceedings*, Mar. 30–Apr. 2, 2017, Kobe, Japan. *IAFOR*, papers.iafor.org/submission34635. Accessed 29 Aug. 2018.

J17 Plays

There are different forms for citing the script of a play and its performance.

J17.1 Script

Citation order:

◆ Author (surname, forename).
◆ Title of play (in italics).
◆ Publisher, year.

Example: print article

In-text citation

The imagery of the fairies (Shakespeare 46) …

Works Cited

Shakespeare, William. *A Midsummer Night's Dream*. Routledge, 1988.

J17.2 Performance

Citation order:

◆ Title of play (in double quotation marks).
◆ By author's name (forename surname),
◆ directed by name of director (forename surname),
◆ performance by name of actor (forename surname),
◆ Company,
◆ Date,
◆ Location.

Example

In-text citation

The portrayal of the fairy realm ("A Midsummer Night's Dream") …

Works Cited

"A Midsummer Night's Dream." By William Shakespeare, directed by Ian Judge, performances by Alex Jennings and Stella Gonet, Royal Shakespeare Company, 1 Mar. 1995, Theatre Royal, Newcastle upon Tyne.

J18 Poems

Citation order:

◆ Author (surname, forename).
◆ Title of poem (in double quotation marks)
◆ Title of publication (in italics).
◆ Publisher, year.

If accessed online, add:

◆ DOI *or* URL and Accessed date.

Example

The image of the country house as a doll's house by Patience Agbabi ...

Agbabi, Patience. "The Doll's House." *The Forward Book of Poetry 2014*. Forward Worldwide in association with Faber, 2013.

Or

Agbabi, Patience. "The Doll's House." *The Poetry Archive*. www. poetryarchive.org/poem/dolls-house. Accessed 23 Nov. 2018.

J19   Research reports

NB If the name of the publisher is the same as the author, omit the author and begin with the title.

Citation order:

♦ Author or department or organisation.
♦ Title (in italics).
♦ Publisher, year.

If accessed online, add:

♦ DOI *or* URL and Accessed date.

Examples

Reports by the Department of Health and by Lovett ...

Department of Health. *Health Inequalities: Progress and Next Steps*. TSI, 2008.
Lovett, Vicky. *Child Development Report: Safeguarding Children*. CPSU, 2015. thecpsu.org.uk/ resource-library/2015/child-development-report/. Accessed 29 Aug. 2018.

J20   Legislation

For UK Acts of Parliament, give the name and the section or paragraph in your in-text citation.

Citation order:

♦ Title of Act including year,
♦ Chapter number.

Example

As determined by the Children Act section 10 (2) ...

Children Act 2004, c. 31.

J21   Organisation or personal internet sites

Citation order:

♦ Author or editor (if available).
♦ Title of page (in double quotation marks).
♦ Title of the website (in italics),

◆ Date last updated.
◆ DOI *or* URL and Accessed date.

Examples

In-text citations

Italy has much to offer, from Roman Pompeii (Nappo) to Renaissance villas (*Palladio's Italian Villas*) …

Works Cited

Nappo, Salvatore Ciro. "Pompeii: Its Discovery and Preservation." *BBC History*, 2011. www.bbc.co.uk/history/ancient/romans/pompeii_rediscovery_01.shtml. Accessed 27 Apr. 2018.

Palladio's Italian Villas. 2005. www.boglewood.com/palladio/emo.html. Accessed 27 Apr. 2018.

J22   Blogs

Citation order:

◆ Author (surname, forename).
◆ Title of article (in double quotation marks).
◆ Title of website (in italics),
◆ Date of post.
◆ URL and Accessed date.

Example

In-text citation

Carillo expressed concerns …

Works Cited

Carillo, Ellen. "Digital Literacy in 'Post-Truth' America." *Behind the Style Blog, MLA Style Center*, 31 July 2018. style.mla.org/digital-literacy/. Accessed 27 Aug. 2018.

J23   Social media

J23.1   Facebook

Citation order:

◆ Author (surname, forename).
◆ Title of post (in double quotation marks).
◆ Title of website (in italics),
◆ Date of post.
◆ DOI *or* URL and Accessed date if not a stable URL.

Example

In-text citation

The event was promoted on social media (Jones).

Works Cited

Jones, Mark. "Guided Walk." *Facebook*, 31 July 2018. www.facebook.com/whickhamhistory/. Accessed 27 Aug. 2018.

J23.2   Twitter

Citation order:

◆ User's name
◆ Twitter handle (in round brackets).
◆ Entire tweet (in double quotation marks).
◆ Twitter (in italics),
◆ Date and time of posting,
◆ Identifier.

Example

In-text citation

Smith tweeted her travel plans.

Works Cited

Smith, Jane (@js24notts). "Hoping to visit Paris." *Twitter*, 22 Jan. 2018, 9:06 a.m., twitter.com/js24notts/status/230954569.

J23.3 Instagram

Citation order:

♦ Name of account holder.
♦ Title of posting (in double quotation marks).
♦ Instagram (in italics),
♦ Date of posting,
♦ URL and Accessed date.

Example

In-text citation

Cathy2001's Harry Potter theme …

Works Cited

Cathy2001. "Potterama." *Instagram*, 22 Jan. 2019, www.instagram.com/p/Bcp_TFnVyf/?hl=en&taken-by=potterama. Accessed 23 Jan. 2019.

J24 Emails

Citation order:

♦ Author of the email (surname, forename).
♦ Title of the email (in double quotation marks).
♦ Received by name of recipient (forename surname),
♦ Date.

Example

In-text citation

Schultz's email to the student …

Works Cited

Schultz, Julia. "Franz Lizst Essay." Received by Helena Braun, 17 Aug. 2018.

J25 Works of art

When citing an original work of art that you have seen (not an image or reproduction of the original) such as a sculpture, painting, photograph or other illustration, start with the name of the artist or creator of the work and include the location.

Citation order:

♦ Artist (surname, forename).
♦ Title of work (in italics).
♦ Year,
♦ Location.

Examples

In-text citations

Her favourite pieces were by Gormley, Rodin and Martin.

Works Cited

Gormley, Anthony. *Angel of the North*. 1998, Low Fell, Gateshead.
Martin, John. *The Bard*. 1817, Laing Art Gallery, Newcastle upon Tyne.
Rodin, Auguste. *The Kiss*. 1882, Musée Rodin, Paris, France.

J26 Installations/exhibits/objects in galleries and museums

If you wish to cite an object (for example, an item in a museum collection), include the creator – if known – and a description, as well as the location and any further identification information.

Citation order:

♦ Creator (if known).
♦ Description of object (without italics or quotation marks).
♦ Date,
♦ Museum,
♦ Location,
♦ Item number (if known).

Examples

This year I have seen fine examples by Chippendale, and a Jade Seal.

Chippendale, Thomas. Rosewood dressing table. c.1760, Lady Lever Art Gallery, Port Sunlight, Merseyside, LL 4012.

Jade Seal. 1368–1644, Durham University Oriental Museum, Durham, DUROM.2017.16.

J27 Exhibitions

Citation order:

♦ Title of exhibition (in italics),
♦ Opening and closing dates,
♦ Location.

Example

Bodies of Evidence revealed what lay beneath the library garden.

Bodies of Evidence: How Science Unearthed Durham's Dark Secret, 9 June. 2018–7 Oct. 2018, Palace Green Library, Durham.

J28 Photographs from the internet

Citation order:

♦ Author (surname, forename) (if available).
♦ Title of item (in italics).
♦ Date of photograph,
♦ Title of website (in italics).
♦ DOI *or* URL and Accessed date if not a stable URL.

Example

Brocklehurst illustrated Sudanese costume.

Brocklehurst, P. *S0000519 – Two Sudanese men in traditional dress*. 1 Jan. 1919–31 Dec. 1920, *Royal Geographical Society Picture Library*. images.rgs.org/gallery.aspx?ID=4&Desig=T&Title=People%20%26%20Culture. Accessed 14 Nov. 2018.

J29 Advertisements

Citation order:

♦ Title of advertisement (in double quotation marks) or description.
♦ Title of publication (in italics),
♦ Date,
♦ Page number.

If online, add:

♦ DOI *or* URL and Accessed date if not a stable URL.
♦ Description (if required).

Examples: print and online advertisements

LionTrust advertised sustainable investment, whilst HSBC offered loans.

HSBC advertisement. *Huffington Post*, 20 Aug. 2018. www.huffingtonpost.co.uk. Accessed 27 Nov. 2018. Pop-up ad.

"LionTrust: Investing in a Changing World." *The Week*, 28 July 2018, p. 17.

J30 Manuscripts/archives

Citation order:

♦ Author (surname, forename) (if available).
♦ Title of item (in italics).
♦ Date,
♦ Name of archive, city,
♦ Manuscript reference.

Examples

In-text citations

Building accounts by Newton and Smirke …

Works Cited

Newton, William. *Letter to William Ord*. 23 June 1785. Northumberland Archives, Woodhorn, MS. Ord 324 E11/4.

Smirke, Sydney. *Report to the Board of Customs*. 16 May 1829, National Archives, Kew, CUST 33/6.

J31 Musical scores

Citation order:

♦ Composer (surname, forename).
♦ Title of score (in italics).
♦ Publisher, year.

Example

In-text citation

His beautiful music (Mozart) …

Works Cited

Mozart, Wolfgang A. *Don Giovanni: Overture to the Opera, K 527*. Dover Music, 1964.

J32 Sound recordings

Sound recordings can be cited in several ways, depending on the containers that you use to hear them (for example, CDs, radio or internet sites such as YouTube and Spotify). You may also cite a recording by the composer or the performer.

J32.1 Complete works

Citation order:

♦ Artist (surname, forename).
♦ Title of full recording (in italics).
♦ Distributor, year.
♦ Format (optional).

Example

In-text citation

The haunting violin accompaniment to Brahms's work …

Works Cited

Brahms, Johannes. *Piano Quintet in F Minor, op.34*. BBC Music, 2015. CD.

J32.2 Songs on an album

Citation order:

♦ Artist (surname, forename).
♦ Title of item (in double quotation marks).
♦ Title of full recording (in italics).
♦ Distributor, year.
♦ Format (optional).

If viewed online, add:

♦ Title of container,
♦ DOI *or* URL and Accessed date if not a stable URL.

Example on CD

In-text citation

Jessie J achieved her second UK number one with "Domino".

Works Cited

Jessie J. "Domino." *Who You Are*. Universal Republic Records, 2011. CD.

Example viewed online

In-text citation

The song by Journey has been covered by many artists.

Works Cited

Journey. "Don't Stop Believing." *Escape*. Columbia, 1981. YouTube, www.youtube.com/watch?v= VcjzHMhBtf0. Accessed 28 Jul. 2018.

J33   Film or video recordings

Citation order:

- ◆ Title (in italics).
- ◆ Directed by
- ◆ Name of director (forename surname),
- ◆ performances by
- ◆ Major performers (forename surname),
- ◆ Distributor, year.

Example

In-text citation

Alien was a truly terrifying film.

Works Cited

Alien. Directed by Ridley Scott, performances by Sigourney Weaver, Tom Skerritt, and John Hurt, MGM, 1979.

If you wish to highlight the work of a specific director or performer, you can begin the citation with the name (surname, first name) of that person, followed by a description of their role.

Example

In-text citation

With *Alien*, Scott combined sci-fi and horror genres.

Works Cited

Scott, Ridley, director. *Alien*. MGM, 1979.

J34   YouTube videos

Citation order:

- ◆ Author's name or poster's username.
- ◆ Title of video (in double quotation marks).
- ◆ Name of website (in italics),
- ◆ Date posted.
- ◆ URL and Accessed date.

Example

In-text citation

Mr Plant's videos demonstrate ancient technologies (Primitive Technology).

Works Cited

Primitive Technology. "Water powered hammer (Monjolo)." *YouTube*, 28 Apr. 2017. www.youtube.com/ watch?v=i9TdoO2OVaA. Accessed 28 July 2018.

J35   Broadcasts

J35.1   Television or radio broadcasts

Citation order:

- ◆ Title of episode (in double quotation marks).
- ◆ Title of programme (in italics),
- ◆ created by (if applicable),
- ◆ performance by (name of lead character),
- ◆ Series or season number, episode number,

♦ Broadcaster,
♦ Broadcast date.

Example

In-text citation

The confrontation with insane Daleks ("Asylum of the Daleks") …

Works Cited

"Asylum of the Daleks." *Doctor Who*, created by Steven Moffat, performance by Matt Smith, series 33, episode 1, BBC One Television, 1 Sept. 2012.

J35.2   Broadcast episode viewed through a streaming service

Citation order:

♦ Title of episode (in double quotation marks).
♦ Title of series (in italics),
♦ Season and episode number,
♦ Distributor, year.
♦ Title of streaming service (in italics),
♦ URL and Accessed date.

Example

In-text citation

Princess Margaret's love life was exposed in "Gloriana".

Works Cited

"Gloriana." *The Crown*, season 1, episode 10, Left Bank Pictures/Sony Pictures Television, 4 Nov. 2016. *Netflix*, www.netflix.com/gb/title/80025678. Accessed 24 July 2018.

J35.3   Broadcast series viewed through a streaming service

Citation order:

♦ Name of creator/writer,
♦ creator/writer.
♦ Title of series (in italics).
♦ Distributor, year.
♦ Title of streaming service (in italics),
♦ URL and Accessed date.

Example

In-text citation

In *The Crown,* Morgan recreated the early years of the Queen's reign.

Works Cited

Peter Morgan, creator. *The Crown*. Left Bank Pictures/Sony Pictures Television, 2016. *Netflix*, www.netflix.com. Accessed 21 Dec. 2018.

J36   Interviews

J36.1   Personal interviews

If you want to cite an interview you have conducted but not published, use the following.

Citation order:

♦ Surname, forename of interviewee.
♦ Personal interview.
♦ Date of interview.

Example

Works Cited

Palanza, Luis. Personal interview. 26 Nov. 2018.

J36.2 Published interviews (print or online)

Citation order:

- Surname, forename of interviewee.
- Title of interview (in double quotation marks, if available).
- Interview with name of interviewer (forename, surname).
- Title of container (in italics),
- Publication details.

Examples

In-text citations

Interviews in newspapers (Riley) and online (Obama) …

Works Cited

Obama, Barak. Interview with Jon Sopel. *BBC News*, 24 Jul. 2015, www.bbc.co.uk/news/world-uscanada-33646543. Accessed 16 Sept. 2018.

Riley, Bridget. "The life of Riley." Interview with Jonathan Jones. *The Guardian*, 5 Jul. 2008, p. 33.

J37 Speeches or lectures

Citation order:

- Surname, forename of speaker.
- Title of speech or lecture (in double quotation marks).
- Title of meeting,
- Date,
- Location.

Examples

In-text citations

After attending Stanton's talk on Wordsworth, students on the literature module attended a lecture by their tutor (Willard).

Works Cited

Stanton, Jane. "Wordsworth's Imagination." Lecture to Durham Book Festival, 18 Sept. 2018, Gala Theatre, Durham.

Willard, Clare. "Wordsworth in Context." Lecture to MA Literature module, 19 Sept. 2018, Durham University.

Sample text

Worsley (*Classical Architecture*) highlighted the variety of styles that eighteenth-century architects employed in their buildings. Initially British architects relied upon the designs of Andrea Palladio, a sixteenth-century Italian architect. His *I Quattro Libri Dell'Archittetura* [*The Four Books of Architecture*] included his re-creations of Roman buildings. As the century progressed, more authentic Roman examples were studied, particularly after the discovery of Pompeii (Nappo). Rich patrons sought designs from Robert Adam, who published his studies of Roman architecture (Adam). With this first-hand knowledge he designed many country houses and public buildings. His work was not always as revolutionary as he claimed (Worsley "Adam as a Palladian" 10), but it certainly impressed clients, for example his work at Kedleston in Derbyshire (Leach 159). Although most patrons favoured classical styles, Horace Walpole suggested that the Gothic style was the national style of England (Walpole, cited in Lang 251). Alexandrina Buchanan suggested that

Gothic style signified ancient lineage and the British Constitution (43).

Sample list of Works Cited

All sources are listed alphabetically in the list of Works Cited, giving all details of author, title and publication. The first line of the reference is not indented, but subsequent lines are indented by ½ inch (1.3cm) so that authors' names are easily identifiable. End each reference with a full stop. The list of Works Cited for the sample text above would look like this.

Works Cited

Adam, Robert. *Ruins of the Palace of the Emperor Diocletian at Spalatro in Dalmatia*. London, 1764. *Eighteenth Century Collections Online*. https://library.dur.ac.uk/record=b2274207~S1. Accessed 21 Dec. 2018.

Buchanan, Alexandrina. "Interpretations of Medieval Architecture." *Gothic Architecture and Its Meanings 1550–1830*, edited by Michael Hall, Spire, 2002, pp. 27–52.

Lang, S. "The Principles of the Gothic Revival in England." *Journal of the Society of Architectural Historians*, vol. 25, no. 4, 1966, pp. 240–267. *JSTOR*, www.jstor-org.ezphost.dur.ac.uk/stable/988353.

Leach, Peter. "James Paine's Design for the South Front of Kedleston Hall: Dating and Sources." *Architectural History*, vol. 40, 1997, pp. 159–170.

Nappo, Salvatore. *Pompeii: Its Discovery and Preservation*. 2012. www.bbc.co.uk/history/ancient/romans/pompeii_rediscovery_01.shtml. Accessed 21 Dec. 2018.

Palladio, Andrea. I Quattro Libri Dell'Archittetura [*The Four Books of Architecture*]. D. De Franceschi, 1570.

Worsley, Giles. "Adam as a Palladian." *Adam in Context: Papers Given at the Georgian Group Symposium 1992*, edited by Giles Worsley, Georgian Group, 1993, pp. 6–13.

---. *Classical Architecture in Britain: The Heroic Age*. Yale UP, 1995.

Section K
Oxford University Standard for the Citation of Legal Authorities (OSCOLA)

Many UK law schools and legal publications use the 4th edition of the *Oxford University Standard for the Citation of Legal Authorities* (OSCOLA). For more information on using OSCOLA, see Meredith, S. and Nolan, D. (2012) *Oxford University Standard for Citation of Legal Authorities*. 4th edn. and the OSCOLA (2006) *Citing International Law Sources Section*. Available at: http://www.law.ox.ac.uk/publications/oscola.php (Accessed: 27 July 2018).

Conventions when using the OSCOLA referencing style

♦ OSCOLA uses numeric **references** in the text linked to full citations in footnotes
♦ Very little punctuation is used
♦ Well-established abbreviations are used for the titles of legal sources such as law reports and parliamentary publications (for example, the journal title *Modern Law Review* is abbreviated to MLR). For details of the accepted abbreviations for legal publications, see the Cardiff University *Cardiff Index to Abbreviations* at http://www.legalabbrevs.cardiff.ac.uk/
♦ OSCOLA assumes that you are referencing UK legal sources. If you are writing about legal material in several countries, use abbreviations of the nations to denote different jurisdictions – for example, Deregulation Act 2015 (UK), Homeland Security Act 2001 (USA)

Authors

♦ In the footnotes, give the author's name as written in the source, with the first name or initial(s) followed by surname – for example, Joan Bell. In the bibliography, reverse this and give the author's surname followed by the initials (not the full first name) – for example, Bell, J
♦ If there are two or three authors, list these in the order given in the source, not alphabetically, with 'and' between the second and third authors
♦ If there are four or more authors, give the name of the first author followed by 'and others'
♦ An organisation can be cited as the author if there are no individual authors
♦ If the source does not have an author, use two em dashes instead (——), but if it is an editorial without a named author, use Editorial instead of the author's name

Examples in footnotes

One author

1. Jane Sendall, *Family Law* (OUP 2018).

Two authors

2. Alan Dignam and John Lowry, *Company Law* (9th edn, OUP 2016).

Three authors

3. Alan Dignam, Andrew Hicks and SH Goo, *Hicks & Goo's Cases and Materials on Company Law* (7th edn, OUP 2011).

Four or more authors

4. FE Forrest and others, *Political Theory* (Ashfield 1999).

Organisation as author

5. European Parliament, 'Cross-border Mergers and Divisions, Transfers of Seat: Is There a Need to Legislate?' (2016) PE 556.960.

No author

——, 'Brexit Referendum: Local Results' (Durham Voice July 2016).

General principles

Although OSCOLA provides examples of many sources, it is not comprehensive. If the type of source is not listed in the OSCOLA guidelines, general principles should be followed.

If the source has an ISBN, cite it like a book and have the title in *italics*. Although older books did not have ISBNs, they had author, title, place of publication and publisher, so would be cited with the title in *italics*.

If the source is recent and does not have an ISBN, use the general principles for secondary sources (OSCOLA p. 33) for the citation order:

♦ Author
♦ Title (in single quotation marks)
♦ Additional information such as report number, publisher, date of publication (all in round brackets)
♦ If online, add <URL> and accessed date

These can be applied to a wide range of sources.

Examples in footnotes

1. Competition & Markets Authority, 'Decision of the Competition and Markets Authority: Online resale price maintenance in the bathroom fittings sector' (Case CE/9857-14, 2016) <https://assets.publishing.service.gov.uk/media/573b150740f0b6155b00000a/bathroom-fittings-sector-non-conf-decision.pdf> accessed 25 August 2018.

2. Roberta Panizza, 'The Principle of Subsidiarity' (Factsheets on European Union, May 2018) <http://www.europarl.europa.eu/ftu/pdf/en/FTU_1.2.2.pdf> accessed 25 August 2018.

3. Crown Prosecution Service, 'Human Trafficking, Smuggling and Slavery' (2018) <https://www.cps.gov.uk/legal-guidance/human-trafficking-smuggling-and-slavery> accessed 25 August 2018.

Online sources

It is very easy to locate legal sources online using library databases and internet searches, but type of publication may be difficult to establish, especially if you have located PDFs of reports, articles or book chapters. Look for authors, publishing organisations, details of any series or larger work that the source may be part of, identification number, ISBNs, DOIs, or titles. If in doubt, apply the general principles on p. 33 of the OSCOLA 4th edition, as in the above examples, giving as much information as you can to help your reader locate the source.

Pinpointing

If you wish to cite a specific page within a source, include this page number at the end of the reference. For example, if you wished to pinpoint something on p. 1357 of a report running from pages 1354 to 1372, you would write:

R v Dunlop [2006] EWCA Crim 1354, 1357.

Repeated references and cross-referencing

If you are referencing in your text a source that you have already cited in the footnotes, you do not need to give the full reference again. If you are referring again to the previous source, you can use **ibid** (note that this is not italicised). If you are referencing a source earlier than the previous one, use the footnote number of the original reference and a short title or author surname. If you are referencing a different page than the earlier footnote, give the new page number at the end of the new footnote.

Examples in footnotes

1. *R v Edwards (John)* (1991) 93 Cr App R 48.

2. Ibid 50.

3. CMV Clarkson, *Criminal Law: Text and Materials* (7th edn, Sweet & Maxwell 2010).

4. *R v Edwards* (n1) 53.

NB Footnote 2 uses ibid as it follows immediately after the same source, but directs the reader to a different page. Footnote 4 refers the reader back to footnote 1 (n1) where the full reference is given, but directs attention to what is written on p. 53.

Referencing several works by the same author

If you have two publications by Smith, give full details of each source the first time that you cite it, and subsequently use their name and a short form of the title of the source.

Examples in footnotes

1. Smith, *Corporate liability*.
2. Smith, 'Shareholder responsibilities'.

How to reference common sources

K1   Books

Citation order:

♦ Author
♦ Book title (in italics and capitalise first letter of each word in title, except for linking words such as and, or, the, for)
♦ Edition, publisher year (in round brackets)

Example in footnotes

1. Alan Dignam and John Lowry, *Company Law* (9th edn, OUP 2016).

K2 Chapters in edited books

Citation order:

♦ Author
♦ Chapter title (in single quotation marks)
♦ in editor (ed)
♦ Book title (in italics)
♦ Edition, publisher year (in round brackets)

Example in footnotes

1. Paul Matthews, 'The Legal and Moral Limits of Common Law Tracing' in Peter Birks (ed), *Laundering and Tracing* (Clarendon Press 1995).

K3 Translated works

Citation order:

♦ Author
♦ Title (in italics)
♦ Name of translator tr, publisher year (all in round brackets)

Example in footnotes

1. Antonio Padoa-Schioppa, *A History of Law in Europe* (Caterina Fitzgerald tr, CUP 2017).

K4 Encyclopedias

Citation order:

♦ Title of encyclopedia (in italics)
♦ Edition, year of issue (in round brackets)

If pinpointing, add volume and page or paragraph number.

Example in footnotes

1. *Halsbury's Laws* (5th edn, 2018) vol 6, para 363.

K4.1 Authored entry within an encyclopedia

Citation order:

♦ Author
♦ Title of entry (in single quotation marks)
♦ Title of encyclopedia (in italics)
♦ Edition, year of issue (in round brackets)
♦ If online, add <URL> accessed date

Example in footnotes

1. M. Schmeeckle, 'Foster Care', *The Wiley Blackwell Encyclopedia of Family Studies* (2016) <https://library.dur.ac.uk/record=b2898148~S1> accessed 29 July 2018.

K5 Works of authority

Older texts that are accepted as definitive guides to the law at the time of their publication use abbreviations (see p. 36 of the OSCOLA guide).

Example

A reference to a quotation on page 329 in the fourth volume of William Blackstone, *Commentaries on the Laws of England* (4 vols Oxford 1765–69)

is abbreviated in footnotes to

1. 4 Bl Comm 329.

K6 Looseleaf services

Citation order:

♦ Title of the source (in italics)

NB You do not need to include publication details.

> **Example in footnotes**
>
> 1. *Blackstone's Criminal Practice.*

If pinpointing in a footnote, include the volume and paragraph number.

> **Example in footnotes**
>
> 2. *Blackstone's Criminal Practice*, part B4, para 100.

K7   Pamphlets

Citation order:

♦ Author
♦ Title (in italics)
♦ Pamphlet series title, number, abbreviation of publisher and year of publication (all in round brackets)

> **Example in footnotes**
>
> 1. John W Jones, *The Nazi Conception of Law* (Oxford Pamphlets on World Affairs no 21, OUP 1939).

K8   Journal articles

Citation order:

♦ Author
♦ Article title (in single quotation marks)
♦ Year (use square brackets if it identifies the volume; use round brackets if there is a separate volume number)
♦ Volume number
♦ Issue number (in round brackets)
♦ Abbreviated journal title
♦ First page number

> **Example in footnotes: with volume number**
>
> 1. AJ Roberts, 'Evidence: Bad Character – Pre-Criminal Justice Act 2003 Law' (2008) 4 Crim LR 303.

> **Example in footnotes: with no volume number**
>
> 2. Po-Jen Yap, 'Defending Dialogue' [2012] PL 527.

K9   Ejournal articles

Citation order:

♦ Author
♦ Article title (in single quotation marks)
♦ [Year] or (Year)
♦ Volume number
♦ Issue number (in round brackets)
♦ Abbreviated journal title
♦ First page number
♦ <URL> *or* <DOI>
♦ Accessed date

> **Example in footnotes**
>
> 1. Cormac Behan and Ian O'Donnell, 'Prisoners, Politics and the Polls: Enfranchisement and the Burden of Responsibility' (2008) 48(3) Brit J Criminol, 31 <doi:10.1093/bjc/azn004> accessed 14 September 2018.

K10   Newspaper articles

Citation order:

♦ Author or Editorial
♦ Article title (in single quotation marks)
♦ Title of newspaper (in italics)
♦ Place of publication, full date (in round brackets)
♦ Page number

Example in footnotes

1. Joanne Hart, 'Tax is no burden for software firm' *Mail on Sunday* (London, 29 July 2018) 48.

K10.1 Online news articles

Citation order:

♦ Author or Editorial
♦ Article title (in single quotation marks)
♦ Title of news source (in italics)
♦ Date (in round brackets)
♦ Section title (if available)
♦ <URL>
♦ Accessed date

Examples in footnotes

1. ——, 'Pop Star Rihanna Wins Image Battle' *BBC News* (22 January 2015) <https://www.bbc.co.uk/news/entertainment-arts-30932158> accessed 19 November 2018.

2. Editorial, 'The rise in youth knife crime should be treated as an emergency' *Independent* (24 June 2018) <https://www.independent.co.uk/voices/editorials/knife-crime-london-stabbing-death-police-investigations-weapons-a8413516.html> accessed 27 July 2018.

K11 Book reviews

Citation order:

♦ Author
♦ Review of
♦ Author and title of book being reviewed
♦ Journal citation or newspaper reference

Example in footnotes

1. John Eekelaar, Review of Anita Bernstein (ed), *Marriage Proposals: Questioning a Legal Status* (2012) 8(2) Int JLC 320.

K12 Websites

Citation order:

♦ Author
♦ Title of web page (in single quotation marks)
♦ Title of website (in italics), date (all in round brackets)
♦ <URL>
♦ Accessed date

Example in footnotes

1. Joshua Habgood-Coote, 'The term "fake news" is doing great harm' (*The Conversation*, 27 July 2018) <https://theconversation.com/the-term-fake-news-is-doing-great-harm-100406> accessed 29 July 2018.

K13 Blogs

Citation order:

♦ Author
♦ Title of post (in single quotation marks)
♦ Title of blog (in italics), full date of post (all in round brackets)
♦ <URL>
♦ Accessed date

Example in footnotes

1. Lorraine, '22 and a Path to Tech Law' (*Life of a London Law Student*, 13 December 2017) <https://lifeofalondonlawstudent.com/> accessed 28 July 2018.

K14   Podcasts

Citation order:

- ♦ Author (if unavailable, use organisation providing podcast)
- ♦ Title of podcast episode (in single quotation marks)
- ♦ Date (in round brackets)
- ♦ <URL>
- ♦ Accessed date

Example in footnotes

1. Emma-Louise Fenelon, 'Episode 36: Secrecy, anonymity and public information' (14 June 2018) <https://itunes.apple.com/us/podcast/law-pod-uk/id1259360349> accessed 29 July 2018.

K15   Radio/television programmes

Citation order:

- ♦ Title (in single quotation marks)
- ♦ Radio or television channel, date of broadcast (all in round brackets)
- ♦ If online, add <URL> accessed date

If you are quoting a speaker in the programme, begin the reference with their name.

Examples in footnotes

1. 'Inside Britain's Moped Gangs' (BBC Three, 21 February 2018) <https://www.bbc.co.uk/iplayer/episode/p05x9kfp/inside-britains-moped-crime-gangs> accessed 1 August 2018.

2. Livvy Haydock, 'Inside Britain's Moped Gangs' (BBC Three, 21 February 2018) <https://www.bbc.co.uk/iplayer/episode/p05x9kfp/inside-britains-moped-crime-gangs> accessed 1 August 2018.

3. 'Law in Action – Facial Recognition Technology' (BBC Radio 4, 26 June 2018) <https://www.bbc.co.uk/programmes/b006tgy1/episodes/downloads> accessed 1 August 2018.

K16   Speeches/lectures

Citation order:

- ♦ Name of speaker
- ♦ Title of speech (in single quotation marks)
- ♦ Additional information, venue and date (in round brackets)

Examples in footnotes

1. Jocelyn Simon, 'With all my Worldly Goods' (Holdsworth Club of the University of Birmingham, 23 May 1964).

2. Natalie Williams, 'Privacy law' (LAW204: Introduction to UK Law, Durham University, 8 November 2017).

K17   Conference papers

- ♦ Author
- ♦ Title of paper (in single quotation marks)
- ♦ Title, location and date of the conference (in round brackets)

If a conference paper has been published, cite the publication. If available online, include <URL> accessed date.

Examples in footnotes

1. Geoffrey Nice, 'What is the point of international human rights?' (JUSTICE Human Rights Conference 2017, London, 13 October 2017).

2. Christian Tietje and Andrej Lang, 'Community Interests in World Trade Law' (European Society of International Law 13th Annual Conference, Naples, 7–9 September 2017). Posted online 16 April 2018 <http://dx.doi.org/10.2139/ssrn.3170152> accessed 29 June 2018.

K18   Theses

Citation order:

♦ Author
♦ Title (in single quotation marks)
♦ Level, university year of award (in round brackets)
♦ If online, add <URL> accessed date

Example in footnotes

1. Sarah Emily Morley, 'Takeover Litigation: the US does it more than the UK, but why and does it matter?' (PhD thesis Durham University 2017) <http://etheses.dur.ac.uk/12228/> accessed 27 July 2018.

K19   Working and discussion papers

Citation order:

♦ Author
♦ Title of working paper (in single quotation marks)

♦ Year (in round brackets)
♦ Working paper series title
♦ Number
♦ <URL>
♦ Accessed date

Examples in footnotes

1. City of London Law Society, 'Fixed and Floating Charges on Insolvency' (2014) Secured Transactions Reform, 2 <http://www.citysolicitors.org.uk/attachments/article/121/20140219%20Secured%20Transactions%20Reform%20Discussion%20Paper%202%20Fixed%20and%20floating%20charges%20v2.pdf> accessed 18 July 2018.

2. Sonia Livingstone, John Carr and Jasmina Byrne, 'One in Three: Internet Governance and Children's Rights' (2016) UNICEF Office of Research – Innocenti Discussion Paper 2016-1 <https://www.unicef-irc.org/publications/pdf/idp_2016_01.pdf > accessed 28 July 2018.

K20   Bills (House of Commons and House of Lords)

Citation order:

♦ Short title
♦ House in which it originated
♦ Parliamentary session (in round brackets)
♦ Bill number (in square brackets for Commons Bills, no brackets for Lords Bills)

Examples in footnotes

1. Transport HC Bill (1999–2000) [8].

2. Transport HL Bill (2007–08) 1.

K21 UK statutes (Acts of Parliament)

A change in the citation of UK legal sources took place in 1963. Before this, an Act was cited according to the regnal year (that is, the number of years since the monarch's accession). You may see references to legislation in this format in early publications.

Example in footnotes

1. Act of Supremacy 1534 (26 Hen 8 c1).

OSCOLA recommends that when citing all legislation (including earlier Acts), you should use the short title of the Act, with the year in which it was enacted, as shown in the example below.

K21.1 Whole Acts of Parliament

Use the short title of an Act, with the year in which it was enacted.

Citation order:

♦ Short title
♦ Year enacted

Example in footnotes

1. Deregulation Act 2015.

K21.2 Parts of Acts

Citation order:

♦ Short title
♦ Year enacted
♦ s followed by section number
♦ Subsection number (in round brackets)
♦ Paragraph number (in round brackets)

Example in footnotes

1. Finance Act 2015, s 2(1)(a).

K22 Statutory Instruments (SIs)

Citation order:

♦ Name/title
♦ SI year/number

Example in footnotes

1. Detention Centre Rules 2001, SI 2001/238.

K23 Command Papers

Citation order:

♦ Author
♦ Title (in italics)
♦ Paper number and year (in round brackets)

Example in footnotes

1. Lord Chancellor's Department, *Government Policy on Archives* (Cm 4516, 1999).

K24   Law reports (cases)

Which case to cite?

In the UK, there is no single publication covering all cases heard in courts. Instead, there are many general reports (such as All England Law Reports) and specialist reports (such as Industrial Relations Law Reports) that publish selections of cases. The same case may be reported in several publications, or not reported at all.

If the case is reported in several publications, there is an order of preference for which one to cite in your work. If possible, use a citation from one of the Law Reports (Supreme Court/House of Lords, Privy Council Appeal Cases, Chancery Division, Family Division, Queen's Bench), but if these are not available, use the citations (in order of preference) from Weekly Law Reports or All England Law Reports. If a case is not reported in any of these, use the citation for the specialist report or newspaper. The titles of publications are abbreviated in OSCOLA. For details of the accepted abbreviations, see Cardiff University's *Cardiff index to legal abbreviations* at http://www.legalabbrevs. cardiff.ac.uk.

Citation order:

♦ Name of parties involved in case (in italics)
♦ Year (use square brackets if the year identifies the volume, use round brackets if each annual volume is numbered and the year is not required to identify the volume)
♦ Volume number and abbreviation for name of report and first page of report

Example in footnotes: with [Year]

1. *Hazell v Hammersmith and Fulham London Borough Council* [1992] 2 AC 1.

NB Date in square brackets because the year identifies the volume required. In this instance, the 2 means that this case appeared in the second volume for the year 1992.

Example in footnotes: with (Year)

1. *R v Edwards (John)* (1991) 93 Cr App R 48.

NB Date in round brackets because there is also a volume number: this is the 93rd volume of Criminal Appeal Reports.

Neutral citations

From 2002, cases have been given a neutral citation that identifies the case without referring to the printed law report series in which the case was published. This helps to identify the case online – for example, through the freely available transcripts of the British and Irish Legal Information Institute (www.bailii.org).

Citation order:

♦ Name of parties involved in case (in italics)

- Year (in square brackets)
- Court
- Number of case in that year

Example in footnotes

1. *Humphreys v Revenue and Customs* [2012] UKSC 18.

This shows that Humphreys v Revenue and Customs was the 18th case heard by the UK Supreme Court in 2012.

If your source uses paragraph numbers rather than page numbers (for example, neutral citations), give the citation followed by the number of the paragraph in square brackets.

Example in footnotes

1. *Humphreys v Revenue and Customs* [2012] UKSC 18 [8].

If citing several separate paragraphs, put each in square brackets separated by a comma.

Example in footnotes

1. *Humphreys v Revenue and Customs* [2012] UKSC 18 [8], [14].

If citing several adjacent paragraphs, put the first and last numbers in square brackets separated by a dash.

Example in footnotes

1. *Humphreys v Revenue and Customs* [2012] UKSC 18 [15]–[21].

The use of neutral citations does not help with locating cases in printed law reports. You will need to add the citation for the law report after the neutral citation.

Example in footnotes

1. *Humphreys v Revenue and Customs* [2012] UKSC 18, [2012] 1 WLR 1545.

This shows that the case was reported in the first volume of the *Weekly Law Reports* for 2012, starting on p. 1545.

Citing names of judges

If you wish to quote something said by a judge, include their name in the text associated with the source you are citing:

Example in footnotes

1. In *R v Jones*,[7] Williams LJ noted …

If the judge is a peer, you would write, for example, 'Lord Blackstone'. If the judge is a Mr, Mrs or Ms, you would write 'Blackstone J' (J for judge); if a Lord Justice or Lady Justice, you would write 'Blackstone LJ'.

Judge's comments in case report

If you wish to pinpoint comments, add the page number and the judge's name after the citation.

Example in footnotes

1. *Donohue v Stevenson* [1932] AC 562, 580 (Atkin LJ).

Unreported cases

Many UK cases are not published in Law Reports. To cite an unreported case, give the party names, followed by the name of the court and the date in round brackets, followed by the case number if available. If the case has a neutral citation, give this after the party names.

> **Example in footnotes**
>
> 1. *R v Tom Hayes* (Southwark Crown Court, 3 August 2015) Case no. T20137308.

K25 *Hansard*

Hansard is the official record of debates and speeches given in Parliament.

Citation order:

◆ Abbreviation of House
◆ Deb (for debates)
◆ Date of debate
◆ Volume number
◆ Column number

> **Example in footnotes**
>
> 1. HC Deb 19 June 2008, vol 477, col 1183.

If you are citing a Commons Written Answer, use the suffix W after the column number.

> **Example in footnotes**
>
> 1. HC Deb 19 June 2008, vol 477, col 1106W.

If you are citing a Lords Written Answer, use the prefix WA before the column number.

> **Example in footnotes**
>
> 1. HL Deb 19 June 2008, vol 702, col WA200.

Use the suffix WS if you are citing a Written Statement.

> **Example in footnotes**
>
> 1. HC Deb 18 September 2006, vol 449, col 134WS.

Use the suffix WH if you are citing a debate in Westminster Hall.

> **Example in footnotes**
>
> 1. HC Deb 21 May 2008, vol 476, col 101WH.

If quoting very old *Hansards*, it is usual, although optional, to include the series number.

> **Example in footnotes**
>
> 1. HC Deb (5th series) 13 January 1907 vol 878, cols 69–70.

In 2007, the earlier system of Standing Committees was replaced by Public Bill Committees. Standing Committee *Hansard* should be cited follows:

> **Example in footnotes**
>
> 1. SC Deb (A) 13 May 1998, col 345.

The new Public Bill Committees would be cited as follows:

> **Example in footnotes**
>
> 1. Health Bill Deb 30 January 2007, cols 12–15.

unless the Bill title is so long that this becomes ridiculous. In this case, use the following:

> **Example in footnotes**
>
> 1. PBC Deb (Bill 99) 30 January 2007, cols 12–15.

Or, where the context makes the Bill obvious, use the following:

Example in footnotes

1. PBC Deb 30 January 2007, cols 12–15.

Since 12 September 2014, written questions and answers have been published in the Written questions and answers database (http://www.parliament.uk/business/publications/written-questions-answers-statements/written-questions-answers/) instead of *Hansard*. This means that the column reference is no longer used. Questions and answers in the database are given a number to include in their citation. At the time of writing (October 2018), there was no guidance from OSCOLA for citing written questions and answers. Adapting the format for pre-September 2014 written questions and answers, we suggest the following.

Example of written question and answer (Commons) in footnotes

1. HC 9 October 2015, PQ 9236.

Example of written question and answer (Lords) in footnotes

1. HL 7 September 2015, HL 1950.

In addition, written ministerial statements (which continue to be published in *Hansard*) are also published in the database.

Example of Commons written statement in footnotes

1. HC 25 June 2015, HCWS 55.

K26   House of Commons briefing papers

Citation order:

♦ Author
♦ Title (in single quotation marks)
♦ Series, number and date of publication (all in round brackets)
♦ <URL>
♦ Accessed date

Example in footnotes

1. Feargal McGuinness, 'Poverty in the UK: Statistics' (House of Commons Library Briefing Paper 7096, 23 April 2018) <https://researchbriefings.parliament.uk/ResearchBriefing/Summary/SN07096> accessed 29 July 2018.

K27   Legislation from the devolved legislatures in the UK

K27.1   Acts of the Scottish Parliament

For Acts of the post-devolution Scottish Parliament, replace the chapter number with 'asp' (meaning Act of the Scottish Parliament).

Citation order:

♦ Title of Act including year
♦ asp number (in round brackets)

Example in footnotes

1. Scottish Elections (Reduction of Voting Age) Act 2015 (asp 7).

K27.2 Scottish Statutory Instruments (SSIs)

Citation order:

♦ Title including year
♦ SSI number

Example in footnotes

1. Tuberculosis (Scotland) Order 2005, SSI 2005/434.

K27.3 Acts of the Northern Ireland Assembly

Citation order:

♦ Title of Act (Northern Ireland)
♦ Year

Example in footnotes

1. Ground Rents Act (Northern Ireland) 2001.

K27.4 Statutory Rules of Northern Ireland

The Northern Ireland Assembly may pass Statutory Instruments. These are called Statutory Rules of Northern Ireland.

Citation order:

♦ Title of Rule (Northern Ireland)
♦ Year
♦ SR year/number

Example in footnotes

1. Smoke Flavourings Regulations (Northern Ireland) 2005, SR 2005/76.

K27.5 National Assembly for Wales legislation

K27.5a Assembly Measures (nawm)

The National Assembly for Wales may pass Assembly Measures (nawm), which are primary legislation but are subordinate to UK statutes.

Citation order:

♦ Title of Assembly Measure
♦ Year
♦ nawm number (in round brackets)

Example in footnotes

1. NHS Redress (Wales) Measure 2008 (nawm 1).

K27.5b Welsh Statutory Instruments

The National Assembly for Wales may also pass Statutory Instruments. As well as the SI number and year, Welsh Statutory Instruments have a W. number.

Citation order:

♦ Title of Order (Wales)
♦ Year
♦ Year/SI number (W. number)

Example in footnotes

1. The Bluetongue (Wales) Order 2003 Welsh Statutory Instrument 2003/326 (W 47).

K28 Law Commission reports and consultation papers

Citation order:

♦ Law Commission
♦ Title of report or consultation paper (in italics)

- Number of report or consultation paper, and year (in round brackets)

Example in footnotes

1. Law Commission, *Double Jeopardy and Prosecution Appeals* (Law Com No 267, 2001).

K29 European Union (EU) legal sources

EU legislation may be legislation, directives, decisions and regulations. The most authoritative source is the *Official Journal of the European Union*.

K29.1 EU legislation

Citation order:

- Legislation title
- Year (in square brackets)
- Official Journal (OJ) series
- Issue/first page

Example in footnotes

1. Consolidated Version of the Treaty on European Union [2008] OJ C115/13.

K29.2 EU directives, decisions and regulations

Citation order:

- Legislation type
- Number and title
- Year (in square brackets)
- Official Journal (OJ) L series
- Issue/first page

Examples in footnotes

Directives

1. Council Directive 2008/52/EC on certain aspects of mediation in civil and commercial matters [2008] OJ L136/3.

Regulations

2. Council Regulation (EU) 2015/760 on European long-term investment funds [2015] OJ L123/98.

Commission Decisions

3. *DS Smith/Duropack* (Case No COMP/M.7558) Commission Decision [2015] OJ C207/3.

K29.3 Judgements of the European Court of Justice (ECJ) and General Court (GC)

Citation order:

- Prefix ('Case C-' for the ECJ or 'Case T-' for the GC)
- Case registration number
- Case name (in italics)
- Year (in square brackets)
- Report citation

If you need to pinpoint within the ECR report, use para(s) after the case number.

Examples in footnotes

1. Case C-111/03 *Commission of the European Communities v Kingdom of Sweden* [2005] ECR I-08789.

2. Case T-8/89 *DSM NV v Commission of the European Communities* [1991] ECR II-01833, para 132.

K29.4 European Case Law Identifier (ECLI)

The European Case Law Identifier (ECLI) was introduced in 2014 to provide a standardised descriptor for cases from the European Court of Justice, the European Court of Human Rights, the European Civil Service Tribunal and the European Patent Office. Several European nations have also adopted the ECLI for cases heard by their courts. ECLI numbers have been retrospectively applied to all EU court cases from 1954 onwards.

An ECLI consists of five parts, separated by colons:

◆ ECLI
◆ The code for the country or jurisdiction
◆ The code for the court that made the judgement
◆ The year of the judgement
◆ An ordinal number or unique number to identify each case

The 4th edition of OSCOLA does not have examples that include ECLIs. Until the 5th edition is published, use an ECLI as you would a neutral citation in a UK case, after the party names and before the case citation.

Example in footnotes

1. Case C-111/03 *Commission of the European Communities v Kingdom of Sweden* ECLI:EU:C:2005:619, [2005] ECR I-08789.

K30 International law sources

Guidance on citing international legal sources is given in OSCOLA (2006) *Citing International Law Sources Section*, available at https://www.law.ox.ac.uk/research-subject-groups/publications/oscola (Accessed: 25 July 2018).

K30.1 United Nations documents

Citation order:

◆ Author
◆ Title
◆ Date (in round brackets)
◆ Document number

Example in footnotes

1. UNSC Res 1970 (26 February 2011) UN Doc S/RES/1970.

K30.2 International treaties

Citation order:

◆ Title of treaty
◆ Date adopted (in round brackets)
◆ Publication citation
◆ Short title (in round brackets)
◆ Article number

If possible, cite from the United Nations Treaty Series (UNTS).

When you mention a treaty for the first time in your text, give the formal and the short title in round brackets. In subsequent references, use the short title.

Example

In-text citation

Britain supported the Convention Relating to the Status of Refugees (Refugee Convention).[1]

Footnote

1. Convention Relating to the Status of Refugees (adopted 28 July 1951, entered into force 22 April 1954) 189 UNTS 137 (Refugee Convention) art 33.

Subsequent footnote example

4. Refugee Convention (n1).

K30.3 International Court of Justice (ICJ) cases

Citation order:

♦ Case name (in italics)
♦ Year (in square brackets)
♦ ICJ report citation or website and date accessed

Examples in footnotes

1. *Corfu Channel Case (UK v Albania) (Merits)* [1949] ICJ Rep 4.

2. *Maritime Dispute (Peru v. Chile)* [2014] ICJ Judgement <http://www.icj-cij.org/docket/files/137/17930.pdf> accessed 14 September 2018.

K31 US legal material

For information on citing and referencing US legal material, see *The Bluebook: a uniform system of citation* (2015) 20th edn. Cambridge, MA: Harvard Law Review Association. A useful online guide is Martin, P.W. (2015) *Introduction to basic legal citation*. Available at: http://www.law.cornell.edu/citation/ (Accessed: 14 September 2018).

K32   Unpublished emails and letters

Citation order:

♦ Form of communication
♦ Author
♦ Recipient
♦ Date (in round brackets)

Examples in footnotes

1. Email from Lord Justice Williams to Theresa May MP (28 June 2018).

2. Letter from Dr J Singh to Mrs T Collins (14 August 2018).

K33   Interviews

Citation order:

♦ Name, position and institution (if relevant) of the interviewee
♦ Location of the interview and date (in round brackets)

Example in footnotes

1. Interview with Jane Stephenson, Professor of International Law, Durham University (Durham, 19 October 2018).

Sample text

The Judge noted the case of *R v Edwards*.[1] The Detention Centre Rules 2001 strengthened this interpretation.[2] An alternative view was suggested by Clarkson.[3] Clarkson highlighted contradictions in the interpretation.[4] Behan and O'Donnell agreed with the Judge's view.[5] They disagreed with Clarkson's opinion on detention.[6] The case left many questions to be resolved.[7]

Sample footnotes

1. *R v Edwards (John)* (1991) 93 Cr App R 48.

2. Detention Centre Rules 2001, SI 2001/238.

3. CMV Clarkson, *Criminal law: text and materials* (7th edn, Sweet & Maxwell 2010) 47.

4. Ibid 56.

5. Cormac Behan and Ian O'Donnell, 'Prisoners, politics and the polls: enfranchisement and the burden of responsibility' (2008) 48(3) Brit J Criminol 31, 37 <doi:10.1093/bjc/azn004> accessed 14 September 2018.

6. Clarkson (n 3) 50.

7. *R v Edwards* (n 1) 49.

Bibliographies

OSCOLA (2012, 4th edn) suggests that for longer assignments such as theses and for books, a separate **bibliography** listing secondary sources (everything except legislation and cases) should be provided. Some law schools require that students provide a separate bibliography with all assignments, so check with your tutor if a bibliography is required as well as footnotes.

Authors' names should have surname followed by initials of given names (not full given names). This should be in alphabetical order by authors' name. Any works without an author should start with a dash, followed by the title. These unattributed sources are listed at the beginning of the bibliography in alphabetical order by the first major word of the title. A sample bibliography for the examples of secondary sources in this section is as follows.

Behan C and O'Donnell I, 'Prisoners, Politics and the Polls: Enfranchisement and the Burden of Responsibility' (2008) 48(3) Brit J Criminol, 31 <doi:10.1093/bjc/azn004> accessed 14 September 2018.

Clarkson CMV, *Criminal Law: Text and Materials* (7th edn, Sweet & Maxwell 2010).

Law Commission, *Double Jeopardy and Prosecution Appeals* (Law Com No 267, 2001).

Lord Chancellor's Department, *Government Policy on Archives* (Cm 4516, 1999).

Matthews P, 'The Legal and Moral Limits of Common Law Tracing' in Birks P (ed), *Laundering and Tracing* (Clarendon Press 1995).

Roberts AJ, 'Evidence: Bad Character – Pre-Criminal Justice Act 2003 Law' (2008) 4 Crim LR, 303.

Note that footnotes end with a full stop, but bibliography entries do not.

Section L
Vancouver referencing style

The Vancouver referencing style is a numeric citation system used in biomedical, health and some science publications. It was first defined in 1978 at the conference of the International Committee of Medical Journal Editors (ICMJE) in Vancouver, Canada, hence its name. The authoritative source for Vancouver referencing is Patrias, K. and Wendling, D. (eds) (2007–2018) *Citing medicine: the NLM style guide for authors, editors, and publishers*. 2nd ed. [Online version last updated 18 May 2018]. Available at: https://www.ncbi.nlm.nih.gov/books/NBK7256/ (Accessed: 12 September 2018).

Conventions when using the Vancouver referencing style

♦ Vancouver uses numeric references in the text, either numbers in round brackets (1) or **superscript** [1]
♦ The same citation number is used whenever a source is cited in your text
♦ These in-text numbers are matched to full numbered references for each publication in a reference list
♦ The reference list gives publications in the order they appear in the text, not alphabetically
♦ Very little punctuation is used
♦ Well-established abbreviations are used for journal titles and US states
♦ There is no agreement among citation authorities about the use of page numbers with in-text citations in Vancouver style. If you wish to use page numbers, we suggest the following format:

Example

In-text citation
Smith (1, p. #) described two examples …

… where # is the page number in source 1.

♦ If using superscript numeric references, use the following format:

Example

In-text citation
Smith[1 (p. #)] described two examples …

Multiple citations

♦ If you have written a section of text based upon several references, these are indicated by listing each source separated by a comma

Example

Several drug trials (3,6,9,12) proved …

Author names

♦ Authors should be cited by surname, then initials

Example

Collinton MS.

♦ Note that there is no comma between the surname and initials, nor any period (full stop) after the initials or spaces between the initials. Indicate the end of the author's name with a full stop

- Authors should be listed in the order shown in the article or book, not alphabetically
- Romanise all author names
- Remove accents and diacritics from letters in author names – for example, ñ should be written as n, and Ø written as O

Multiple authors

- Many science publications are the result of collaborative work, resulting in multiple authors who require citation. If you have six authors or fewer, list all of them, separating their names with a comma. Use a full stop to indicate the end of the authors' names. If there are more than six authors, *Citing medicine* suggests citing the first six authors followed by et al. or 'and others'

Example

Bourne AD, Davis P, Fuller E, Hanson AJ, Price KN, Vaughan JT, et al.

Organisations as authors

- Names of organisations are spelt out, not abbreviated

Example

General Medical Council.

No authors identified

- If no authors or editors are listed, use the title of the book, journal article or website

Editors

- Unlike other citation styles shown in *Cite them right*, the Vancouver system never abbreviates the word 'editor'

Example

Redclift N, Gibbon S, editors. Genetics: critical concepts in social and cultural theory. London: Routledge; 2017. 4 vols.

Edition

- The abbreviation ed. is used for edition

Example

Bradley JR, Johnson DR, Pober BR. Medical genetics. 9th ed. Malden, MA: Blackwell Science; 2018. 160 p.

Dates

- Dates are given as 'Year' for books or 'Year month (abbreviated) day' for articles

Article titles

- Article titles follow immediately after the author names
- The article titles are in standard text and are not enclosed in quotation marks, nor italicised or underlined
- Capitalise the first word of the article title, **proper nouns** and initials
- For non-English titles, write the title as in the journal article, but give a translation in square brackets immediately after the original form
- Use a full stop to indicate the end of the article title

Journal titles

- Journal titles are abbreviated. If the correct abbreviation is not included in the journal article you have used, check the *National Library of Medicine List of Serials Indexed for Online Users* (http://www.nlm.nih.gov/tsd/serials/lsiou.html). Use a capital letter for each word of the abbreviated title – for example, Annu Rev Cell Biol is the accepted abbreviation for *Annual Review of Cell Biology*

Book titles

♦ Only the first word and any proper nouns or acronyms are capitalised, and the title is neither underlined nor italicised
♦ Book titles should be written in their original language. Non-English titles should be followed by a translation of the title in square brackets

Example

Cite them right: the essential referencing guide.

Reference list and bibliography

♦ The reference list should only include sources you have cited in your text. List any sources you read but did not cite in your work in a separate bibliography

How to reference common sources in your reference list

L1   Books

Citation order:

♦ Author/editor
♦ Title (capitalise only the first letter of the first word and any proper nouns)
♦ Edition (only include the edition number if it is not the first edition)
♦ Place of publication: publisher; year of publication
♦ Number of pages (optional)

Example: single author

Reference list

1. Bleakley A. Patient-centred medicine in transition: The heart of the matter. Switzerland: Springer; 2014. 267 p.

Example: up to six authors

Reference list

2. Nussbaum R, McInnes R, Willard H. Genetics in medicine. 8th ed. Amsterdam: Elsevier; 2015. 560 p.

Example: more than six authors

Reference list

3. Bourne AD, Davis P, Hanson AJ, Price KN, Vaughan JT, Williams V, et al. Health systems. London: Fuller Ltd; 2008. 212 p.

L1.1   Multi-volume works

Citation order:

♦ Author/editor (if available)
♦ Title
♦ Place of publication: publisher; year
♦ Number of volumes.
♦ Number of pages (optional)

Example: whole publication

Reference list

4. British Pharmacopoeia 2018. London: The Stationery Office; 2017. 5 vols.

Example: reference within a specific volume

Reference list

5. British Pharmacopoeia 2018. Vol. 2. London: The Stationery Office; 2017.

L2 Ebooks

Citation order:

♦ Author/editor
♦ Title of ebook (capitalise only first letter of first word and any proper nouns)
♦ Edition (only include the edition number if it is not the first edition)
♦ [Internet]
♦ Place of publication: publisher; year of original publication
♦ Cited year month day (in square brackets)
♦ Available from: URL

Example

Reference list

6. Templeton AR. Population genetics and microevolutionary theory [Internet]. Hoboken (NJ): John Wiley and Sons; 2016 [cited 2018 Dec 23]. 262 p. Available from: http://library.dur.ac.uk/record=b2111435~S1

L3 Edited books

L3.1 Whole books

Citation order:

♦ Name of editor(s) of book
♦ editor(s)
♦ Title of book
♦ Place of publication: publisher; year of publication
♦ Number of pages (optional)

Example

Reference list

7. Knowles MA, Selby PJ, editors. Introduction to the cellular and molecular biology of cancer. Oxford: Oxford University Press; 2005. 288 p.

L3.2 Chapters/sections in edited books

Citation order:

♦ Author(s) of the chapter/section
♦ Title of chapter/section
♦ In
♦ Name of editor(s) of book
♦ editor(s)
♦ Title of book
♦ Place of publication: publisher; year of publication
♦ Page numbers (preceded by p.)

Example

Reference list

8. Hart I. The spread of tumours. In: Knowles MA, Selby PJ, editors. Introduction to the cellular and molecular biology of cancer. Oxford: Oxford University Press; 2005. p. 278–88.

L4 Journal articles

L4.1 Articles in print journals

Citation order:

♦ Author(s)
♦ Title of article
♦ Abbreviated title of journal
♦ Date of publication as year month day;
♦ Volume (issue): page numbers (not preceded by p.)

Example

Reference list

9. Consonni D, De Matteis S, Lubin JH, Wacholder S, Tucker M, Pesatori AC, et al. Lung cancer and occupation in a population-based case-control study. Am J Epidemiol. 2010 Feb 1; 171(3):323–33.

L4.2 Articles in ejournals

Citation order:

♦ Author(s)
♦ Title of article
♦ Abbreviated title of journal
♦ [Internet]
♦ Date of publication as year month day
♦ Cited date (in square brackets)
♦ Volume (issue): page numbers (not preceded by p.)
♦ Available from: URL DOI

Example
Reference list

10. Amr S, Wolpert B, Loffredo CA, Zheng YL, Shields PG, Jones R. Occupation, gender, race and lung cancer. J Occup Environ Med [Internet]. 2008 Oct [cited 2018 Feb 23]; 50(10):1167–75. Available from: https://europepmc.org/abstract/med/18849762 doi:10.1097/JOM.0b013e31817d3639

L5 Preprints

Preprints may be drafts of articles or working papers made available online to other researchers so that new research is available as soon as possible. They are published before peer-reviewing, so may differ significantly from later published articles. You should make it clear to your reader that you are citing a preprint, not a published article.

Citation order:

♦ Author
♦ Title of preprint
♦ Identifier
♦ [Preprint]
♦ Year
♦ Cited date (in square brackets)
♦ Available from: URL DOI

Example
Reference list

11. Nelson PC. The role of quantum decoherence in FRET. arXiv: 1809.05622 [Preprint]. 2018 [cited 2018 Sep 22]. Available from: https://www.cell.com/biophysj/fulltext/S0006-3495(18)30107-3 doi:10.1016/j.bpj.2018.01.010

L6 Systematic reviews

Citation order:

♦ Author (surname followed by initials)
♦ Title of review
♦ Year month day of review
♦ In:
♦ Title of database
♦ [Internet]
♦ Place of publication: publisher year
♦ File size
♦ Available from: URL DOI
♦ Year, issue number
♦ Record No.: CD …

Example
Reference list

12. Pasquali S, Hadjinicolaou AV, Chiarion Sileni V, Rossi CR, Mocellin S. Systemic treatments for metastatic cutaneous melanoma. 2018 Feb 6. In: The Cochrane Database of Systematic Reviews [Internet]. Hoboken (NJ): John Wiley & Sons, Ltd. c1999–2018. 3.28MB. Available from: https://www.cochranelibrary.com/cdsr/doi/10.1002/14651858.CD011123/full doi:10.1002/14651858.CD011123. pub2/pdf Record No.: CD011123

L7 Newspaper articles

L7.1 Articles in print newspapers

Citation order:

♦ Author
♦ Article title
♦ Newspaper title
♦ Edition, if applicable (in round brackets)
♦ Date
♦ Section (if applicable)
♦ Page and column

Example

Reference list

13. Vasquez T. Pharmacy company's R & D aims. Boston Globe (3rd ed.). 2018 Nov 17: C4 (col. 2).

L7.2 Articles in online newspapers

Citation order:

♦ Author
♦ Article title
♦ Newspaper title and edition (if applicable)
♦ [Internet]
♦ Date
♦ Cited date (in square brackets)
♦ Section (if applicable)
♦ Page and column or approximate location (number of screens in square brackets)
♦ Available from: URL

Example

Reference list

14. Merrick J. Robots are not the enemy. Independent [Internet]. 2015 Sept 15 [cited 2018 Nov 30]: Voices [about 3 screens]. Available from: https://www.independent.co.uk/voices/robots-are-not-the-enemy-its-time-to-stop-this-panic-about-them-replacing-us-10502464.html

L8 Theses or dissertations

Citation order:

♦ Author
♦ Title
♦ Publication type (in square brackets)
♦ Place of publication: publisher; year
♦ Number of pages (optional)

Example

Reference list

15. Harston DN. Formation of cancer cells [dissertation]. Sheffield: University of Northampton; 2014. 236 p.

L9 Conference papers

Citation order:

♦ Author(s)
♦ Title of conference paper
♦ Title of conference (capitalise all initial letters, except for linking words)
♦ Date as year month day(s)
♦ Location

If published, add:

♦ Details of place
♦ Publisher or journal reference

Example

Reference list

16. Valberg PA, Watson AY. Lack of concordance between reported lung cancer risk levels and occupation-specific diesel-exhaust exposure. 3rd Colloquium on Particulate Air Pollution and Human Health; 1999 Jun 6–8; Durham (NC).

L10 Scientific or technical reports

Citation order:

♦ Author(s)
♦ Title of report
♦ Place of publication: publisher; year
♦ Number of pages (optional)
♦ Report series and number

Example

Reference list

17. Breslow NE, Day NE. Statistical methods in cancer research. Vol 1. Analysis of case-control studies. Lyon, France: International Agency for Research on Cancer; 1980. 48 p. IARC Scientific Publication no. 32.

L11 Research data collections

Citation order:

♦ Title of data series
♦ Title of data collection or programme (capitalise all initial letters, except for linking words)
♦ Organisation hosting data
♦ Cited date (in square brackets)
♦ Available from: URL

Example

Reference list

18. Tumour incidences, Nebraska 1973–83. Surveillance Epidemiology and End Results (SEER) Data 1973–2006. National Cancer Institute (USA). [cited 2018 Aug 23]. Available from: http://seer.cancer.gov/resources/

L12 Organisation or personal internet sites

Citation order:

♦ Author
♦ Title of internet site
♦ [Internet]
♦ Year that the site was published/last updated
♦ Cited date (in square brackets)
♦ Number of screens or pages (in square brackets)
♦ Available from: URL

Example

Reference list

19. Macmillan Cancer Support. Lung cancer [Internet]. London: Macmillan Cancer Support; 2019 [cited 2019 Feb 23]. Available from: https://www.macmillan.org.uk/information-and-support/lung-cancer

NB For **web pages** where no author can be identified, you should use the title of the web page.

Example

Reference list

20. WhyQuit.com [Internet] 2012 Aug 13 [cited 2015 Aug 23]; [50+ screens]. Available from: http://whyquit.com/

L13 Blogs

Citation order:

- Author
- Title
- [Internet]
- Place of publication: publisher; year
- Cited date (in square brackets)
- Available from: URL

Example

Reference list

21. Dr No. Bad medicine [Internet] Leicester: Chris Sinclair; 2018 [cited 2018 Aug 23]. Available from: http://www.badmed.com/

L14 Maps

Citation order:

- Author
- Title
- Medium (in square brackets)
- Place of publication: publisher; year
- Description, including size in cm
- Colour/black and white
- Series and number

Example

Reference list

22. Ordnance Survey. Kendal to Morecambe [map]. Southampton: Ordnance Survey, 1982. 1 sheet: 1:50,000; 80 x 80 cm.; colour. Landranger series; 97

L15 Standards

Citation order:

- Publishing organisation/institution
- Standard number
- Title
- Place of publication: publisher; year

Example

Reference list

23. British Standards Institution. BS EN 12155:2000. Curtain walling. Watertightness. Laboratory test under static pressure. London: BSI; 2000.

L16 Patents

Citation order:

- Inventor
- Assignee
- Title
- Patent country and document type
- Country code and patent number
- Date issued

Example

Reference list

24. Padley S, inventor. Thompson Hydraulics Ltd, assignee. Pressure isolating valve. United Kingdom patent GB 2463069. 2015 Nov 21.

L17 Photographs

Citation order:

- Artist
- Title
- Medium (in square brackets)
- Place of publication: publisher; year
- Physical description

Example

Reference list

25. Ikhanov T. Sclerosis in human liver [Photograph]. Kiev: Ukrainian Institute of Medicine; 2015. 1 photograph: colour, 10 × 20cm.

L18   Tables/figures

Cite the source in which the table, graph or figure appears, and include the number and title of the table, graph or figure before page numbers.

L18.1   Graph in a book

Citation order:

♦ Author/editor of book
♦ Title of book
♦ Edition (if not first edition)
♦ Place of publication: publisher; year
♦ Figure/table (number), figure/table caption
♦ Page number

Example

Reference list

26. Hocking S, Sochacki F, Winterbottom M. OCR AS/A level Biology A. 2nd ed. London: Pearson; 2015. Figure 3, Calibration curve for known concentrations of glucose solution vs transmission of light; p. 77.

L18.2   Figure in chapter of an edited book

Citation order:

♦ Author(s) of chapter
♦ Title of chapter
♦ In:

♦ Author/editor of book
♦ Title of ebook
♦ Edition (if not first edition)
♦ [Internet]
♦ Place of publication: publisher; year
♦ Figure (number), figure caption
♦ cited year month day (in square brackets)
♦ Page number or location (in square brackets)
♦ Available from: URL

Example

Reference list

27. Matthews NH, Li WQ, Qureshi AA. Epidemiology of Melanoma. In: Ward GH, Farma JM editors. Cutaneous melanoma: Etiology and therapy [Internet]. Brisbane: Codon Publications; 2017 Dec 21. Figure 2, Worldwide age-standardized annual incidence of melanoma by age; [cited 2018 Aug 21]; [Chapter 1]. Available from: https://www.ncbi.nlm.nih.gov/books/NBK481862/

L18.3   Table in a journal article

Citation order:

♦ Author(s)
♦ Title of article
♦ Abbreviated title of journal
♦ [Internet]
♦ Date of publication as year month day
♦ Volume number (issue number if available): page numbers (not preceded by p.)
♦ Table (number), caption, page number
♦ Cited date (in square brackets)
♦ Page number
♦ Available from: URL *or* DOI

Example

Reference list

28. Ferlay J, Colombet M, Soerjomataram I, Dyba T, Randi G, Bettio M, et al. Cancer incidence and mortality patterns in Europe: Estimates for 40 countries and 25 major cancers in 2018. Eur J Cancer [Internet]. 2018 Aug 9; 103:1–32. Table 7, Estimated number of new cancer cases (hundreds) by sex, cancer site and country, 2018; [cited 2018 Aug 23]; p. 8. Available from: https://www.sciencedirect.com/science/article/pii/S0959804918309559 doi:10.1016.2018.07.005

L19   Equations

Cite equations within the source that you read.

Citation order:

♦ Author
♦ Title of source
♦ Publication details, including date
♦ Page number or precise location within source

Example of equation in journal article

In-text citation

Fradelizi and Meyer[30] noted that for $z>0$ …

Reference list

29. Fradelizi, M, Meyer, M. Some functional inverse Santaló inequalities. Advances in Mathematics [Internet]. 2008 [cited 2018 Feb 23]; 218(5):1430–52. Available from: https://www.sciencedirect.com/science/article/pii/S0001870808000844 doi:10.1016/j.aim.2008.03.013

NB In this instance, we suggest that you place the in-text reference (the superscript number) close to the authors, rather than with the equation, where it may be mistaken for part of the equation.

L20   Legislation

Citation order:

♦ Title of legislation, including year.

Example

Reference list

30. Human Tissue Act 2004.

L21   Legal cases

Citing medicine notes that legal cases have established citation formats and recommends that these be used.

Citation order:

♦ Party names
♦ Legal citation
♦ Available from: URL

Example

Reference list

31. Grant & Anor v The Ministry of Justice [2011] EWHC 3379 (QB). Available from: https://www.bailii.org/ew/cases/EWHC/QB/2011/3379.html

L22   Personal communications

Citing medicine notes that as emails and letters are personal communications, they should usually be noted in your text but not in the reference list. Provide the author's name, the date of the email, and note that it will not be included in your reference list by including the word unreferenced. You should obtain permission from the sender of the email to quote them in your work.

L22.1 Emails

Example

In-text citation

32. In an email to this author, N. Johnson (Nov 12, 2018, unreferenced) …

L22.2 Letters

Example

In-text citation

33. In her letter, T. Stone (Nov 1, 2018, unreferenced) …

L23 Poster presentations

Citation order:

♦ Author
♦ Title of poster
♦ Poster presentation at:
♦ Name of event
♦ Date (year month day(s))
♦ Location

If viewed online, add:

♦ Available from: URL

Example

Reference list

34. Collins B. Real men get checked. Poster presentation at: American College of Surgeons Cancer Programs Conference; 2017 Sep 8–9; Chicago (IL). Available from: https://www.facs.org/~/media/files/ quality%20programs/cancer/ conference/2017/collins.ashx

L24 Audiovisual sources

L24.1 Radio/television broadcasts

Citation order:

♦ Title of programme
♦ Title of series
♦ Format (in square brackets)
♦ Place of publication: channel
♦ Date of broadcast

Examples

Reference list

35. Complexity in biology. Inside science [Radio broadcast]. London: BBC Radio 4; 2018 Sep 6.

36. Oceans of wonder. Blue Planet II [Television broadcast]. London: BBC One; 2018 Jan 5.

L24.2 Movies

Citation order:

♦ Title
♦ [Motion picture]
♦ Place of publication: publisher; year

Example

Reference list

37. Children of men [Motion picture]. New York: Universal Studios; 2006.

L24.3 Streaming videos

Citation order:

♦ Title
♦ [Online streaming video]
♦ Place of publication: publisher; year
♦ Cited date (in square brackets)
♦ Available from: URL

Example

Reference list

38. Chasing coral [Online streaming video]. Los Gatos, CA: Netflix; 2017 [cited 2018 Sep 8]. Available from: https://www.netflix.com/gb/title/80168188

L24.4 Sound recordings

Citation order:

♦ Author/artist (if available)
♦ Title of recording
♦ Title of publication
♦ Format (in square brackets)
♦ Date of publication
♦ Cited date (in square brackets, if online)

Examples

Reference list

39. British Library. Hedgehog. Erinaceus europaeus. British wildlife recordings [Internet]. 1960s–1990s [cited 2018 Aug 4]. Available from: https://sounds.bl.uk/Environment/British-wildlife-recordings

40. Sound Effects Vol. 2 – Nature and Animals [CD]. Bristol: Environmental studios; 2006.

L25 Interviews

Citation order:

♦ Interviewee
♦ Interviewed by: name of interviewer
♦ Date

Example

Reference list

41. Johnson C. Interviewed by: Roberts D. 2018 Oct 14.

L26 Course materials in virtual learning environment

Citation order:

♦ Author
♦ Title of lecture
♦ Format (in square brackets)
♦ Module name
♦ Institution; date
♦ Cited date (in square brackets)
♦ Available from: URL

Example

Reference list

42. Singh R. Protein classification [lecture notes]. BIOL3014, Durham University; 2018 Mar 3 [cited 2018 Apr 2]. Available from: http://duo.dur.ac.uk

Sample text

More than 38,000 people are diagnosed with lung cancer every year in the UK. (1) Studies elsewhere have investigated links between occupation or socio-demographic status and cancer (2,3), but smoking is the biggest single cause of lung cancer in the UK. (1) Some researchers have analysed populations to establish incidences of tumours. (4) Tumours may spread from the lungs to elsewhere in the body. (5, p. 280) Charities and self-help groups provide advice and moral support to victims. (1,6)

Sample reference list

1. Macmillan Cancer Support. Lung cancer. [Internet]. 2018 [cited 2018 Aug 23]; [29 screens]. Available from: http://www.macmillan.org.uk/Cancerinformation/Cancertypes/Lung/Lungcancer.aspx

2. Valberg PA, Watson AY. Lack of concordance between reported lung

cancer risk levels and occupation-specific diesel-exhaust exposure. 3rd Colloquium on Particulate Air Pollution and Human Health; 1999 Jun 6–8; Durham (NC).

3. Amr S, Wolpert B, Loffredo CA, Zheng YL, Shields PG, Jones R. Occupation, gender, race and lung cancer. J Occup Environ Med [Internet]. 2008 Oct [cited 2018 Aug 23]; 50(10):1167–75. Available from: doi:10.1097/JOM.0b013e31817d3639

4. Tumour incidences, Nebraska 1973–83. Surveillance Epidemiology and End Results (SEER) Data 1973–2006. National Cancer Institute (USA). [cited 2018 Aug 23]. Available from: http://seer.cancer.gov/resources/

5. Hart I. The spread of tumours. In Knowles MA, Selby PJ, editors. Introduction to the cellular and molecular biology of cancer. Oxford: Oxford University Press; 2005. p. 278–88.

6. WhyQuit.com. [Internet] 2012 Aug 13 [cited 2018 Aug 23]; [50+ screens]. Available from: http://whyquit.com/

Glossary

Address bar: Also known as location or URL bar, it indicates the current URL, web page address, path to a local file or other item to be located by the browser.

Bibliography: A list of all the sources you consulted for your work arranged in alphabetical order by author's surname or, when there is no author, by title. For web pages where no author or title is apparent, the URL of the web page would be used.

Citation: The in-text reference that gives brief details (for example, author, date, page number) of the source you are quoting from or referring to. This citation corresponds with the full details of the work (title, publisher and so on) given in your reference list or bibliography so that the reader can identify and/or locate the work. End-text citations are commonly known as references.

Common knowledge: Facts that are generally known.

Digital object identifier (DOI): A numbered tag used to identify individual digital (online) sources, such as journal articles and conference papers.

Direct quotation: The actual words used by an author, in exactly the same order as in their original work, and with the original spelling. See Section C for details of how to set out all quotations in your text.

Ellipsis: The omission of words from speech or writing. A set of three dots (…) shows where the original words have been omitted.

End-text citation: An entry in the reference list at the end of your work, which contains the full (bibliographical) details of information for the in-text citation.

et al.: (From the Latin *et alia* meaning 'and others'.) A term most commonly used for works having four or more authors (for example, Harvard author-date system). The citation gives the first surname listed in the publication, followed by *et al.*

Footnote/endnote: An explanatory note and/or source citation either at the foot of the page or end of a chapter used in numeric referencing styles (for example, MHRA). These are not used in Harvard and other author-date referencing styles.

ibid.: (From the Latin *ibidem* meaning 'in the same place'.) A term used with citations that refer to an immediately preceding cited work. It is not used in the Harvard system, where works appear only once in the alphabetical list of references.

Internet: The global computer network that provides a variety of information and communication facilities, consisting of interconnected networks using standardised communication protocols.

In-text citation: Often known as simply the citation, this gives brief details (for example, author, date, page number) of your source of information within your text.

op. cit.: (From the Latin *opere citato* meaning 'in the work already cited'.) A term used with citations that refer to a previously cited work. It is not used in the Harvard system, where works appear only once in the alphabetical list of references.

Paraphrase: A restating of someone else's thoughts or ideas in your own words. You must always cite your source when paraphrasing (see Section C for details and an example).

Peer review: A process used in academic publishing to check the accuracy and quality of a work intended for publication. The author's draft of a book or article is sent by an editor to experts in the subject, who (usually anonymously) suggest amendments or corrections. This process is seen as a guarantee of academic quality and is a major distinction between traditional forms of publishing, such as books and journals, and information on web pages, which can be written by anyone, even if they have no expertise in a subject.

Plagiarism: Taking and using another person's thoughts, writings or inventions as your own without acknowledging or citing the source of the ideas and expressions. In the case of copyrighted material, plagiarism is illegal.

Proper noun: The name of an individual person, place or organisation, having an initial capital letter.

Quotation: The words or sentences from another information source used within your text (see also *direct quotation*).

Reference: The full publication details of the work cited.

Reference list: A list of references at the end of your assignment that includes the full information for your citations so that the reader can easily identify and retrieve each work (journal articles, books, web pages and so on).

Secondary referencing: Citing/referencing a work that has been mentioned or quoted in the work you are reading (see Section A for more details and an example).

Short citation: This is used in numeric referencing systems, including MHRA and OSCOLA, instead of *op. cit.* When a work is cited for the first time, all bibliographic details are included in the footnotes/endnotes and in the bibliography reference. If a work is cited more than once in the text, the second and subsequent entries in the footnotes/endnotes use an abbreviated, short citation, such as the author and title (as well as a specific page reference), so that the reader can find the full bibliographic details in the bibliography.

sic: (From the Latin meaning 'so, thus'.) A term used after a quoted or copied word to show that the original word has been written exactly as it appears in the original text, and usually highlights an error or misspelling of the word.

Summarise: Similar to paraphrasing, summarising provides a brief account of someone else's ideas or work, covering only the main points and leaving out the details (see Section C for more details and an example).

Superscript number: A number used in numeric referencing styles (including Chicago, MHRA and OSCOLA) to identify citations in the text, which is usually smaller than and set above the normal text, that is[1].

URL: The abbreviation for uniform (or universal) resource locator, the address of documents and other information sources on the internet (for example, http:// …).

Virtual learning environment (VLE): An online teaching environment that allows interaction between tutors and students, and the storage of course documents and teaching materials (see Section E.6 for more details).

Web page: A hypertext document accessible via the world wide web (www), the extensive information system on the internet, which provides facilities for documents to be connected to other documents by hypertext links.

Works Cited: The Modern Language Association's (MLA) equivalent of a reference list that provides full details of the sources cited in your text.

Further reading

Avoiding plagiarism

Cardiff University Information Services (no date) *Is it plagiarism quiz*. Available at: https://ilrb.cf.ac.uk/plagiarism/quiz/ (Accessed: 17 December 2018).

Carroll, J. (2013) *A handbook for deterring plagiarism in higher education*. 2nd edn. Oxford: Oxford Centre for Staff and Learning Development.

Cottrell, S. (2019) *The study skills handbook.* 5th edn. London: Red Globe Press.

Williams, K. and Davis, M. (2017) *Referencing and understanding plagiarism.* 2nd edn. London: Red Globe Press.

Referencing

American Psychological Association (2009) *Publication manual of the American Psychological Association*. 6th edn. Washington, DC: American Psychological Association.

APA style blog (2018) Available at: http://blog.apastyle.org/ (Accessed: 17 December 2018).

The Bluebook: a uniform system of citation (2015) 20th edn. Cambridge, MA.: Harvard Law Review Association.

Chicago manual of style (2017) 17th edn. Chicago: University of Chicago Press.

Chicago manual of style online (2018) Available at: www.chicagomanualofstyle. org/home.html (Accessed: 17 December 2018).

IEEE (2018) *IEEE referencing guide.* Available at: http://ieeeauthorcenter.ieee. org/wp-content/uploads/IEEE-Reference-Guide.pdf (Accessed: 17 January 2019).

International Committee of Medical Journal Editors (ICMJE) (2015) *Recommendations for the conduct, reporting, editing and publication of scholarly work in medical journals.* Available at: www.icmje.org/ icmje-recommendations.pdf (Accessed: 17 December 2018).

Meredith, S. and Nolan, D. (2012) *Oxford University Standard for Citation of Legal Authorities*. 4th edn. Available at: www. law. ox.ac.uk/published/OSCOLA_4th_edn_ Hart_2012.pdf (Accessed: 17 December 2018).

MLA Style Center (2018) Available at: https://style.mla.org/ (Accessed: 13 September 2018).

Modern Humanities Research Association (2013) *MHRA style guide: a handbook for authors, editors, and writers of theses*. 3rd edn. Available at: www.mhra.org.uk/ Publications/Books/StyleGuide/index.html (Accessed: 17 December 2018).

Modern Language Association (2016) *MLA Handbook for Writers of Research Papers*. 8th edn. New York, NY: Modern Language Association of America.

Neville, C. (2016) *Complete guide to referencing and avoiding plagiarism.* 3rd edn. (London: Open University Press).

Patrias, K. (2007–2018) *Citing medicine: the NLM style guide for authors, editors, and publishers*. 2nd edn. [Online version updated 18 May 2018]. Available at: www. nlm.nih.gov/citingmedicine (Accessed: 17 December 2018).

Williams, K. and Davis, M. (2017) *Referencing and understanding plagiarism.* 2nd edn. London: Red Globe Press.

Index for the Harvard referencing style

NB To avoid confusion when referencing, this index does not list items specific to the alternative referencing styles (Sections F–L).

Index entries are arranged alphabetically letter by letter, with numbers referring to pages. Bold numbers indicate glossary entries.